TRANSLINGUAL PRACTICE

Translingual Practice: Global Englishes and Cosmopolitan Relations introduces a new way of looking at the use of English within a global context. Challenging traditional approaches in second language acquisition and English language teaching, this book incorporates recent advances in multilingual studies, sociolinguistics, and new literacy studies to articulate a new perspective on these areas. Canagarajah argues that multilinguals merge their own languages and values into English, which opens up various negotiation strategies that help them decode other unique varieties of English and construct new norms.

Incisive and groundbreaking, this will be essential reading for anyone interested in multilingualism, World Englishes and intercultural communication.

Suresh Canagarajah is Edwin Erle Sparks Professor in Applied Linguistics and English at Pennsylvania State University.

One more to Amma
For shaping us
In so many silent, unseen,
And yet unrecognized ways

TRANSLINGUAL PRACTICE

Global Englishes and Cosmopolitan Relations

Suresh Canagarajah

Routledge
Taylor & Francis Group

LONDON AND NEW YORK

First published 2013
by Routledge
2 Park Square, Milton Park, Abingdon, Oxon OX14 4RN

Simultaneously published in the USA and Canada
by Routledge
711 Third Avenue, New York, NY 10017

Routledge is an imprint of the Taylor & Francis Group, an informa business

British Library Cataloguing in Publication Data
A catalogue record for this book is available from the British Library

Library of Congress Cataloging in Publication Data
Canagarajah, A. Suresh.
Translingual practice : global Englishes and cosmopolitan
relations / Suresh Canagarajah.
p. cm.
Includes bibliographical references.
1. Multilingualism--Social aspects. 2. English language--Globalization.
3. Intercultural communication. 4. Second language acquisition.
5. Sociolinguistics. I. Title.
P115.45.C36 2012
306.44'6–dc23
2012026893

ISBN: 978-0-415-68398-2 (hbk)
ISBN: 978-0-415-68400-2 (pbk)
ISBN: 978-0-203-07388-9 (ebk)

Typeset in Bembo
by Taylor & Francis Books

CONTENTS

ACKNOWLEDGEMENTS

It is difficult to list the many scholars who have influenced the ideas in this book either through direct conversations or indirectly through their own work. Even when I depart from their work, I am indebted to them for opening up new orientations through their publications and inspiring my research and thinking. My students have also not been passive listeners of my research and ideas. They have shaped my thinking in so many ways through their classroom interactions.

It is similarly difficult to list the many people who have provided the spiritual, psychological, and social resources that sustain one's research. Knowledge construction and academic writing are not activities of the mind alone.

I must restrict myself to the more immediate contributors to this book. I thank Dwight Atkinson, Martin Dewey, Alan Firth, Bonny Norton, Mukul Saxena, Jean-Jacques Weber, and Xiaoye You for reading versions of this manuscript during various stages of its evolution and offering useful suggestions. The limitations of course remain mine.

A resident fellowship at the Stellenbosch Institute of Advanced Studies in the summer of 2011 enabled me to write the first draft of this book.

I thank Nadia Seemungal of Routledge for being very supportive throughout the writing of this manuscript. I thank her for offering me the space to represent boldly some of the unconventional ideas and goals for this book.

Nanthini, Lavannya, Nivedhana, and Wiroshan continue to provide the stability at home that gives me the luxury to imagine more ways of changing the world.

PERMISSIONS

The author and publisher would like to thank the following copyright holder for permission to reproduce an extract from the following:

Galang

Words and Music by Maya Arulpragasm, Ross Orton, Stephen Mackey and Justine Frischmann

Copyright © 2003, 2005 ISLAND MUSIC LTD., IMAGEM LONDON LTD. and EMI MUSIC PUBLISHING LTD

All Rights for ISLAND MUSIC LTD. in the US and Canada Controlled and Administered by UNIVERSAL-POLYGRAM INTERNATIONAL PUBLISHING, INC.

All Rights for IMAGEM LONDON LTD. in the U.S. and Canada Controlled and Administered by UNIVERSAL MUSIC- Z TUNES LLC

All Rights for EMI MUSIC PUBLISHING LTD. in the U.S. and Canada Controlled and Administered by EMI BLACKWOOD MUSIC INC.

All Rights Reserved. Used by Permission

Reprinted by Permission of Hal Leonard Corporation

They that have frequent intercourse with strangers, to whom they endeavour to accommodate themselves, must in time learn a mingled dialect, like the jargon which serves the traffickers on the *Mediterranean* and *Indian* coasts. This will not always be confined to the exchange, the warehouse, or the port, but will be communicated by degrees to other ranks of the people, and be at last incorporated with the current speech.

Samuel Johnson (1755, p. 3)

1

INTRODUCTION

وَمَنْ يَهِيب صُعُودَ الجِبَالِ ~~~ يَعِشْ أَبَدَ الدَّهْرِ بَيْنَ الحُقَر

As I type each word in this literacy autobiography, storms of thoughts stampede to be considered and mentioned. Which experiences should I value, which shall I consider, and which should I ignore. My literacy situation is unique as only a few number of students [...] share the same status. As I click the keys on the keyboard, an illustration of my literacy development shunt me to continue my ongoing learning adventure from my academic communities, my home, and my life experiences.

That is how a Saudi Arabian student, whom I will call Buthainah, begins her literacy autobiography for an assignment in my course on teaching second language writing. For many readers, this kind of writing—which I label *codemeshing*—will be irritating. The mixing of languages (Arabic and English), the novel idiomatic expressions ("storms of thoughts stampede," and "my literacy development shunt me") and the grammatical deviations from standard written English ("a few number of students," and the missing question mark) will go against many assumptions readers hold dear about writing in specific and communication in general. They violate our assumption that a text should be constructed in only one language at a time and that its meaning should be transparent. This expectation is partly motivated by a broader assumption we hold about all communication. We believe that for communication to be efficient and successful we should employ a common language with shared norms. These norms typically come from the native speaker's use of the language. We also believe that languages have their own unique systems and should be kept free of mixing with other languages for meaningful communication. I consider these assumptions as constituting a *monolingual orientation* to communication.

Despite the power of the monolingual orientation in social and educational institutions today, we increasingly see texts such as Buthainah's that emerge from language contact in everyday life, whether in writing, conversation, or multimedia.

It is not that such communication is particularly new. There is a long history of texts and talk that have meshed languages (as I will show in Chapter 3). Recent forms of globalization have given more visibility to such forms of communication. Transnational contact in diverse cultural, economic, and social domains has increased the interaction between languages and language groups. Migration has involved people taking their heritage languages to new locales and developing repertoires that were not traditionally part of their community. Technological developments have facilitated interactions between language groups and offered new resources for meshing languages with other symbol systems (i.e., icons, emoticons, graphics) and modalities (i.e., images, video, audio) on the same "page." All these developments pose interesting possibilities and challenges for communicating across language boundaries. They are engendering new communicative modes as people adopt creative strategies to engage with each other and represent their voices.

It is from these perspectives that we should understand Buthainah's writing. I have conducted interviews with her to understand her motivations for writing in this manner. In an essay that narrates the development of her literate competence in Arabic, English, and French, she considered a merging of all her linguistic repertoires as most effectively representing her identities and objectives. She told me that the objective of her writing was not to merely convey some information about her multilingual literacy development, but to demonstrate or "perform" it. There was no better way to do this than to mesh the languages that were part of her literate and communicative life. Writing solely in English, and in a variety that is not hers (i.e., privileged "native speaker" dialects), would be unsuitable for such purposes. Her English shows the creative influences of her multilingual and multicultural background. I find *codemeshing* (which I define and discuss more fully in Chapter 6) emerging as an important mode of writing for multilingual scholars and students to represent their identities in English (Canagarajah, 2006a).

Despite the seeming novelty and difficulty of this writing, Buthainah's peers, constituting both international and Anglo-American students, negotiated her essay effectively for meaning in the classroom. Once her peers had figured out her rhetorical objectives, they didn't find it difficult to shift from the monolingual orientation of traditional classroom literacy to an alternate style of reading. In fact, for the most part they were quite successful in co-constructing meanings from her unconventional language usage. As I will narrate in Chapter 7, it became evident that they were drawing from communicative practices in the contact zones outside the classroom where they had developed the competence for such literate activity. Popular culture and multimedia communication involve many similar textual practices in contemporary life.

To understand the texts that develop such competencies in popular culture, consider the Sri Lankan hip hop artiste M.I.A.'s recording of *Galang*. With a backdrop in the music video where "*eppiTi*" (i.e., "what's up?") is written in Tamil script, M.I.A. raps:

London Calling
Speak the Slang now

Boys say Wha-Gwan
Girls say Wha-What *[x2]*

Slam Galang galang galang
Ga la ga la ga la Land ga Lang ga Lang
Shotgun get you down
Get down get down get down
Ge-d Ge-d Ge-d Down G-down G-down
Too late you down D-down D-down D-down
Ta na ta na ta na Ta na ta na ta

Blaze a blaze Galang a lang a lang lang
Purple Haze Galang a lang a lang lang
Blaze a blaze Galang a lang a lang lang
Purple Haze Galang a lang a lang lang

The linguistic hybridity of the performance draws from the artiste's own sociocultural in-betweenness. The references to guns and the visuals relating to tigers (i.e., the symbol of the resistance group Tamil Tigers) and palmyrah trees (part of the topography of Jaffna, the Tamil homeland) in the music video remind one of the Tamil people's struggle for a separate state in Sri Lanka. M.I.A. is an outspoken sympathizer with the aspirations of her ethnic community. However, a refugee, now located in inner-city London, she experiences a similar context of violence. She is making connections between both locations through her rap. Hence "London calling." The Tamil word *eppiTi* might be a rough translation for the Guyanese patois *gwan*, for "what's going on?" *EppiTi* is a common conversation opener in Tamil, an utterance someone would use in a phone call from London to Jaffna. *Galang* is a Jamaican creole word meaning variously "go along," "behave yourself," or simply "be cool." The rap urges listeners to face oppressive conditions with ease. *Lang ga langa* is slang for marijuana and, combined with "purple haze," suggests the possibilities in psychedelic drugs to transcend the violence in people's immediate environment. (To reinforce that point, *gwan* is also a British slang for cannabis.) In addition to Tamil and various forms of Caribbean creole, there are also uses of Black English, as in the omission of the auxiliary verb or inflected verb forms ("Shotgun get you down") and references to *slam* and *slang*. Such practice of borrowing words from the languages of out-group members for purposes of temporary identity representation and community solidarity has been labeled (crossing) in sociolinguistic literature (see Rampton, 1999a).

Why does M.I.A. cross in and out of codes of diverse communities in this fashion? Once again, we have to consider the performative dimensions of the lyric and go beyond meaning as a paraphrasable product. The language reflects the communities M.I.A. comes into contact with in her diaspora life. The rap builds solidarity among diverse migrant communities sharing the metropolitan urban space. Sri Lankans, Jamaicans, and Guyanese, not to mention underclass British and Black Americans, are able to share in a communicative and artistic experience in a hybrid language that is similar and yet different (i.e., localized varieties of English). The language and the rap unite them in the common struggles they face living in an urban environment. Furthermore, the hybrid language connects diaspora Tamils with their community members in their homeland in their struggle for self-affirmation. The fact that the rap adopts English and flows across transnational spaces also provides an opportunity for the Tamil aspirations to receive a hearing in locations outside the Tamil homeland. Non-Tamil communities are able to express solidarity with Tamils through the rap. I have read reviews of this rap and other performances of M.I.A. on the Internet, and I can confirm that non-Tamils are able to interpret her rhetorical intentions and social meanings quite well, adopting interpretive strategies that involve combining the words with the visuals and other multimodal resources in the music video.

Such hybrid modes of communication are found not only in written and multimedia communication, but they also feature in everyday face-to-face conversation. Talk doesn't have to be in a single language; the interlocutors can use the respective languages they are proficient in. This kind of practice is becoming necessary in contact situations where speakers don't always find a common code for their conversation. David Block narrates an interesting example where he spoke in Catalan and his cab driver spoke in Italian when he was in Rome, and they still managed to accomplish their goals quite well. The conversation was so smooth that Block emphasizes that "there was very little need for repair or repetition" (Block, 2010, p. 24). Though this instance is easy to explain, as their languages are part of the Romance family and share certain commonalties, there are other instances of people using traditionally disparate codes to still achieve intelligibility and meaning. For example, as my own Sri Lankan Tamil community now constructs new homes outside its traditional homelands, it is developing new conversational strategies. Increasingly, children are not developing advanced proficiency in their heritage language of Tamil, but adopting languages of their new "homes," such as English, French, and German. How then does intergenerational communication take place within the family when the elders don't have proficiency in some of these new languages? Consider my conversation with an East London family (English words are in bold font, Tamil in regular, and translations in italics). The teenager Rajani's mother and uncle are troubled that she hasn't developed competence in her heritage language[1]:

1. ASC: makaL tamiL kataikka maaTTaa enRu **worry** paNNuriinkaLoo?
   *Do you **worry** that your daughter can't speak Tamil?*
2. Mother: **worry** paNNi enna, onRum ceiya eelaatu enna? viLankum taanee avavukku?
   *We can't achieve anything by **worry**ing, can we? Isn't the fact that she understands enough?*
3. Uncle: caappaaTu atukaLilai **she is more**.
   She is more *[conservative] in food and things like that.*
4. Mother: oom. maTRatu paavaaTai caTTai atukaL pooTa konca naaL pooTaamal iruntava, piraku orumaatiri **friends** aakkalooTai ceerntu **skirt** pooTa atukaL itukaL ellaam viruppam.

Yes. She was earlier disinterested in wearing skirt and things like that. After joining some **friends,** *she now likes to wear* **skirt** *and stuff.*

5. ASC [to mother]: **Temple** atukaL ellaam?
   What about **temple** *and things like that?*
6. Rajani: **Not regularly, but yeah.**
7. ASC [to Rajani]: **Hmm would you maintain Tamil culture and language in the future?**
8. Rajani: **Culture, culture yes. I can't see myself speaking in Tamil now, because I think I have left it too late. xxx it's hardly useful, to choose between English, so.**
9. Mother: pirayoosanam illai enRu colluvaa @@@
   She says it is useless.
10. Rajani: **No, I am just saying. It's the truth though. You don't speak so much in Tamil, so.**

It is interesting that Rajani is able to participate in this conversation by using her receptive competence in Tamil and productive skill in English. For example, when the uncle and mother seem to exaggerate her interest in traditional cultural practices, Rajani intervenes on line 6 to say that she doesn't go to temple too regularly. Though the occasional English codemeshed items might have helped her a bit (see my use of the English word "temple" on line 5), she would have needed Tamil receptive competence to understand the drift of the conversation. Again, when the mother slightly criticizes her daughter on line 9 for saying that she finds Tamil useless, Rajani defends herself in English. Note that the mother too has receptive competence in English to understand her daughter's statements and respond appropriately in Tamil. Interestingly, the family's definition of what it means to "know" Tamil is also changing. The mother is satisfied with her daughter's receptive competence in Tamil that enables Rajani to perform her ethnic identity (see line 2). In this manner, diaspora Tamils are able to bond as a family and enjoy community without a shared single language. I found Sri Lankan Tamil youth adopting bits and pieces of Tamil, woven into the other European languages they speak, for intergenerational contact and community solidarity (see Canagarajah, 2013). This conversational strategy is so significant that there would be serious damage done to family relationships and community identity in diaspora settings without it.

This conversational strategy is becoming known as "polyglot dialog" (Posner, 1991). Its prevalence and effectiveness in global contact zones today is easy to explain. It is enabled by the "receptive multilingualism" (Braunmüller, 2006) we all have. We understand more languages than we can speak. Using our receptive skills we can understand the interlocutor's language, in the same way that the interlocutor uses his/her competence to understand our own language. And the conversation proceeds. Besides, communication involves more than words. In many cases, speakers use the context, gestures, and objects in the setting to interpret the interlocutor's utterances. This form of polyglot dialog increasingly characterizes lingua franca English encounters also. As speakers bring their diverse varieties of English (e.g., Indian or Sri Lankan English) to the interaction, they are developing conversational strategies to communicate with each other without shifting to a shared variety (i.e., whether native speaker varieties or one of their own). While using their own varieties, they adopt strategies to negotiate intelligibility and co-construct situational norms with speakers of other varieties.

The communicative modes I have referred to above with terms such as code-meshing, crossing, and polyglot dialog require a new orientation to language studies. We have many other terms used by diverse scholars to represent their insights into cross-language relations in the global contact zones. Jørgensen (2008) coins _poly-lingual languaging_ to refer to children's playful shuttling between languages in Europe. Blommaert (2008) uses _hetero-graphy_ for African literacy which involves a mix of different languages and semiotic systems. Pennycook (2010) adopts _metrolinguistics_ for urban communication in which people adopt languages not traditionally associated with their communities for new identities. The Council of Europe (2000) has used _plurilingualism_ to refer to the functional competence in partial languages it is aiming to develop among school children. I adopt the umbrella term _translingual practice_ to capture the common underlying processes and orientations motivating these communicative modes.

Toward a different paradigm

How does the translingual orientation differ from the dominant monolingual orientation? The label translingual highlights two key concepts of significance for a paradigm shift. Firstly, communication transcends individual languages. Secondly, communication transcends words and involves diverse semiotic resources and ecological affordances. Let me explain.

To understand the first claim, we need to appreciate the following points which will be developed further in the coming chapters:

- "Languages" are always in contact with and mutually influence each other. From this perspective, the separation of languages with different labels needs to be problematized. Labeling is an ideological act of demarcating certain codes in relation to certain identities and interests.
- Users treat all available codes as a repertoire in their everyday communication, and not separated according to their labels.
- Users don't have separate competences for separately labeled languages (as it is assumed by traditional linguistics), but an integrated proficiency that is different in kind (not just degree) from traditional understandings of multilingual competence.
- Languages are not necessarily at war with each other; they complement each other in communication. Therefore, we have to reconsider the dominant understanding that one language detrimentally "interferes" with the learning and use of another. The influences of one language on the other can be creative, enabling, and offer possibilities for voice.
- Texts and talk don't feature one language at a time; they are meshed and mediated by diverse codes, which may not always be evident on the surface.

- In the context of such language diversity, meaning doesn't arise from a common grammatical system or norm, but through negotiation practices in local situations.
- Though language patterns (in the form of dialects, registers, and genres) and grammatical norms do evolve from local language practices sedimented over time, they are always open to renegotiation and reconstruction as users engage with new communicative contexts. Patterns and norms have to be situated (or "relocalized"—Pennycook, 2010) in every ecological context of use to be meaningful
- At its most basic, then, communication involves treating languages as "mobile resources" (Blommaert, 2010, p. 49) that are appropriated by people for their purposes; these resources index meaning and gain form in situated contexts for specific interlocutors in their social practice.

To understand the second notion that defines translingual practice—that is, that communication transcends words—we have to appreciate the following assumptions:

- Communication involves diverse semiotic resources; language is only one semiotic resource among many, such as symbols, icons, and images.
- All semiotic resources work together for meaning; separating them into different systems may distort meaning, violating their ecological embeddedness and interconnection.
- Language and semiotic resources make meaning in the context of diverse modalities working together, including oral, written, and visual modes.
- Semiotic resources are embedded in a social and physical environment, aligning with contextual features such as participants, objects, the human body, and the setting for meaning.
- Therefore, treating language as a tightly knit system that stands free of other semiotic resources, detached from the environment, a self-standing product, and autonomous in status distorts meaning-making practices. Though it is important for linguists to focus on language for analytical purposes, such considerations should be informed by its multimodality.

To appreciate the significance of the term translingual, it is important to ask why *multilingual* (i.e., the obvious contrast to monolingual) is not adopted in this book. The term *multilingual* typically conceives of the relationship between languages in an additive manner. This gives the picture of whole languages added one on top of the other to form multilingual competence. This orientation may lead to the misleading notion that we have separate cognitive compartments for separate languages with different types of competence for each (an assumption which has been critiqued by Cook, 1999, among others). Similarly, in society, *multilingual* often connotes different language groups occupying their own niches in separation from others. What should be clear is that the term *multilingual* doesn't accommodate the dynamic interactions between languages and communities envisioned by translingual. In other words, the multilingual orientation to language relationships is still somewhat influenced by the monolingual paradigm. It has rightly been dubbed "separate bilingualism" (Creese and Blackledge, 2008) or "two solitudes" (Cummins, 2008) to reflect the ways in which the languages are kept separate. The term translingual conceives of language relationships in more dynamic terms. The semiotic resources in one's repertoire or in society interact more closely, become part of an integrated resource, and enhance each other. The languages mesh in transformative ways, generating new meanings and grammars.

In adopting translingual, I would also like to break away from the binary mono/multi or uni/pluri, a dichotomy that has led to reductive orientations to communication and competence. From this perspective, I also treat *monolingual* as positioned differently in relation to competence and communication as traditionally defined. If languages are always in contact and communication always involves a negotiation of mobile codes, we have to ask if the term monolingual has anything more than an academic and ideological significance. Communities and communication have always been heterogeneous. Those who are considered monolingual are typically proficient in multiple registers, dialects, and discourses of a given language. Even when they speak or write in a single "language," they still have to communicate in relation to diverse other codes in the environment. That very "language" is constituted by resources from diverse places. Consider how "English" includes words and grammatical structures from Scandinavian, Latin, French, and other languages. Therefore, all of us have translingual competence, with differences in degree and not kind. To turn Chomsky (1988) on his head, we are all translinguals, not native speakers of a single language in homogeneous environments. In this sense, the binaries "native/non-native" also distort the translingual competence of all people. These binaries treat certain languages as owned by and natural to certain communities, when languages are in fact open to being adopted by diverse communities for their own purposes.

Translingual practice will find manifestation in diverse ways in communicative modes and media. Though they find expression in the hybrid modes I have articulated above—such as in codemeshing, crossing, and polyglot dialog—they also find expression in texts that may resemble a narrower range of hybridity, including those approximating "standard" language norms. We must keep in mind that "standard" language is also an ideological construct, and accommodates considerable hybridity. What is important is that users negotiate both the diverse semiotic resources in their repertoire and the context to produce a text that is rhetorically most appropriate and effective for the situation. In some institutionalized contexts, the textual product may require a limited level of hybridity, based on the conventions and norms in those institutions. However the practices and processes that go into its production are no less translingual. Translingual practice applies more to the strategies of engaging with diverse codes, with the awareness that the shape of the final textual products will vary according to the contextual expectations. While translingual practice might find expression in codemeshing for multilinguals in certain contexts, in others it might find representation in a text that approximates and reconfigures "standard English." The translingual paradigm then does not disregard established norms and conventions as defined for certain contexts by dominant institutions and social groups. What is more important is that speakers and writers negotiate these norms in relation to their translingual repertoires and practices. We will find that such translingual negotiations lead to subtle variations of established norms, as appropriate for one's interests and contexts, and gradual norm changes. Translingual practice therefore calls for a sensitivity to similarity-in-difference (i.e., appreciating the common practices that generate diverse textual products) and difference-in-similarity (i.e., appreciating the mediated and hybrid composition of seemingly homogeneous and standardized products).

As mentioned earlier, translingual practice serves as an umbrella term for many communicative modes which scholars are finding in diverse domains and fields, that suit their orientations. The following is a more elaborate list of emerging terms:

In composition: translingual writing (Horner, Lu, Royster, and Trimbur, 2010), codemeshing (Young, 2004; Canagarajah, 2006a) and transcultural literacy (Lu, 2009);

In new literacy studies: multiliteracies (Cope and Kalantzis, 2000), continua of biliteracy (Hornberger, 2003), and hetero-graphy (Blommaert, 2008);

In sociolinguistics: fused lects (Auer, 1999), ludic Englishes and metrolinguistics (Pennycook, 2010), poly-lingual languaging (Jørgensen, 2008), and fragmented multilingualism (Blommaert, 2010);

In applied linguistics: translanguaging (Creese and Blackledge, 2010), dynamic bilingualism and pluriliteracy (Garcia, 2009), plurilingualism (Council of Europe, 2000), and third spaces (Gutiérrez, 2008).

All these terms share the common assumptions articulated above and help to develop a translingual paradigm in communication, literacy, and pedagogy. However, there are also minor differences relating to the objectives and assumptions of the respective scholars.

Many of the terms above are used for specific domains of communication. So, for example, translingual writing, codemeshing, transcultural literacy, pluriliteracies, and third spaces are used in pedagogical contexts relating to literacy. Terms like multiliteracies, continua of biliteracy, and hetero-graphy are used for multimodal and multilingual literacies, unlike the previous set that refers to reading or writing in a more traditional sense. There are more serious theoretical differences behind some of the other terms above. Terms like metrolinguistics, fragmented multilingualism, and ludic Englishes have been presented as an urban and late modern phenomenon in the context of recent forms of globalization. However, I don't treat translingual practice as new or recent. Though we have fascinating new communicative modes in contemporary times, especially in the context of new technology, I treat the practices of meaning-making as arising from a common underlying human competence. In fact, there is evidence of such practices in past modes of communication in precolonial and non-Western communities. I favor recovering a knowledge of these occluded communicative practices, and theorizing the continuities. In fact, in Chapter 3 I will show that these practices are not new to the West either. They have always been there in everyday communication and literacies, though unacknowledged by the dominant discourses and institutions. It is the ideologies of monolingualism that are new in both academic and institutional life. My approach also deviates from terms such as translanguaging, dynamic bilingualism, and pluri-lingualism which have hitherto been defined largely in cognitive terms. Scholars in applied linguistics who favor these terms have been more concerned with defining translingual practices as involving a different type of cognitive competence. Working against the Chomskyan model, they have developed the implications of multi-competence (Cook, 1999) and theorized multilingual competence as qualitatively different from monolingualism (Franceschini, 2011). Although this is an important project, it faces the danger of treating translingual practice as a solitary mental activity. I argue that we have to treat meaning-making as a social practice that engages holistically with ecological and contextual affordances. Though there are implications for cognition, I define this form of competence in fundamentally social and practice-based terms later in the book (in Chapter 9). I also have reservations against terms like fragmented or truncated multilingualism (Blommaert, 2010). These terms treat translingual practice as deficient. They assume a purported "whole" language as the norm, forgetting that wholeness is a social and ideological construction that people provide to their language resources. We must also be wary of terms that celebrate hybrid textual products, such as codemeshing. As mentioned earlier, it is possible to generate diverse products that approximate dominant norms and still manage to represent multiple identities. The translingual orientation therefore focuses on practices and processes rather than products in my approach.

We have to ask if we really need new labels to talk about translingual communicative practices. What about existing terms like *codeswitching* and *code mixing*? Traditionally, codeswitching was distinguished from code mixing on the basis that the former required bilingual competence (Romaine, 1989). It was assumed that one required fairly advanced competence in both relevant languages to switch between them in contextually appropriate ways with rhetorical and social significance. Code mixing constitutes borrowings which are appropriated into one's language so that using them doesn't require bilingual competence. Borrowed words are treated as part of the appro-priating language so much so that they are not identified as belonging to an alien language. There are several problems with these distinctions. Borrowings can be rhetorically significant, as in the examples we found from M.I.A.'s lyrics. And also, to codeswitch, bilingual competence is not always needed. Rajani's mother and uncle don't have advanced proficiency in English, and yet they can switch into English phrases as needed in their conversation. At this point, it becomes difficult to distin-guish between code mixing and codeswitching. More importantly, there is an assumption that the codes involved in the mix or the switch come from separate and whole languages. In translingual practice, one can adopt language resources from different communities without "full" or "perfect" competence in them (as traditionally defined), and these modes of hybridity can be socially and rhetorically significant.

It is important to note that codeswitching and mixing are themselves changing in definition as scholars try to relate to contemporary forms of multilingualism. Some now acknowledge that one can codeswitch without bilingual competence (Auer, 1999), and others doubt the difference between borrowing, mixing, and switching as they see them all as having rhetorical significance (Eastman, 1992). Though this expansion of meanings is salutary, it is important to note that scholars still operate within a monolingual framework as they perceive the codes involved as coming from and leading to distinct language systems. Consider Auer's (1999) integration of these terms into a cline. His model projects that codeswitching leads to code mixing when the switched items become more integrated into the borrowing language. As they develop further in time, mixing leads to fused lects, which constitute a new hybrid language. At this point in the cline, the languages in contact have sedimented into a new grammatical system where the appropriated codes lose their social or rhetorical distinctiveness. In contrast to this approach, translingual practice holds that it is possible for words to be meshed into another language and still play significant functions for voice, values, and identity. Since Auer seems to assume autonomous language systems, his model treats codes as constituting rhetorically significant switching or insignificant lects based on their level of embeddedness in the languages they are meshed into. For translingual practice, which adopts a more dynamic orientation to language systems and semiotic resources, mobile codes can freely merge to take on significant meaning and new indexicalities in practice. Also, while sedimentation is real, the evolving language "system" is still open to being appropriated for new contexts and purposes with new meanings. Thus, despite the advances in the definitions of codeswitching and code mixing, the assumption of separately systematized languages prevents scholars from accommodating the full range of meanings and practices which inform translingual orientation. Though translingual orientation is distinctive from other existing terms then, we can still make a space for using codeswitching and mixing in a qualified way in specific contexts. In cases of clear grammatical sedimentation, with certain language varieties identified by appropriate local ideologies, we can distinguish which "language" a word gets borrowed from or a phrase gets switched into.

New questions to be explored

As we treat communicative practices from a translingual orientation, there are new questions for language-related fields, such as applied linguistics, sociolinguistics, rhetoric/composition, and literacy. There are two foci to this exploration in this book: one is research-based, and the other is pedagogical. To describe the research focus first, we need more knowledge on the strategies people adopt to produce and interpret translingual modes of communication. Though many scholars have identified this important communicative practice in diverse domains, we haven't gone far beyond the product-oriented level of describing their form and features. We need more insights into the production, reception, and circulation of these texts, and the implications of these processes for the meanings that are co-constructed in spatio-temporal context. This book focuses on describing the communicative strategies that make up translingual practice, thus moving beyond product to process, and exploring the implications for meaning construction, language acquisition, and social relations.

The pedagogical implications of these translingual practices also need more exploration. Some scholars have started complaining that advances in theorization of translingual practices have far outstripped pedagogical implementation (see Creese and Blackledge, 2010; Tardy, 2011). How do teachers translate theory and research findings for their classrooms in order to develop competence in these practices among their students? This book treats as one of its important goals the development of the language proficiencies needed for global citizenship. However, I don't consider the pedagogical domain as a passive and secondary site where research and theory are applied after the fact. The pedagogical domain is itself a site of complex translingual practices and generates useful insights into communicative practices. Students bring to the classroom the translingual practices they engage in outside the classroom. Furthermore, pedagogy is a very challenging domain where the relevance of new communicative orientations will be hotly contested and scrupulously tested, helping us examine their practicality and usefulness. The notion of bounded languages, with neatly patterned grammatical structures of their own, has been an asset for product-oriented teaching. The norms and standards that come with monolingual orientation have served as a benchmark for language assessment and social stratification for a long time. The translingual orientation disturbs these arrangements. Interestingly, a publisher was hesitant to offer a contract for this book purely on pedagogical grounds. The editor wrote to me her fears, summarizing the concerns of her reviewers, saying "to work on the development of code meshing strategies with students could be undermining rather than empowering in academic ELT contexts, and could confuse teachers who are more familiar with promoting language as used within academic genres as well as students who are under pressure to conform to conventions of academic writing if they are to get the recognition they deserve." This book takes up this challenge. I show the classroom as a potent site where students may develop a critical attitude toward existing norms but also develop the repertoires and strategies required for social success. I develop pedagogies that teachers may find useful to help students communicate along, against, and beyond the dominant norms without disregarding them. It is possible to modify, appropriate, and renegotiate dominant norms as one adopts them.

The pedagogical focus of this book is on my primary areas of teaching: English language and literacy. As a lingua franca with a dominant global status and imperial history, English invites a special consideration in communication and pedagogy. English is the language most people in the world use for contact purposes. There is a unique place for this language in global contact zones, as people adopt this language to engage with diverse communities. We have to ask how English is participating in these translingual practices. As people all over the world appropriate the resources of English according to their own norms and values, accommodate them into their existing language repertoires, and shuttle between English and diverse local languages for communication, the translingual orientation also explains their competence and practices better. However, there is an interesting paradox in this approach that needs to be addressed. If the translingual orientation questions the separation of languages, how is it possible that we can limit the discussion to English language teaching alone?

Doesn't this treatment reify the status of English as a separate language? To some extent, this book makes a concession to the existing institutional and pedagogical arrangements that structure teaching into separate languages. However, my research treatment and pedagogical recommendations go on to situate the development of English proficiency in relation to repertoire building with other codes and languages. I am also pragmatic in acknowledging dominant language ideologies that posit a homogeneous language called "English." Despite the well-motivated theoretical assumptions driving this book, social and educational institutions consider English to be a separate language and define proficiency in terms unique to English. I prefer to engage with these attitudes and ideologies, to critique them, and also to suggest how translingual practice might provide a more complex understanding of competence for global citizenship. In fact, as I mentioned above, translingual practice is not incapable of generating products that approximate socially sanctioned norms in some contexts for strategic reasons. The translingual orienation enables one to develop repertoires and practices that allow shuttling between different norms.

A second concern relating to my choice of pedagogical focus is the orientation to literacy. If the translingual orientation transcends the separation of modalities, it might be asked if it is possible to address literacy separately from conversation, digital communication, and other language events. This book will develop an integrated orientation to language skills and modalities in its focus on literacy. For me, translingual strategies in conversations have implications for writing. For this reason, I focus equally on conversational strategies in contact situations and show their implications for literacy events. I go on to define texts in more holistic terms as emerging from diverse semiotic resources and social interactions, drawing from the fullest range of ecological resources.

Before I move on to pedagogical considerations in Chapter 9, I first explore what we mean by proficiency, communicative success, and meaning-making in translingual practice. I begin by situating the new communicative orientation in a broader theoretical framework. In the next chapter, I outline the theoretical developments that have contributed to defining communication in monolingual and monolithic terms. I ask what assumptions led to the monolingual orientation, and what social conditions account for its dominance. I then outline the social conditions that compel us to seek new explanatory models for emergent communicative modes. I introduce the theoretical constructs that help develop the alternative paradigm of translingual practice.

In Chapter 3, I adopt a historical orientation. I recover traditions of translingual communication and literacy in precolonial East and premodern West. I show also that while modernity and colonization promoted ideologies intended to suppress translingual practices, earlier communities treated languages as mobile semiotic resources and freely appropriated them for their contact purposes. Even after colonization, the dominant codes and literacies imposed on peripheral communities have been appropriated locally. The imposed codes and literacies became part of local translingual practice. I identify communicative processes and attitudes from the past that are conducive to theorizing and teaching translingual practice in the present.

In Chapter 4, I turn to models of English language in the contact zone. As scholars theorize the changes English is going through in its global spread, they are still adopting a largely monolingual orientation. Global English is treated as a bounded system with shared norms at different levels of national, regional, or international scales. Scholars are designing normative models that contain the pluralization of English or occlude the processes of mobility and diversity. I review current models such as World Englishes, English as an International Language, and English as a Lingua Franca, and redefine English as a form of translingual practice.

Such an orientation involves perceiving English not as a language held together by a commonly shared or systematized grammar, but perceiving communication as involving heterogeneous and changing norms. When grammatical norms are treated as ontological constructs, with an objective reality of their own, this may hide the inherent diversity in all communication and the practices that generate meaning. Therefore, the focus should not be on shared form, but on the pragmatic strategies people use to negotiate difference and achieve intelligibility. In Chapter 5, I formulate the strategies that facilitate communicative success through an analysis of an interaction between multilingual students in English. This formulation helps to take further the practice-based models of other scholars in global English studies.

In Chapter 6, I turn to writing. I consider the difficult question that writing is less open to pluralization of norms as it is a high-stakes and gatekept activity. Multilingual students and scholars are especially concerned about avenues for voice in English academic writing. I demonstrate how the translingual practice of codemeshing may enable multilingual users to both recognize the dominant conventions and also insert qualified changes for voice. I consider how such hybrid texts may initiate pluralization of texts from within, in relation to the existing norms, without sacrificing one's prospects for success in academic contexts. I show the implications for the high-stakes activity of academic publishing.

How can we help students engage in such forms of translingual textual production and reception? As texts offer different modalities and resources for meaning-making, they have to be negotiated in slightly different ways from conversations. I expand the negotiation strategies of conversational interactions offered in Chapter 5 to redefine literacy in Chapter 7. Based on an ethnography of a writing classroom, I identify the strategies that students themselves adopt from their socialization in multilingual environments. These are the strategies they already use to negotiate texts in contemporary contact zones outside the classroom.

From the microlevel analysis of texts and talk in classrooms and interpersonal negotiations, I turn to the big picture in Chapter 8. I adopt a spatiotemporal orientation to context to consider the dynamics of language mobility. I analyze the ways migrants recontextualize translocal spaces to make their English index new meanings and values. I argue for a treatment of geopolitical spaces as negotiable and generative of new norms and conventions, against a static and deterministic view of context.

I focus on the question of language learning in Chapter 9. Understandably, competence would work differently in my framework from traditional models that have theorized language acquisition in terms of separated and autonomous languages.

Dichotomies such as native/non-native, learner/user, and interlanguage/target language have dominated studies on language acquisition to elevate the competence of the "owners" of a language and denigrate those of others. The chapter will theorize language development in a more dynamic fashion that integrates everyday learning ✓ and use of the repertoires people bring with them, before making relevant pedagogical recommendations.

I conclude the book with an exploration of what translingual practice implies for cosmopolitan relations in the global contact zones. <u>Translingual practice results from and enables global citizenship</u>. Though we have made considerable progress in understanding how language is further diversifying in the context of globalization, we have more work to do in understanding how we can communicate across these differences. What strategies and dispositions enable us to enjoy effective cosmopolitan relationships that allow us to be different and yet collaborative? The concluding chapter takes this question forward and offers a model of cosmopolitanism that enables people to retain their differences and achieve community in global contact zones.

A note on terminology

Finally, I must explicate the terms used in this book. When one develops a new paradigm, there are challenges created for the language used to discuss it. The assumptions motivating the earlier constructs can militate against their use for a discussion of the new paradigm. However, it is difficult to completely change all the terms and metaphors informing the language of a field or a subject. Often, the only terms we have for discussion belong to the previous paradigm. It is sometimes difficult to discuss the new paradigm without using existing terminology. Furthermore, not all the assumptions motivating the earlier set of terms are fully explicit. It is common, therefore, for scholars arguing for new paradigms to unwittingly slip into metaphors colored by traditional assumptions. For example, while Rampton (1999a) argues for a post-structuralist orientation to language, his construct *crossing* may give the impression that he believes in bounded and owned languages which are crossed into and out of. Though I don't claim to have ironed out all the implications of the terms and metaphors used in this book, I do explain the rationale for the central terms. In general, I tend to be sparing in my use of neologisms, having always disliked convoluted poststructuralist prose featuring terms under erasure or freshly minted.

The most glaring challenge in this book is the need to use labeled languages (such as Tamil or English) or English varieties (such as Sri Lankan English or Nigerian English) when the translingual approach holds that we are dealing with language resources ✓ that are mobile, fluid, and hybrid. However, using these terms is not just a practical necessity for analytical reasons, it is also motivated by my theoretical position. The translingual orientation posits that while language resources are mobile, they acquire labels and identities through situated uses in particular contexts and get reified through language ideologies. Therefore, labeled languages and language varieties have a reality for social groups. More significantly, they are an important form of identity for these groups. Rather than treating these labels as false consciousness then, I hold such labels and identities as having an empowering and affirmative function for social groups. The main difference is that I don't treat these labeled languages and varieties as having an ontological status. They don't have an objective reality out there. They are constructs that are always open to reconstitution and relabeling. However, this is not an abstract philosophical distinction I am making here. There are profound differences for language use and relationships, as the pages to follow will show. For example, the translingual orientation will motivate groups to rethink other constructs such as sole language ownership, language purity, and proficiency.

The same argument applies to the notion of *community*. Although I use the term community in the book, I develop the position in Chapter 2 where I treat all contexts as contact zones and heterogeneous. While the translingual orientation challenges the notion of communities as bounded, territorial, and homogeneous, this doesn't mean that people don't enjoy collective identities based on the diverse considerations that bring them together. People provide tentative coherence to their communities through symbolic and ideological resources. Though communities at national, regional, and even global terms are possible, we mustn't think of them as ontological. These are changing, relational and, most of all, inherently heterogeneous, as they are always socially constructed. In the final chapter, I go on to theorize about how we might affirm diverse local communities and still construct translocal cosmopolitan identities through suitable uses of our language resources.

To move to constructs at a more microlevel of consideration, the translingual orientation generates challenges relating to language/learner identities. The terms *native/ non-native* have been critiqued, as they are based on birthright in specific languages. However, I need a way to distinguish those who traditionally claim native ownership over the language and others who claim English as an additional language in their repertoire, as I intend to demonstrate how both groups may adopt similar translingual practices to negotiate intelligibility. I also have the practical need to discuss how language learners have been discussed in previous scholarship in order to demonstrate the limitations and move the field to a different orientation to both groups. Therefore, I still use the term *native English speaker* (abbreviated as NES) for the former and *multilinguals* for the latter. However, I go on to demonstrate that both groups of speakers have the capacity to use English in relation to the other codes in society and their personal repertoires. When I refer to their capacity for translingual practice, I label both groups as *translinguals*.

The use of the terms *practices* and *products* of communication also requires an explanation. Communicative products (in the form of form, texts, modes, or genres) don't enjoy an objective ontological status from a translingual perspective. All that we have in communication are practices. However, for analytical purposes, we must discuss constructs like grammar or norms, and language patterns such as dialects, registers, and genres. The translingual perspective posits that language practices lead to sedimentation of certain forms/patterns via repeated situated use over time, and their gradual shaping into grammars, norms, and other products. The caveat is that these norms and products are constituted by practices and are always reconstructed to be meaningful. If we adopt the orientation that these norms and products are always changing, variable, and constructed, it will make a difference in how we orientate to language use and learning, as the chapters that follow make clear.

Finally, we need to adopt some clarity over the status of *shared norms* in a book that emphasizes the inherent diversity and heterogeneity of all communication. The notion of sedimentation suggests that certain relatively shared norms do develop over time. However, the fact that they don't have an ontological status would dictate that we don't base our explanations or ground communication on shared or homogeneous norms. In fact, what we consider as shared may mask a lot of diversity which our ideological spectacles may not allow us to acknowledge. In Chapter 8, I will demonstrate that there might be greater scope for temporary shared norms at the local level, with less sharedness at the translocal level. In both contexts, however, sharedness is achieved and not given. Furthermore, at both levels, a reliance on sharedness may create the wrong expectation in communication, as interlocutors would rule anything they think of as unshared as erroneous or deviant. The objective of the book is to consider how diversity is normal and how sharedness is socially achieved. Though evolving norms can guide communication in future interactions and provide a measure of efficiency in communication, it is important to treat meanings and norms as co-constructed so that interlocutors are open to negotiating difference. In this book, therefore, the focus is more on the uses that are non-shared, "deviant," and "erroneous"—not because nothing is ever shared, but because the negotiation of such usage explains the basic practice in all communication. In other words, it is sharedness and homogeneity that are the exception. Difference is the norm on which communicative success is built.

Conclusion

My orientation to language and literacy is informed by my own background and investments in this topic. It is unwise for any author or scholar to overlook the ways in which their experiences shape their thinking and research. However, we have to adopt appropriate measures to triangulate our findings, make certain that we offer suitable evidence for our arguments, and adopt enough transparency in the research and writing process for readers to make their own interpretations. Research in the post-Enlightenment context is not based on claims of objectivity, but on honesty about one's values and responsibility toward the academic and larger community. As readers will see, my positions on language and literacy are based on a disciplined collection of data and its rigorous analysis. I have adopted a range of qualitative methods—featuring discourse analysis, ethnography, and sociolinguistic interviews—in a range of contexts to study translingual texts and talk.

Before I offer a reading of my data, let me be upfront about my biases. I am a multilingual speaker of English from a former British colony, Sri Lanka. I grew up in a community with rich translingual practices, as we shuttled across languages and cultures, even as the relationship between the groups became charged. I was surrounded by Sinhala, Tamil, Malay, and creole versions of Dutch and Portuguese, in addition to English. I consider it a mission to rediscover the South Asian tradition of translingual communication and cosmopolitanism that was historically practiced but increasingly suppressed by monolingual ideologies entering the region. As I have turned out to be a teacher and scholar of English, trained in the research centers of the West and currently teaching in an American institution, I am intrigued by the tensions between the dominant constructs in academic discourses and lived experiences in non-Western communities. My status as a migrant in the West, as part of the Sri Lankan Tamil diaspora which fled its traditional homeland in the 1980s, provides an additional investment to a search for effective cosmopolitan practices. Compelled to think of my identity in transnational terms, I am motivated to develop healthy forms of global citizenship. These tensions and investments shape my exploration of translingual life at the contact zone.

2

THEORIZING TRANSLINGUAL PRACTICE

It is quite understandable that readers are skeptical of much new-fangled terminology in academia these days. Terms like *translingual practice* may similarly sound outlandish and unnecessary. However, we must be open to the fact that the terms and labels we already use in linguistics are not innocent. They are informed by competing orientations to language and society. In this chapter, I first show how the existing terms belonging to the monolingual orientation are informed by values and philosophies that gained dominance during a particular historic period in relation to particular social conditions. These values in fact became dominant very recently—specifically, eighteenth-century modernity. They are also associated with a particular geographical and cultural location—namely, Western Europe. Though traces of these values have been evident in previous periods and places, a confluence of social and philosophical developments accounts for their rise to dominance in eighteenth-century Europe. After delineating the values that make up the monolingual paradigm and identifying the social and philosophical movements that account for their dominance, I will introduce the emergent orientations to language informed by a practice-based view of translingual communication that favors cosmopolitan social relationships.

The monolingual orientation

The monolingual paradigm is built upon a set of interrelated assumptions that became solidified in Western Europe around the eighteenth century. Roy Harris considers this orientation "a western myth" (Harris, 2009, p. 43) and Michel de Certeau calls this "an occidental ambition" (de Certeau, 1984, p. 133). de Certeau locates its rise in "the ideology of the Enlightenment" (de Certeau, 1984, p. 166). He associates this orientation with the rise of empirical science, industrialization, and bureaucracy. Collectively, these movements display a positivistic orientation to reality, transforming experiences into manageable and disciplined knowledge. The monolingual orientation seemed to promise efficiency, control, and transparency, features valued by the Enlightenment.

What follows is a brief narrative on the rise of the monolingual orientation. The range of social and philosophical movements that go into the construction of this orientation did not always work in concert, and did not go without challenge. There are also diverse points of the origins to this story. However, I am going to simplify the story for purposes of clarity.

Put simply, the monolingual orientation is made up of the following ideas:

- Language = Community = Place.
- 1 language = 1 identity.
- Language as a self-standing system.
- Languages as pure and separated from each other.
- The locus of language as cognition rather than social context, or mind rather than matter.
- Communication as based on grammar rather than practice, and form isolated from its ecological embeddedness.

The following are the key movements that played a role in formulating and popularizing the above notions:

- Romanticism
- Enlightenment and Modernity
- Industrialization
- Nation-State formation
- Structuralism
- Colonization and imperialism.

An important starting point in the story is the Romantic movement. Johannes Gottfried Herder and other thinkers of this period defined the essence of a community through its language. Language embodied the innermost spirit, thought, and values of the community. And what made each language unique was the spirit of the community it embodied and the collective experiences in a place. Both language and community were rooted in a place, which helped territorialize them in a specific location. This equivalence of language, community, and place has been widely called the "Herderian triad" (see Bauman and Briggs, 2000; Blommaert and Verschueren, 1992). The organic connection between all three elements, typical of the Romantic Movement, has many serious implications for communication and social life.

Firstly, the Herderian triad made each language unique and even separate. Each language was stamped with the essence of the particular community it was associated with. The language was capable of naturally expressing only the values and thoughts belonging to that community. This idea made the community the owners of the language. Others were illegitimate users. They may not be able to express the thoughts of their community life and values in someone else's language. The Herderian triad also territorializes language. A language that moves to another place is in alien territory. It cannot express the spirit of the other community or become part of that place.

This ideology also has implications for community. One's language and territory made a community homogeneous and pure. If individuals in the community were open to influences from elsewhere, the thinking made clear that the spirit of the community couldn't be expressed best in other languages. Those who were closest to the soil of the land were most representative of the community. In this sense, there was a mystical spirit from the territory that found expression in the language and the community. Languages borrowed from other communities couldn't embody that spirit well. This way, communities were also separated from each other, with their own values and location. Communities were thus bound together as homogeneous units with their own internal harmony and essence. Mobility makes people out of place.

The Herderian triad also leads to places being colonized for one language or another. Each language is associated with the geographical space it is located in. That is the expected or even authorized language for that place. Another language can be defined as an interloper and prevented from being used in that place. This orientation can potentially limit the range of languages that can be used in a place in social interactions. It gives justification for a community to exert its own language on others sharing its place. Since there are always diverse communities in a place, we can guess how this orientation can become a colonizing activity. The language of the dominant community can be imposed on others. Minority languages and communities in a place, in addition to newly entering languages, lose their claim to that place and probably get suppressed.

Ideologies such as the Herderian triad answered many of the needs European communities had around that time. Though Herder himself didn't theorize these connections—and, in fact, may have opposed some of these consequences— the Herderian triad spawned other discourses that facilitated these connections. These discourses helped in the resistance by local communities against the dominance of the Holy Roman Empire and the feudal social formation. Local communities developed distinct identities, in separation from the collective identity in the Empire. Language helped give identity and boundedness to each community. Furthermore, the Herderian triad gave a way for each community to feel proud of their own vernacular. There was something natural and right about the connection of the community with its own language and place. The territoriality of this connection also made each community claim a natural right to its own place. We can guess how these ideologies strengthened the nationalism and nation-state formation that was underway.

However, in order to make this connection between language, community, and place operational, languages had to be invented. If language is basically a fluid set of "mobile resources," we can understand the challenges in formulating a stable and homogeneous set of "immobile languages" (Blommaert, 2010, p. 43) to represent the community and place. Though efforts at language standardization, purification, and codification in many communities are often considered heroic efforts of progress, we have to also consider the ulterior motivations behind them. This is often an arbitrary process of grouping diverse semiotic resources together, attaching a label to name them, and claiming ownership of them. As in the case of English, it was not always achieved in one decisive act. Consider how English began as a set of mobile resources belonging to three tribes in North Europe. After these dialects migrated to the British Isles, they gradually got labeled as a single language and territorialized as the language of England. The efforts of those like King Alfred, Samuel Johnson, and others constituted this protracted effort to construct a language out of the disparate codes involved in the contact between diverse tribes. Even though Johnson acknowledged the importance of migration and contact that would continue to hybridize English (as reflected in the epigraph to this book), his lexicographical effort was meant to standardize it. Language standardization also happened with the assistance of schools, textbooks, mass media, and other institutions to make a selected set of codes index elite values, mostly according to class and regional hierarchies—an ideological and social process which Agha (2003) calls ["enregisterment."] It is fascinating how a collection of mobile semiotic resources achieves a uniform identity, restricted to a new home, and made to identify one group of people. The rest is history. English is now the language of the English and of England. The connection is circular and self-perpetuating, that is, the language identifies the people and the place; the place and people identify the language.

There are also implications for identity in these developments. The Herderian triad defines a person a native of a single language. There is one language, belonging uniquely to one's speech community, which defines one's identity. It also roots a person to a community and a place. Furthermore, it gives legitimacy to the so-called native speaker, and gives him/her the authority to define how the language is to be used. We are thus authorities of the language we own. On the other hand, this move also makes us interlopers in other languages. Others who use our language are interlopers into ours. One's identity is thus inextricably tied to one language, one place, and one community. The identity and authority we develop in a native language come with a price, however. Individuals are fixed as belonging to this or that identity. We are supposed to be born into that identity, based on the language, community, and place that locates our birth. In terms of language, we have the ability to speak our "native" language intuitively and enjoy authority in it. On the other hand, we are supposed to be incompetent or inauthentic in the languages of other communities. What might mark our variations and differences in using the other languages are treated as deficiencies and evidence of our alienation. Our right to use semiotic resources categorized as belonging to another language, place, or community comes into question.

The notion that language characterizes the inner essence of a people gets further interiorized and gains a cognitive dimension in Enlightenment thinking. As the mind gains more priority over the heart or soul of the Romantics, the seat of language also changes in the discourses of those like Descartes and Locke (see Bauman and Briggs, 2000). Associating language with the mind generates some new implications. Language is tied to thinking. It becomes the medium of human reason, elevating us from other animals. As we seek to demonstrate the logic of the mind, we also show the systematicity and logic of our language. This philosophical move also comes at a price. Language is removed from the material and social settings in which it functions in the fullest ecological context to produce meaning. Language becomes separated and systematized from other environmental affordances. We lose the notion that languages are mobile, heterogeneous, and hybrid resources that combine with other semiotic resources to make meaning in context. Enlightenment thinkers postulate an abstract and autonomous language system in an abstract and autonomous cognitive system for meaning-making activity. We are left with the notion that it is the cognitive domain of language that is superior, and its social and material manifestations secondary. This orientation will lead later to making distinctions on the rational and logical nature of certain languages, with damaging consequences for communities perceived to own less developed languages. More advanced languages indicate more advanced minds.

Such Cartesian thinking leads to further forms of interiorization of language in the hands of Chomsky, a self-proclaimed disciple of Descartes. The Chomskyan influence entrenches the dualistic way of looking at language, that is, mind over matter, cognition over context, individual over society. With language and the ability to communicate located in mind, certain other implications follow, that is, language is incorruptible by the environment or society; language doesn't need environment or society for its meaning-making potential; the capacity for language and meaning is innate; and all languages have a universal grammar deriving from our innate cognitive dispositions. This development leads to a lack of significance for the diversity of language. The dark side of this thinking is that the "universal" values and grammar of language are theorized in terms of the values of the dominant communities.

A major development in the gradual systematization of language is its definition as a self-standing system. Structuralism develops this orientation to language as autonomous. Though starting from an orientation to language in the work of Saussure, Structuralism became a broader movement beyond linguistics. Not only language and text, but mind, society, and culture are also treated as *sui generis*. These domains had their inner consistency and maintained themselves without the need for factors outside their system to run or define them. Their autonomy was established by the fact that elements within each domain defined themselves in relation to each other. They thus made a tightly woven and integrated system. If one element was taken out, the whole system would crumble. This was a good philosophical move to make the codification of language permanent and rigid. However, it also isolated language from other semiotic resources, modalities, and environmental affordances.

Structuralism has helped turn language into an objectively analyzable product. Such a move lends itself to the analytical need to conveniently circumscribe the domain of analysis. Language had to be isolated from other domains such as society, culture, individuals, and politics and even the inquirer for a proper understanding. These assumptions reduced language to an abstract, passive, detached, and static product. Even time had to be collapsed into the structure—that is, elevating synchrony over diachrony—for proper analysis. These philosophical moves thus complemented the Enlightenment orientation to inquiry as objective, empirical, and positivistic.

These orientations also turned language into a transparent system. Language provided access to external and psychological reality. It served as a conduit to reality and truth which, for Enlightenment thinkers, was absolute and attainable. This expectation leads to efforts to use and theorize language in ways that would give access to uniform, value-free, and universal meaning. There is an effort to define language in a way that the diverse spatial and temporal contingencies would not have any bearing on its meaning-making potential. These are convenient philosophical moves in the context of industrialization, science, capitalism, and bureaucracy. The efficiency needed for these movements for what they define as progress leads to molding language as a transparent and efficient medium. Language has to serve the ends of quantification and control. The sharedness and universality of norms is one way to ensure this transparency and objectivity of meaning.

The ownership of languages, their separation from each other, and their superiority based on their access to truth and knowledge can understandably set off a contest over which language is most conducive to progress. In many cases, this question is simply an excuse for certain communities to lay claim over other territories and communities, which have been conveniently defined in antagonistic terms. Such considerations can lead to comparison, competition, and conquest. As we have already seen, these processes first start within the nation-state. Minority languages within the nation-state are defined as irrelevant or inferior. They can then be suppressed or left to die.

The story of colonization and imperialism takes off from the discourses and conditions set in motion by the previously reviewed movements. The European nations which take pride in their superiority and in the ways in which their languages serve scientific/technological progress now move beyond their nation-states to impose their languages on other communities. Notions such as one language being more efficient as a shared resource for meaning-making by everyone at the global level, and superior languages helping in human development while backward languages made redundant, are examples of such technocratic discourses that assist in this imperialistic activity. Thomas Macaulay's "Minute on Indian Education" (1835), which offers a justification for teaching English in South Asia, is a good example of the thinking described above. He argues that English embodies superior knowledge resources, offers a more complex and rational language for development, and connects local communities with other advanced communities. Therefore, he argues that English should be preferred over the local languages, including regional linguae francae such as Arabic and Sanskrit, enabling local people to develop their own languages on the model of English. We have come a long way from the mobile resources of the three tribes who migrated to the British Isles. These fluid codes have been solidified into a monolithic language, territorialized as the language of a developed country, defined as cognitively more advanced, and exported to other countries as a product. The language aspires to serve as a global medium of efficient communication in the network of communities centered around the technologically more developed Europe.

Changing social conditions, emergent communicative modes

The discourses I have described above lead to constructing a form of transnational connectedness, which scholars have labeled *modernist globalization* (see Hall, 1997). Keeping in mind that globalization is not a new phenomenon and that there have been other models of globalization preceding the developments I have articulated since the eighteenth century, modernist globalization can be defined as being enabled by the ideologies of the European Enlightenment and based on spreading its values to other communities. It might appear ironic that the Herderian triad, based on celebrating the territoriality and homogeneity of local communities, should lead to translocal connections of this nature. However, it is not difficult to understand the implications. When communities take pride in their uniqueness, separateness, and superiority, they attempt to impose themselves on others with good moral justification. The translocal connection that discourses of modernist globalization promoted is unilateral, segregated, and hierarchical. It was motivated by a belief in the superiority of Western European communities (the center), and their power to integrate less powerful communities (the periphery) in a dependent network of relationships. Knowledge, values, and technology were expected to travel one way from the center to the periphery, with the latter providing the raw materials to build the social and economic institutions of the former.

However, social processes are messy and unpredictable. We shouldn't also discount the agency of human beings, even those from less developed communities, to resist and renegotiate social processes for their own interests. What has become clear in more recent years (perhaps since the 1980s) is another discourse on globalization which encourages different geopolitical relationships. We are now cognizant that the very channels and networks built to impose the one-sided flow of knowledge and values of modernity have served as the means to spread the knowledge and values of those on the receiving end (Chambers, 2002). Current discourses theorize globalization as more bi- or even multi-directional, with cultural and material resources flowing through multiple paths and constructing social spaces which are more diverse and power hierarchies that are less neat (see Appadurai, 1996). The technologies and institutions of modernist globalization have led to increased migration, internationally collaborative production networks, and more rapid flow of information. Advances in digital technology have further reduced time/space differences and intensified the levels of contact and collaboration between communities. It is not that these developments are creating a more egalitarian relationship between global communities; scholars like Hall (1997) theorize that even these developments can be manipulated by powerful groups and institutions for their own advantage. However, as geopolitical inequalities and power differences are uneven, they are negotiable by diverse communities for their own advantage. The revised geopolitical relations and discourses have been called *postmodern globalization* (Hall, 1997).

If modernist globalization was associated with the values of territoriality and homogeneity, postmodern globalization celebrates mobility and diversity. These developments have led to social conditions which are different from those promoted by the Herderian triad. The multilateral flow of people, things, and ideas across borders has made more visible mixed forms of community and language in highly diversified geographical spaces. Scholars are constructing new terms to describe life in these social spaces. *Super-diversity* is a term being used to describe the layered, meshed, and overlapping relationships between communities in many urban spaces (Vertovec, 2007). This social formation is markedly different from the earlier orientation to ethnic communities occupying their own niches even as they lived beside and interacted with other communities maintaining their boundedness. In super-diversity, the boundaries are difficult to discern. A term I use more in this book is *contact zones.* Introduced by Mary Louise Pratt (1991), this notion reminds us that we have to shift our focus from communities to the spaces where diverse social groups interact. There are patterns of interaction and communication that are yet to be theorized for contact zones, as we have been preoccupied with the formation and maintenance of bounded communities. It is becoming clear that *contact zones* is not an antonym for *communities*. All spaces are contact zones. As "communities" are treated as less homogenous and bounded, we are forced to understand the patterns of contact within and between social groups.

There are serious implications for language and communication behind all these developments. The discourses of modernist globalization attempted to keep languages separate, even as the dominant European languages spread to new lands and communities. The relationship between languages was expected to be hierarchical and segregated, as we see in Macaulay's proposal. However, in the social relations facilitated by postmodern globalization, languages relate to each other in fluid ways and, therefore, become more hybrid in form. These social and ideological developments explain the prominence of codemeshing, crossing, and polyglot dialog which I presented in the introductory chapter. The big question now is how to account for successful communication and meaning-making in postmodern contexts of translingual contact. It is becoming clear that the monolingual models we constructed under the influence of modernist ideals are inadequate for our purposes. Models based on fixed systems, grammatical competence, and homogeneous communities are not useful when we are dealing with plural languages and interlocutors. Unpredictability and diversity are the norm in postmodern globalization, conditions that modernist and monolingual discourses treated as the exception or attempted to control through their models and institutions.

Devising new paradigms to explain how communication works in contact zones is not just a theoretical need. People are always and already employing alternate practices to make meaning in the context of the mobile and multiple semiotic resources in their everyday life. Explicating the communicative strategies people have been adopting is the objective of this book. To give a preview of what is to come, we will see that people are not relying on ready-made meanings and forms (as posited by Structuralist language models) for communicative success in contact zones. Rather than moving top down to apply predefined knowledge from their language or cognitive system, people are working ground up to collaboratively construct meaning for semiotic resources which they are borrowing from diverse languages and symbol systems. They are co-constructing meaning by adopting reciprocal and adaptive negotiation strategies in their interactions. They are also not relying on words alone for meaning. They are aligning features in the environment, such as objects, bodies, setting, and participants to give meaning to words. All these strategies point to the need for an analytical trajectory diametrically opposed to the one adopted by modernity. We have to move away from system, cognition, and form to focus on *practice* in order to explain how communication works in the contact zone.

Emergent theoretical orientations

The term *practice* is becoming so clichéd in our field that we have to be mindful of the distinction being proposed in this book. Pennycook (2010), in his *Language as a Local Practice*, provides a useful theoretical perspective on the difference practice makes in communication. He takes care to emphasize that *practice* is not *function*. From the latter perspective, language is supposed to have a predefined form and meaning that is applied to an already existing social context to perform its functions. A practice-based *Practice + Generative* perspective, on the other hand, is open to form, functions, and meaning being generated through social activity. From this perspective, practice is not passive and secondary, but generative. The dichotomy between practice and its contrasting constructs (i.e., system, cognition, form) is also challenged, and their connections are perceived in more interactive and dynamic terms. The social and material context of practice also needs to be reconsidered. Context is often opposed to the cognitive, structural, and ideational locus of form. While the latter set of terms are treated as unchanging, primary, and basic, context is supposed to be a passive location for the application of cognition, structure, or abstract principles. A practice-based perspective views context (or locality) as itself generative. The features and conditions in the local context have implications for the meanings and forms that are generated. The process of communication also reflexively alters context, changing the terms of engagement and meaning. The meanings and forms that are thus created are situational, arising from the modes of alignment between participants, objects, and resources in the local ecology. We must note, therefore, that communication as a translingual practice involves a fundamental shift from the way communication has been theorized in modernist and monolingual orientations.

However, the practice-based perspective doesn't mean that the other competing constructs, such as form/grammar, structure/system, community, and cognition are disregarded. They have a role to play in translingual practice, but they don't remain autonomous and primary, nor do they have the same roles and definitions as in traditional models. They are redefined and reconfigured according to practice-based perspectives. Several scholars have started working against monolingual and modernist assumptions to develop alternate models. I introduce them below and indicate where I depart, in order to develop a model of translingual practice.

The model of integrationist linguistics developed by Roy Harris (2009) and his collaborators has contributed immensely to challenging the view of language as a fixed system with predefined meanings. The model posits that linguistic resources are interrelated and combine with other semiotic resources to make meaning. These resources don't come with fixed meanings, but gain referentiality through use. The model has also questioned the notion of standard language and theorized these norms as arbitrary social impositions. The framework has inspired many scholars today to deconstruct models of languages and language ideologies at various points in history to bring out the ulterior motives of colonizing and missionary agencies in the past (Pennycook and Makoni, 2005) and commercial and nation-state interests since then (Blommaert, 2010). However, integrationist linguistics works better as a model for deconstruction than reconstruction. In other words, it offers useful tools and perspectives for questioning dominant myths of languages as pure and fixed structures, but doesn't proceed too far in offering insights into the ways in which people do make meaning from fluid repertoires of semiotic resources in social practice. The school's overly philosophical orientation works somewhat against this reconstructive project. It hasn't developed an empirical tradition to observe language practice in social contexts in order to theorize the social dimensions of meaning-making.

Pennycook (2010) borrows from performative theorists such as Judith Butler (1990) and Michel de Certeau (1984) to theorize how form and meaning arise in and through social practice. He argues that form and meaning get sedimented, as language resources get used repeatedly and habitually in specific local contexts. Codes attain grammatical status and also begin to signify certain meanings by convention. This is a useful perspective on how the grammatical and referential value of languages changes over time and in different contexts. The theorization is also admirably from the ground up, as it doesn't resort to predefined forms or homogeneous communities to anchor meaning. It has the capability to explain how diverse interlocutors can adopt a heterogeneous mix of resources and still achieve meaning through local practice and sedimentation. However, this very ground up social constructionist perspective leads to some oversight. In moving completely away from language as fixed systems to the other end of the continuum, the perspective overlooks the interactional nature of communication. How does local practice relate to previously sedimented forms and norms that have arisen from the history of prior usage? Is meaning fully unilateral in arising from practices ground up, or is it a more dialectical process of negotiating dominant norms and conventions in terms of local practices? To appreciate this question, we have to ask if some language norms evolve from prior sedimentation to govern talk. This has implications for power. Does power arise afresh from each context of communication or are there power structures that exist relatively independently of language? What strategies do people use in local contexts to negotiate dominant ideologies and power structures as they create new meaning? To address these questions, we need a more social interactionist perspective than the theorization of de Certeau or the analytical approach of Pennycook would allow. We need to consider how people engage with each other, tailor their language uses reciprocally, display uptake, resist dominant conventions, and co-construct meanings in relation to existing norms and ideologies in actual interactions.

The school of language ideology (see Kroskrity, 2000; Silverstein, 1996; Agha, 2003) provides a more pragmatic and social orientation on the role of power and ideology in shaping meaning and communication. It throws more light on the process of

sedimentation by exploring how people's social values and assumptions (i.e., ideologies)
shape what counts as language, grammatical, and meaningful. Mobile semiotic resources
thus get organized (one might say arbitrarily) into fixed grammars and languages.
From this point of view, it is possible to explain the reality of notions such as standard
language, language purity, and grammatical systems. They are given coherence by the
language ideology of specific groups or communities of speakers. Therefore it is
important to analyze and theorize how people formulate and negotiate these language
ideologies (and forms and structures motivated by these ideologies) as they use diverse
semiotic resources in translingual practice. In this sense, translingual practice is not
easy, free, or egalitarian. At a more micro-level, the language ideology school also
adopts the construct *indexicality* to theorize how fluid and mobile resources begin to
point to (i.e., index) meanings. Semiotic resources index meanings through situated
use in relation to existing language ideologies. This process is similar to sedimentation.
However, the language ideology school also provides a social and ideological
perspective, as it explores how indexicalities require uptake from others in relation to
the values and ideologies which they bring to the interaction. Though these meanings are not set in stone—in fact, the usefulness of indexicality is that it can help
explain how meanings change for the same word or token in different times and
places—it also shows that they are not totally free or fluid either.

Despite the value of language ideology for an understanding of translingual practice,
there are also ways in which the school adopts a less complex notion of power and
social structure for my purposes. Blommaert's (2010) recent application of this school's
constructs for Global Englishes in his *Sociolinguistics of Globalization* reveals some
of the problematic issues. Though Blommaert is open to the fact that English can
gain new indexicalities in different communities, he also adopts a view of power and
ideology that is unilateral and treats the indexicals from certain less powerful communities as being unsuitable for mobility. His notion of "orders of indexicality"
applies power in a somewhat hierarchical and stratified manner, as I will explain
further in Chapter 8. Native speaker and developed communities define these orders
of indexicality on their terms. Though these norms are polycentric and accommodate
orders of indexicality from less developed communities, there is a strong sense in
Blommaert's treatment that the latter's resources are powerless and even deficient.
We don't see much negotiability of hierarchy, power, and dominant language
ideology in Blommaert's treatment. The data presented in the coming chapters shows
how the less powerful still adopt creative strategies to negotiate the dominant ideologies
and indexicals in their favor. They are quite successful in persuading more powerful
interlocutors to change their footing, renegotiate their norms, and reconstruct
meanings and form in context. To accommodate this possibility, I will adopt a notion
of social spaces and orders of indexicality as less rigidly stratified and more negotiable,
even though power-ridden. In fact, we have to acknowledge that there are competing language ideologies and indexicals in global social spaces, and that those of the less
powerful social groups cannot be written off.

A model that allows us to treat translingual practices as constrained by power and
yet open to renegotiation is Pratt's contact zones perspective, mentioned earlier. Pratt

Contact zones ✓

defines contact zones as "social spaces where cultures meet, clash, and grapple with each other, often in contexts of highly asymmetrical relations of power, such as colonialism, slavery, or their aftermaths as they are lived out in many parts of the world today" (Pratt, 1991, p. 34). She theorizes contact zones as social interactions between groups positioned differentially in power. However, their contact is generative. It produces new "literate arts of the contact zone" (Pratt, 1991, p. 40). The new genres evolving in these zones are translingual, showing the meshing of different or competing norms. Pratt demonstrates through fascinating examples how the new norms and genres evolving in the contact zones provide possibilities for resistance and voice for less powerful groups. She takes care to acknowledge, however, that these literate arts are also risky and prone to failure. Nothing is guaranteed. However, the possibilities she provides for renegotiating power and finding spaces for voice are salutary. The model thus accommodates a notion of power that is able to better explain the strategic interactions that renegotiate norms and indexicals, generating new meanings and patterns. Despite its usefulness, Pratt's metaphor of contact zones, originally introduced in a lecture and then published as a brief essay, requires further fleshing out. We need a closer analysis of contact zone interactions. How do different communities negotiate these interactions? What strategies do they adopt? What processes explain the emergence of the literate arts of the contact zone? These issues require empirical analysis, which the following chapters provide.

Pratt's model initiates a useful shift from a "linguistics of community" to a "linguistics of contact" (Pratt, 1987). She thus makes us attend to the liminal spaces between social groups, where the Herderian triad had made us obsessed with bounded communities. However, if we pay close attention to Pratt's metaphors in her definition (i.e., clash, grapple, etc.), we find that her model perceives contact zone negotiations as conflictual and stressful. We are finding, however, that in many such spaces people also collaborate and help each other succeed in their interactions. We have to now ask if there are possibilities of community from a practice-based perspective. Or should we consider community to be passé in postmodern globalization? The model

Communities of practice

communities of practice (Lave & Wenger, 1991; Wenger, 1998) helps us theorize how flexible and fluid communities can be formed with open and changing memberships in contact zones for translocal collaboration and communication. Communities of practice (CoP, for short) are not based on traditional essentialized features that construct homogeneous communities, such as race, ethnicity, language, or religion. In CoP, people from any of these backgrounds can come together for functional purposes. It is the practices they engage in to accomplish their shared objectives that make them a community. Through these practices, they also develop some communicative repertoires that are reified through their mutual engagement. We might consider this process of reification similar to the sedimentation and indexicalization discussed by the previously mentioned schools. The difference in CoP is that it provides a way of looking at these repertoires as helping construct tentative communities. These communities are relational, overlapping, and interconnected. In this way, they are not bounded and separate as in the Herderian triad. They are also open to change through influences from other CoPs, as members shuttle in and out of communities.

This model can also be applied to ethnic or national groups in postmodern globalization, as members shuttle in and out of communities and manage their sometimes conflicting identities in a "nexus of multimembership" (Wenger, 1998, p. 159). Community solidarities are still important for people, and CoP provides a way to reconstruct these relationships in a non-essentializing manner for postmodern globalization. The model thus provides a complex orientation to the processes involved in community formation, change, and reconstruction, as individual members move from the periphery to core membership, get apprenticed by old timers, sometimes facing possible non-participation and marginalization, or change the practices and repertoires of the CoP in light of their values and interests.

Despite these insights that enable us to theorize community formation in the contact zones, CoP is not very sensitive to power differences between communities. That CoPs are themselves situated in power, with their norms and practices shaped by dominant institutions and ideologies, also needs to be addressed better. The sharedness of the repertoires shouldn't be also exaggerated. Though reification does occur, members can conduct business through resources that are different and unshared. What ensures meaning are communicative practices and strategies, not uniform repertoires. At some point in the theorization of this model, there is a slippage from practices to repertoires as being primary for cohesion and meaning. We need to emphasize the primacy of practices and treat repertoires as resultant. Furthermore, CoP is defined so much in terms of consensus that it is not always appreciated how the inner tensions and differences can be constructive. The model also doesn't give too much consideration to subjective factors such as members' attitudes, values, and ideologies in the conduct of their practices. Without a suitable disposition, there is nothing to guarantee that members will collaborate and not exploit the community for their own agendas. On the other hand, attitudes of resistance can complicate the cohesion and consensus of a CoP, leading to its creative reconstruction.

That repertoires have to be shared and uniform for a community, cognition, or system to work effectively is an assumption widely held, not excluding even the practice-based model of CoP. Dynamic systems theory explains how a system can work without homogeneity. A system constituting differences is not only possible, but it can also provide richer outcomes for that reason (Cilliers, 2010). The theory also explains how a system can be both changing and still have structure, be fluid yet stable, and layered, multimodal, and be multiscalar yet functional. These are important considerations when we perceive systems of language (such as dialects, genres, registers, and discourses) as being patterned and structured while being open to change and further pluralization. In a similar way, communities can be held together by dissimilar semiotic resources and values. The theory can also help explain language competence as enabling successful communication and yet remain open to further learning, change, and reconstitution (see Larsen-Freeman, 2011). The possibility of a translingual competence constituted by a stable and yet open orientation to plural semiotic resources will be taken up in Chapter 9. The theory explains how it is possible for translinguals to speak and yet keep learning at the same time; have still-evolving proficiencies in specific languages for specific functions and yet be functional; and use a set of indexicals and still be open to changing their meaning as they use them.

Thus dynamic systems theory offers an important corrective to Chomskyan and monolingualist orientations to language and competence based on homogeneity. Yet it places so much emphasis on redefining the system—especially on building the system in such a way that it can stand on its own and account for success in communication and meaning—that it overlooks the social and the pragmatic. It is not the system that guarantees meaning but the practices in social activity. Meaning-making requires the work of creative and active social agents to employ the disparate and conflictual elements of a language or cognitive system. If this area of consideration is not addressed, the model will lead to binaries that again favor the mentalist, autonomous, and the abstract. It will locate language and competence in the mind of an individual, and play into the traditional dichotomies of mind versus matter, individual versus society, and form versus practice.

Interestingly, there are scholars in the sociocognitive tradition who are redefining the mind in a manner that gives importance to the environment and practice (see Atkinson, 2011b). There are two key realizations characterizing this approach. Firstly, cognition is embedded. Thinking occurs not separated from the environment but in engagement with it. Cognition works in and through social and environmental ecology. This understanding leads to the second realization: cognition is extended. It doesn't occur within the mind alone. The environment and others help us think. Our thinking cannot be complete or successful without participation of other people, resources, and things. The process for such cognitive operations is *alignment*. The mind develops connections between objects, people, and words to achieve meaning and coherence. This process is *adaptive*—yet another term that resembles sedimentation, indexicalization, or reification of the schools reviewed above. The mind develops certain patterns of alignment even as the configuration of the mind, world, and language relationships always keeps changing. In other words, the meaning-making potential of language and human competence emerges through processes of alignment and adaptation, and does not reside in the system of language or cognition.

This orientation to cognition helps us develop a practice-based explanation for one's competence in translingual communication. In essence, translingual competence constitutes not grammatical competence, but performative competence, that is, what helps achieve meaning and success in communication is our ability to align semiotic resources with social and environmental affordances. We bring with us a capacity for social practice that enables us to give meaning to words and construct patterns out of disparate grammars by seeking alignment between cognitive, social, and physical contexts. It is this capacity for practice that also helps us negotiate social structures, ideological complexes, and power inequalities through language. In other words, we can realign our positioning toward others and the environment as we seek a voice through language. More importantly, alignment explains how we can use resources that are disparate, incomplete, and even conflictual, and systems that are not tight, whole, or uniform, and still communicate. It is not those self-standing language or mental systems that guarantee meaning. It is our capacity to achieve alignment that does so. As we shuttle across different communities and locations, then, we are able to align diverse semiotic resources with our changing social and physical contexts for successful communication.

Conclusion

Though I have developed a theoretical orientation to translingual practice in relation to recent schools of language, cognition, and society, we mustn't think of this paradigm as constructing new practices. I will show in Chapter 3 that communicative *not* practices outside the West and in the past were informed by similar assumptions and *new* approaches. Translingual practices in South Asia, Africa, South America, and other *practice* indigenous communities go back many centuries before modernity and colonization. ↓ Furthermore, despite the power of monolingualist discourses, translingual practices *new* have also been alive in the grass-roots and everyday contexts in the West, although *theory* perhaps unacknowledged and hidden always. What we have are new theories, but not new practices. What we considered as legitimized knowledge in the Western academy has left out the important experiences and practices of millions of people outside the centers of research and scholarship. There has been a disconnect between scholarship and everyday communicative practices. The attempt in the preceding pages is to align our language philosophies with long-standing communicative practices.

Before I conclude this chapter, it is important to make more explicit the assumptions behind the historical and geopolitical comparisons offered above. To begin with, modernist globalization and postmodern globalization shouldn't be interpreted as standing for different social realities and communicative practices. Translingual social relations and communicative practices have always existed, although perhaps unacknowledged and discouraged in some times and places. Modernist ideologies and globalization discourses favored monolingual practices and policies. However, discourses have socially reproductive effects. They are not mere ideas in one's head. Therefore, discourses of modernist globalization also attempted to suppress translingual relations and reproduce bounded and hierarchical social structures, with qualified success. However, recent developments in globalization encourage different social relations and institutions and have generated new communicative modes, media, and technologies. These developments have also generated new theoretical discourses that favor hybridity, fluidity, and diversity in communication. However, at the level of practices, people's strategies of making meaning have been essentially the same in both forms of globalization. Human communicative practices are simply finding new realization in the new media available around us in contemporary globalization. It is for this reason that I argue that we don't have to reinvent the wheel in theorizing or formulating the communicative practices required for contemporary communication. We can develop them by learning from the past, especially from the premodern West and the precolonial East.

As we move in the next chapter to focus on the social and language relations of South Asia, we have to also clarify the relationship between the East and the West. For historical and cultural reasons, the West has constructed ideologies that favor monolingual orientations and bounded notions of community and identity. Despite these ideologies, language practices at the everyday level have been translingual even in the West. However, we mustn't treat lightly the effects of ideologies on social relations and communicative practices. The monolingual ideologies have also subtly distorted and even suppressed vibrant practices over time. Such ideologies have also had their effects in the East via colonization. Thus monolingual ideologies, and social policies and practices based on them, are not hard to find in the East today. However, the position adopted in the book is that at the level of practices in everyday life, both in the East and West, translingual practices have been always present.

We mustn't therefore read my description of language practices in South Asia in the next chapter as somehow "natural" to that region. I am not essentializing translingual practices as naturally belonging to the East and alien to the West. In both regions, these practices are constructs of different language ideologies. The focus should be on the language ideologies and dispositions that favor different communicative practices in South Asia, without treating the communicative practices as somehow special to the region. However, when modernist language ideologies in the West have adopted a monolingualist orientation and distorted or suppressed translingual practices, a consideration of South Asia is useful. The description of language practices there shows how communication can work under alternate language ideologies and attitudes. It provides a different vision of social relations and communicative life. Such revisionist historiography is an attempt by postcolonial scholars to retrieve practices and knowledge that are losing their vibrancy under modernist and monolingual ideologies.

3

RECOVERING TRANSLINGUAL PRACTICES

Siva gets up in the morning and prays to all his Hindu Gods before he goes to the village market to open his vegetable stall. He prays most of all for negotiation strategies. He has to negotiate not only the price, but the languages of those who come to the market from neighboring villages. As he opens his stall, he sees a white-skinned man walking toward him. He prepares himself for some very intense negotiations, as this man probably brings language and values he has never encountered before. He tucks up his sarong and looks with anticipation at the foreigner. He observes the foreigner looking at the bananas. So, he asks *"paLam veeNumaa?"*[1] He points to the bananas when he says *paLam*. The foreigner reaches into his pocket, takes out a book, and hastily checks a few things. Then he says *"paLam price enTai?"* as he takes out a couple of rupee notes from his other pocket. From his gestures, Siva figures out what the word "price" meant. However, he was confused by the foreigner's use of the Tamil word *enTai*. The word means "my." From the context, Siva assumes that the foreigner probably wanted to say *enna*, which means "what" (i.e., to mean "What is the price of the fruit?"). Siva knows that in these contact zone encounters one has to be supportive and collaborative. If one is obsessed with issues of language correctness, he/she faces the danger of damaging the interaction and probably losing the transaction. Besides, Siva knows how to use ecological resources to make meaning in translingual contexts. He can combine clues such as gestures, objects, setting, topic, and other features to help in intelligibility and communicative success.

So, letting pass the incorrect word and adopting the sentence structure the foreigner had himself used, Siva replied, *"paLam price two rupees."* That this sentence structure doesn't follow the SVO structure of Tamil doesn't bother him. That it doesn't follow the grammatical rules of English, he wouldn't have known. What was important to him was to co-construct grammatical norms that worked for both of them in this context. Siva had the ability to quickly decode the preferred structures and patterns of the interlocutor and collaborate with him to achieve intelligibility.

Though the foreigner had first seemed to rely on a phrase book or bilingual dictionary rather than negotiation strategies, he too quickly learnt from Siva how to negotiate language face-to-face in the immediate context. He put his phrase book inside his pocket, and said "*paLam* price too much," as he turned to go to the next vendor. From his gestures, Siva knew that the interaction was about to end. He wanted to reduce the price by fifty cents in order to revive the bargaining. But he now faced a problem. He didn't know how to say "One rupee and fifty cents" in English. He knew the English words for only numbers one through ten, which he had learnt from a passing sailor some years back. What should he do now? Siva remembered that the bananas only cost him 75 cents each. It is enough to get a 25 cent profit and go through with the deal. In such contact zone negotiations, one has to make the best of one's resources for the situation. Even compromises are needed. There is no point in looking for words and resources one doesn't have. So he said, "*PaLam* price one rupee." The foreigner handed over the note to Siva. The transaction was completed without any more words. As the foreigner was about to leave, Siva tried out his newly coined syntax one more time. This time he substituted a new noun in the topic slot: "*kiLangu* price not much." But the foreigner was in no mood to buy the potatoes Siva was pointing at. He walked away.

Siva felt proud of the new English words and sentence structures he had added to his repertoire. That this was a hybrid language that mixed Tamil and English didn't bother him. What was more important was the ability to treat words as resources to accomplish one's communicative and social objectives. He turned to his wife seated at the back of the stall and announced proudly, "Look! I made a quick rupee and also learnt a new *moLi*."

Translingual connections across time and space

That is the day in the communicative life of my compatriot, a South Asian villager. What we find demonstrated are communicative practices developed from ancient times. Since we lack published records of local communicative practices before colonization, I have had to reconstruct the modes of interaction as they emerge from the insights offered by South Asian applied linguists (Annamalai, 2001; Bright, 1984; Bhatia and Ritchie, 2004; Khubchandani, 1997; Mohanty, 2006; Pattanayak, 1984). It is unfortunate that local translingual practices haven't received adequate representation in scholarship. Colonization led to the imposition of Western language ideologies on local communities. In many cases, even the few available translingual literate products were destroyed. Baca (2009) describes how centuries of non-alphabetic writing in Mexico were put on fire by the conquering Spanish as they considered the texts ignorant or immoral. These texts didn't confirm their own notions of literacy. Though vestiges of the oral communicative practices are still around in many local communities, they are losing their vibrancy under the monolingual ideologies of Western dominance.

Translingual practices have received considerable attention in scholarly circles recently. However, they are often treated as a new development, ignoring the fact that such practices have been around in other times and places. Contemporary scholars think that translingual practices came into being because of developments such as globalization, migration, digital communication, and transnational economic and social networks, which encourage intense language contact. Therefore, Rampton's (2008) book on crossing highlights late modernity in its title: *Language in Late Modernity: Interaction in an Urban School*. Rampton contextualizes his treatment of crossing in relation to the new developments in community construction: "Western societies are actually in a new era, where among other things, aestheticized multi-modal texts recruit people into 'life-style' communities, into 'neo-tribes without socialisation' where centres of authority are hard to find and where entry is a matter of the consumer's desire, personal taste, shopping skills and purchasing power" (Rampton, 1999a, p. 425). As suggested by the title of Rampton's book, many scholars also treat translingual practices as an urban phenomenon (e.g., Pennycook's 2010 term is "metrolinguistics").

It is true that in modern sociolinguistics the city is treated as the locus of diversity while villages are treated as homogeneous. However, in South Asia and other non-Western regions, rural life has involved considerable translingual interactions, as tribes and villages of close proximity came into contact in markets and temples. Furthermore, scholars like Calvert (1998) argue that there were more fluid forms of multilingualism in premodernity rather than in contemporary times. Postmodern social conditions and discourses didn't *create* translingual practices. They have only created more visibility for them. Furthermore, ironically, they have also sparked an interest in precolonial oriental practices and led to their recovery from suppression under modernist ideologies. It is perhaps a useful rhetorical strategy to make a case for past traditions of translingual practice by pointing to present-day needs and concerns. I framed my introduction to this book around the current translingual practices in migrant and diaspora contexts for this reason.

The description of precolonial South Asia should not be read as an effort to glorify the practices of the past. In fact, new technologies provide novel ways in which social and communicative practices may be realized. Consider the ways in which diverse languages and modalities can be combined in web-based digital texts. The hyperlink embeds pages within pages in a fascinating form of intertextuality. The "page" was relatively more static and rigid in past times, even though it did incorporate diverse languages and modalities. Consider also the way in which texts are able to travel across distant communities, thanks to the Internet and digital media. This almost instant, simultaneous, and multilateral shuttling of people and texts calls for complex practices of translingual production and reception. Though communicative practices remain vibrant, if not more dynamic, language ideologies today are more restrictive. The dominance of monolingual and colonizing language ideologies means that people's attitudes toward these communicative practices are also more negative. A return to the past can help us recover lessons and insights for our times. We can learn more about the interpretive practices, negotiation strategies, and communicative relationships people adopted in contact zones for intelligibility and meaning.

There is now a burgeoning literature and scholarship on translingual practices in Africa (Makoni, 2002), Polynesian islands (Dorian, 2004), South America (de Souza, 2002), and Mexico (Baca, 2009). In this chapter, I focus mostly on the region I come from, South Asia. The Indian linguist Khubchandani (1997) has provided a book-length treatment of the way communication works in South Asia. Though I draw from his account for my description, his insights are supported by other linguists from the region which I have cited above. Still, as the documentation of these practices is scant, my description will be somewhat generalized. We have to remember that there are many different language and ethnic groups in South Asia, each with slightly different traditions.

South Asianists consider language diversity as "natural" to the ecology of the region. Tej Bhatia and William Ritchie state: "In qualitative and quantitative terms, Indian bilingualism was largely nourished naturally rather than by the forces of prescriptivism" (Bhatia and Ritchie, 2004, p. 794). As evidence for this, they point to the status of the whole of South Asia as a *linguistic area*—"that is, an area in which genetically distinct languages show a remarkable level of similarity and diffusion at the level of grammar" (Bhatia and Ritchie, 2004, p. 795). Though such claims border on essentializing such practices, I consider the scholars are suggesting that such a linguistic diffusion is extraordinary, compared to other regions of the world. Debi Prasanna Pattanayak notes: "If one draws a straight line between Kashmir and Kanyakumari and marks, say, every five or ten miles, then one will find that there is no break in communication between any two consecutive points" (Pattanayak, 1984, p. 44). Other scholars more sensibly attribute this linguistic synergy to language dispositions and ideologies in the region, that is, an "accepting attitude, which has brought about the assimilation of features from Dravidian, Indo-Aryan, Islamic, and even Christian and European cultures into a single system, complex, but integrated" (Bright, 1984, p. 19). Such features are a testament to the adaptive strategies of the local communities, which enhance their repertoires when new languages come into contact with them, rather than rejecting or suppressing them.

I first describe everyday conversational interactions in contact situations. I show how such interactions achieved intelligibility and communicative success even when multiple languages were involved. I then go on to discuss literacy practices in these communities. Much against the dominant orientation in modernist linguistics that communicative success is based on shared norms, I show how intelligibility can be achieved when there are few or no formal similarities to begin with. Of course, this perspective on language is explained by the different orientation to community, communication, and learning in the region at that time. The chapter wouldn't be complete without consideration of the contact with the West and modernity during colonization, and the ways in which the newly entering languages and language ideologies were negotiated. To guard against essentializing translingual practices as Oriental, I will add a brief note on the translingual practices in past Western communities as well. Hopefully, this chapter will encourage scholars to recover translingual traditions from archival research in diverse communities in the West and in the East.

Everyday interactions and translingual dispositions

It is important to understand the language dispositions in South Asia in order to understand how they facilitate the language practices there. Linguistic diversity is at the heart of South Asian communities. There is constant interaction between language groups, and they overlap, interpenetrate, and mesh in fascinating ways. Not only do people have multiple memberships, they also hold in tension their affiliation with local and global language groups as the situation demands. Khubchandani uses an indigenous metaphor, *Kshetra,* to capture this sense of community. *Kshetras* "can be visualized as a rainbow; here different dimensions interflow symbiotically into one another, responsive to differences of density as in an osmosis" (Khubchandani, 1997, p. 84). *Kshetra* (which can be translated as "region") encapsulates the wide lingua-cultural variation found in a plural society. According to Khubchandani, this concept represents "the feeling of oneness among diverse people in the region, creating in them 'a sense of collective reality'" (Khubchandani, 1997, p. 9). He sees the concept of *Kshetra* as being different from the Western model of *region,* which refers to an amalgamated area with diverse people yoked together by statutory policy. The unity that develops out of this diversity and continuity of affiliations Khubchandani calls a "superconsensus" (Khubchandani, 1997, p. 84). As is clear from Khubchandani's metaphor of a rainbow, this kind of unity accommodates much diversity. Similarly, though there are vertical differences—that is, power and status differences—superconsensus provided a way for the community to accommodate these inequalities and negotiate them effectively for social harmony. Unlike communities where individual differences have to be sacrificed for group identity, South Asian communities preserve their group differences while also developing an overarching community orientation with other groups.

Furthermore, community for South Asians is not based on a shared language or culture. Community is shared space. Therefore, it can accommodate many language groups living in the same geographical area. Such communities assume diversity and contact within this area. Language diversity is the norm and not the exception. In such communities, people are always open to negotiating diverse languages in their everyday life. Their shared space will typically feature dozens of languages in every interaction. They don't assume that they will meet people who speak their own language most of the time. This mindset prepares them for negotiating different languages as a fact of everyday life. When they meet a person from another language group, furthermore, they don't look for a common language that will facilitate their interaction. In most cases, such a search would be futile. Therefore, the interlocutors usually start the interaction with their own languages. Both parties retain their own preferred language resources in the conversation. Note how Siva boldly starts with his Tamil "*paLam veNumaa?*", assuming that the ecological factors and ongoing negotiation will make the meaning clear to the outsider as the interaction proceeds.

In this sociolinguistic milieu, language attitudes are also different. Individuals and communities are so radically multilingual that it is difficult to identify one's mother tongue or native language. People develop simultaneous childhood multilingualism, making it difficult to say which language comes first. Khubchandani points out that, "Identification through a particular language label is very much a matter of individual social awareness" (Khubchandani, 1997, p. 173). Language identity is relative to the communities and languages one considers salient in different contexts. Therefore, the language identity label is applied in a shifting and inconsistent manner. Siva would shuttle between a couple of related languages, such as Tamil, Kannada, and Malayalam (all border languages in South India), so that he wouldn't be able to claim one rigid language identity or declare one as his native language.

Such dispositions explain the different language practices found here. In a specific speech event, one might see the mixing of diverse languages, literacies, and discourses. It might be difficult to categorize the interaction as belonging to a single language. Languages are treated as resources and used freely in combination with others for people's communicative purposes. Khubchandani explains: "The edifice of linguistic plurality in the Indian subcontinent is traditionally based upon the *complementary* use of more than one language and more than one writing system for the same language in one 'space,'" (Khubchandani, 1997, p. 96; emphasis in original). If social spaces feature complementary—not exclusive—use of languages, mixing of languages and literacies in each situation is the norm, not the exception. This becomes clear in Siva's interaction with the foreigner. Siva is unfazed about using English and Tamil words in a syntactic structure that shows the influence of both, in his conversation.

Because of the intense language contact in the region, languages themselves are influenced by each other, losing their "purity" and separateness. Many local languages serve as contact languages, and develop features suitable for such purposes. They develop a hybridity of grammar and variability of form. Khubchandani says: "Many Indian languages belonging to different families show parallel trends of development ... [They] exhibit many phonological, grammatical and lexical similarities and are greatly susceptible to borrowing from the languages of contact" (Khubchandani, 1997, p. 80). He goes on to say that differences "between Punjabi and Hindi, Urdu and Hindi, Dogri and Punjabi, and Konkani and Marathi can be explained only through a pluralistic view of language" (Khubchandani, 1997, p. 91). Though he does not elaborate, the "pluralistic view of language" would raise many enigmas for traditional linguistics: How do we classify and label languages when there is such mixing? How do we describe languages without treating them as self-contained systems? How do we define the system of a language without the autonomy, closure, and tightness that would preclude openness to other languages? As we can see, local communities probably held a different orientation to language. They treated languages as open systems that changed in response to situated practices. The notion of translingual practice would accommodate their orientation better than modernist linguistics.

It is clear that this linguistic pluralism had to be actively negotiated to construct meaning. In these communities, meaning and intelligibility are intersubjective. The participants in an interaction produce meaning and accomplish their communicative objectives in relation to their purposes and interests. In this sense, meaning is socially constructed, not pregiven. Meaning does not reside in the language; it is produced in practice through negotiation strategies. Two of the strategies Khubchandani identifies are *serendipity* and *synergy*: "Individuals in such societies acquire more *synergy* (i.e., putting forth one's own efforts) and *serendipity* (i.e., accepting the other on his/her own terms, being open to unexpectedness), and develop positive attitudes to variations in speech (to the extent of even appropriating deviations as the norm in the lingua franca), in the process of 'coming out' from their own language-codes to a neutral ground" (Khubchandani, 1997, p. 94; emphasis in original). "Synergy" captures the creative agency subjects must exert in order to work jointly with the other participant to accomplish intersubjective meaning. Contemporary applied linguists discuss this strategy under the label of "alignment" (Atkinson, *et al.*, 2007). Beyond just synergy between interlocutors, alignment also emphasizes the need for interlocutors to connect other ecological features such as the body and the environment to make meaning. "Serendipity" involves an attitudinal readiness to accept "deviations as the norm." To adopt this attitude, one must display "positive attitudes to variation," and be "open to unexpectedness." Subjects have to be radically other-centered. They have to be imaginative and alert to make on the spot decisions in relation to the forms and conventions employed by the other.

We see these attributes in Siva's interaction. He is prepared to interpret words in context, to the extent that *enTai* is still functional despite its incorrectness. Siva is able to align this incorrect Tamil word and other new English words with ecological resources to generate meaning. Recall how Siva used the gestures (the interlocutor's movements and gaze) and objects (money and fruit) to aid in meaning-making. Similarly, novel syntax structures are made normal through collaborative interaction with the interlocutor. Consider the structure "Topic+ 'price' + Comment" that Siva and the foreigner construct to facilitate their interaction. Consider also their mixing of English and Tamil in their sentences. In some cases, this involves overlooking correctness and even unintelligible items in a spirit of collaboration. See how Siva ignores the wrong use of *enTai* by the foreigner. If both interlocutors had focused on correctness of form, or relied on grammar to achieve communicative success, they would not have proceeded far. It is because they focused on negotiation strategies that they could succeed in their transaction. What therefore enables people to communicate is not a shared grammar, but communicative practices and strategies that are used to negotiate their language differences. Furthermore, these strategies are not a form of knowledge or cognitive competence, but a practice, that is, a resourcefulness that speakers employ to deal with the unpredictable communicative situations they encounter.

We must note that the interlocutors negotiate their differences to construct norms that work for them in a locally situated manner, in their particular conversation. These are intersubjective norms; they are co-constructed. While these norms will work for the interlocutors in that particular context, they may not work for another set of interlocutors. Siva should not assume that the "Topic+ 'price' + Comment" structure will be understood by the next person who comes to his stall from another language group. Norms have to be co-constructed in the specific context, as befits the interlocutors and their purposes. In this sense, preconstructed grammar will not always help in multilingual contact situations. The interlocutors have to co-construct the grammar that will be operational in their interaction. Grammar, therefore, is emergent in these contexts (see Hopper, 1987), as it is clear from the unique syntax Siva and the stranger co-construct in the course of their interaction.

The norms that are thus operational in these interactions are hybrid, and accommodate the languages which the different interlocutors bring to the interaction. Such hybrid language resources have the possibility of becoming forms of pidgins and creoles over time through sedimentation. As we saw earlier, Khubchandani mentions that there are many such hybrid languages in South Asia, whose identities and origins are difficult to locate as they have gone through deep mixing. While in other communities, language loyalties and ideologies will lead to these resources becoming new and separate languages in their own right, in South Asia they are kept open for further negotiation, appropriation, and creolization. In Siva's case, if the mixed vocabulary and syntax have the potential of becoming a variety for use with buyers who visit the market from the West, Siva will still be open to renegotiating these forms rather than using them as ready-made crutches for communication.

In such communities, language acquisition also works differently. Since the languages one will confront in any one situation cannot be predicted, interlocutors cannot go readily armed with the resources they need for an interaction. Therefore, language learning and language use work together. People learn the languages as they use them. They decode the other's grammar as they interact, make inferences about the other's language system, and take these into account as they formulate their own utterances. It should have been evident that Siva was doing some language learning on the spot, as he figured out the meanings of the words which the buyer was using. He was also sensitive to the preferred syntax of the buyer in order to use it consistently and assist in meaning-making. Khubchandani argues that when modernist linguistics is able to theorize language acquisition as based on "directed effort" (i.e., something predictable, with learners armed with a stock of forms and strategies that can make them competent for successful communication), in the South Asian community learning is "an effortless integral activity; discourse centres around the 'event' with the support of ad hoc 'expression' strategies" (p. 40). South Asians recognize that "the 'tradition inspired' standardized nuances of another language or culture" (p. 93) of modernist pedagogies cannot help them engage in the mix of languages and dialects they encounter in each situation.

Also the objective of language learning is different for South Asians. They don't aim to master a language for all purposes and functions. They acquire the resources that are sufficient for the functions they want that language to perform. There is no need to develop proficiency in all the languages for the same purposes—or the same language for all purposes. That is considered redundant. South Asians adopt different resources for different contexts and objectives. From this perspective, the objective of their acquisition is repertoire-building rather than "total" competence (if at all possible) in individual languages. They prefer to develop a range of codes for a range of purposes. Siva is interested in developing the words and structures he needs for market interactions. He is not aiming to develop competence in English as an all-purpose language or advanced grammatical competence for its own sake. When he boasts to his wife that he learned a new language through this interaction, he does mean it. What he has learnt counts as knowledge of a language—a knowledge that is functional and contextual.

If Siva's disposition and practices are different, they derive from his socialization in a region with a different language ideology. Pollock (2006), through his exhaustive archival research, provides a fascinating perspective on the ways South Asian language ideologies contrasted with those of Europe during the emergence of the vernacular around the eleventh century. He points out that while European communities had an emotive and invested relationship with their languages, South Asian ideologies ✓ were different. He points out that, "nowhere in South Asia before colonialism did the emotive and naturalizing trope 'mother tongue' find expression. Nowhere do we hear a discourse of friendship or love toward the vernacular; there is nothing comparable to what Dante called the 'natural love of one's own speech'" (p. 473). This emotional tie with the language leads to other ideologies of ownership, purity, and even nativeness, which are also different in South Asia.

Sheldon Pollock points out that while European discourses associated languages with ethnic identity, and treated them as a marker of their purity, discourses in South Asia didn't link languages to primordial claims of blood. Studying European discourses of the High Middle Ages, once literacy vernacularization was fully underway, Pollock observes what has been called "ethnic origin" discourses (Pollock, 2006, p. 474). He characterizes these discourses as follows: "a concern with origins, purity of descent, and exclusion of mixture, as well as a sense of historical necessity and a growing conception of peoples as the subject of history—and therefore, perhaps inevitably, of peoples and languages in competition" (Pollock, 2006, p. 475). However, in texts of the similar period in South Asia, he doesn't find the presence of such discourses. Not only is the language/ethnicity connection not made in South Asia, there is also an absence of genetic connections between language and the community: "It is equally impossible to locate evidence in South Asia for the linkage of blood and tongue so common in medieval Europe, or for cultures as associations restricted by so-called primordial ties" (Pollock, 2006, p. 475).

The attitudes to multilingualism and language diversity are also different in South Asia. Pollock finds the story of Babel interpreted in Europe to taint multilingualism with sin and guilt. It is this mindset that he attributes to the fact that "European cultural politics over much of the vernacular millennium can arguably be interpreted as expiation of this sin through a project of reduction and hence of purification" (Pollock, 2006, p. 476). Part of this purification was how nations conquered others and forced them to accept their language as the sole medium of communication. In South Asia on the other hand, "Diversity was not a sign of divine wrath, nor was multilinguality a crime that demanded punishment" (Pollock, 2006, p. 477). This language ideology explains the accepting attitude the other South Asian linguists have described above.

There were also differences in attitudes to language and power in South Asia and Europe. During the rise of the vernacular in Europe, Pollock sees a "new symmetry between regional power and regional language" (Pollock, 2006, p. 481). Tellingly, this is also paralleled by language purification ideologies. However, the political associations of language in South Asia were different: "No Indian text before modernity, whether political or grammatical, even acknowledges any conjuncture of these two elements. Nor did the concern with language purity ever find institutional embodiment, whether in the political or the civil sphere" (Pollock, 2006, p. 481). Another marker of this political difference is that "No language in southern Asia ever became the target of direct royal regulation; sanctions were never imposed requiring the use of one and prohibiting the use of another" (Pollock, 2006, p. 573). As we know from European history, imposition of a uniform language within communities and penalizing conquered communities for not using the conqueror's language were common practices.

The contrasting language ideologies don't appear surprising from the perspective of the Herderian triad introduced in Chapter 2. What is surprising is that many of these discourses emerged much earlier in European history. Without essentializing all of Europe as characterized by such language ideology, we can safely say that such discourses constituted the dominant tendency there, just as the dominant discourses in South Asia were different. In practice though, both then and now, plurilingual practices have been present at the ground and everyday level in Europe. We mustn't also exaggerate the seemingly egalitarian nature of South Asian language relations. Everyone knows the reality of caste inequalities in India. However, Dirks (2001) shows through his painstaking historical research that caste distinctions were much more layered and fluid in precolonial times, leading to the situational negotiation of roles and powers based on a range of social and contextual factors. The rigid stratification of caste is an Orientalist discourse, partly to simplify the work of the colonial administrators. Similarly, the sectarianism we see in the region now will also be attributed by many to the post-colonial developments in the region, including policies like "divide and rule" and the reproduction of the Western ideologies of exclusive ownership and identity.

Precolonial literacy practices

We now know that literacy in precolonial communities was similarly influenced by translingual practices. What we are finding is that these literacies were, in many cases, hybrid, multimodal, and non-Alphabetic. They were quite different from the *graphocentric* literacy of Europe and modernity (Mignolo, 2000). The graphocentric tradition is monolingual (one language per text), monosemiotic (alphabets preferred over other sign systems such as icons, symbols, or images), and monomodal (visual preferred over oral, aural, and other multimodal channels). European modernity developed the ideology that words were the most accurate and objective representation of ideas. The types of truth and knowledge represented in precolonial literacies, however, have to be understood differently. Needless to say, this form of literacy also involved different forms of reading and writing. I illustrate these literacies from selected traditions below.

To begin with the South Indian *manipravala* tradition, the Dravidians (my proto-ethnic group) mixed their language with Sanskrit at a time when Sanskrit was the elite and privileged language for learned and formal purposes. The practice was more pronounced and better studied in Tamil. By mixing Tamil with Sanskrit, Tamils were appropriating Sanskrit for their purposes of writing. This was a time when Sanskrit had the cachet as the medium for serious purposes. However, by mixing Tamil, the Tamils upgraded their regional language, making it a suitable medium for serious purposes. This literacy had profound implications for power, cultural development, and community relations. By appropriating Sanskrit for their purposes, Tamils were democratizing a learned, literary, and elite language. Resources from Sanskrit were made more widely available to the local community. This literacy also creolizes local cultures. Furthermore, Tamil was being gradually made a suitable medium for religious, political, and learned discourses, elevated from its regional and localized status.

Pollock considers the label *manipravala* as made up of the words pearl and coral, presumably metonymic of the two materials constituting it. Pearl represents the more cultivated Sanskrit, and coral stands for the plainer Tamil. Furthermore, Pollock considers *manipravala* to be a third language beyond Tamil and Sanskrit (Pollock, 2006, p. 409). However, the eleventh-century grammatical treatise *Viracoliyam* defines *manipravala* as "a kind of style in which words of two languages, like Sanskrit and vernacular, are mixed" (quoted in Pollock, 2006, p. 322). I tend to agree with the latter definition and treat *manipravala* as a form of codemeshing rather than a new language. Pollock dates the earliest occurrences of the *manipravala* style at around the eighth century AD. It appears in texts written to commemorate the achievements and patronage of local Kings (a genre known as *meykiirtti*). The mixing of Sanskrit gave the texts a much needed grandeur, elevation, and pomposity that the vernacular failed to index. The mixing is also metonymic of the merging of the cosmopolitan (Sanskrit) and the regional (Tamil). Though such texts initially appeared in the political and literary domains, they spread later to become employed in exegetical prose by the theologians of Vaishnavism (a denomination of Hinduism) in the twelfth and thirteenth centuries. In this sense, contrary to the stereotype that Sanskrit is a religious language, and that religion was the main domain of its spread, Pollock shows that the presence of the style was more widespread. Pollock especially draws attention to *manipravala*'s presence in political discourse and courtly grammar.

This literacy practice evolved over time, becoming also more institutionalized. Pollock argues: "*Manipravala* embodied the very process of localization of the Sanskrit universal, in both political discourse and literature, that was occurring across southern Asia from this moment on [i.e., eleventh century AD], with the vernacular at first supplementing Sanskrit and later taking on an ever-increasing proportion as vernacularization gained power and confidence" (Pollock, 2006, p. 322). It appears that there was a cline in the level of meshing. From vernacular being mixed into Sanskrit matrix texts, Sanskrit was mixed into vernacular matrix texts as regional languages became more assertive. We also learn that there were grammars for such Sanskrit/ vernacular meshing. *Margam*, a Kannada grammatical text, says: "Words should enter [into a poem] in accordance with the thought [of the poet] and should not be permitted to counteract it. The beauty of the language of the culture-land [must be maintained] in [the use] of Kannada words. Propriety must be observed for Sanskrit words in due measure, and no stumbling over [Sanskrit] words with their harsh phonemes should be permitted. The composition thereby achieves sweetness and becomes strong, growing forth like the sprout of a vine. Such is the Way of the One Endowed with Consistent Political Wisdom" (quoted in Pollock, 2006, p. 366). Note that the incorporation of the cosmopolitan language Sanskrit is conducted in terms of the vernacular and the interests of the local community. The grafting metaphor and use of the botanical analogy show that the meshing was expected to be organic. The meshing also has rhetorical implications. The grammar states that the meshing should complement thought. There are also aesthetic considerations, beyond knowledge or information transmission. Beauty is defined in terms of local language and literacy traditions. The fact that such grammars for *manipravala* existed in Tamil and other Dravidian languages suggests their acceptance into formal mainstream circles. This form of hybrid literacy was closely studied, theorized, and institutionalized. Obviously, there was an ideology conducive to such forms of codemeshing.

Texts of such nature had to be read differently. Though these texts were written in the Brahmi script of the Tamils, and not the Devanagari script of Sanskrit, alphabets had to be invented in Tamil to accommodate the special sounds from Sanskrit. In some ways, this was a bilingual text. The Sanskrit parts were not translated, and readers had to negotiate both languages in their reading. Though *manipravala* was initially a literacy for the learned who had proficiency in both languages, this form of literacy has continued to percolate to lower social rungs as well. Not everyone would have had proficiency in Sanskrit to understand it fully. At any rate, both groups would have had to rely on many negotiation strategies to decode such bilingual texts. This literacy practice still continues in the Tamil community. Today, in both popular/creative writing and scholarly texts, Tamil writers mesh English (and French, in regions formerly colonized by the French) freely with Tamil (for examples, see Canagarajah, 2009). The English meshings are not translated into Tamil. This means that readers have to perform a bilingual reading. In creative writing, the English which is meshed are simple words and phrases. However, the mixed forms will often be printed in the Roman script, contrasting with the Brahmi script of Tamil. In academic texts, writers might quote in English or French extensively. They might also use citations and technical terms in the Roman script. In some academic texts, it would be difficult to say whether the text is meant to be primarily in English or Tamil, as the codemeshing is quite extensive.

The role of Sanskrit in literacy invites a consideration of lingua franca in the South Asian region. Pollock (2006) argues that the lingua franca in this region functioned differently from linguae francae in other regions. Sanskrit was not imposed on local communities by force or conquest, as was the case with English and Latin in many communities. Furthermore, Sanskrit allowed itself to be appropriated freely and meshed with vernaculars in usage. As a result, communities took over Sanskrit and used it in their own way. From this perspective, the regional lingua franca didn't stifle the codemeshing practices of local communities. It in fact participated in those practices. As we now know, there was considerable resistance on the part of other linguae francae, such as Latin or English, to be taken over by local communities and democratized or transformed in character. They had to be learnt in terms of native speaker norms. In fact, these privileged languages were disseminated only to a few to maintain their elite status. Their teaching was carefully controlled. This practice and policy also preserved the other linguae francae from pollution or distortion.

Interestingly, Pollock points out that the etymology of the name "Sanskrit" suggests that it is not tied to any particular community. "Sanskrit" means "perfected." It was considered a more institutionalized medium compared to the regional vernaculars. This means that the language is not owned by any one particular community. This was true of the way Sanskrit spread in the region. Local communities appropriated it for their literate purposes, mediated by their own vernacular values and languages. English and Latin, on the other hand, were associated with particular communities. Their names connote their community origins. The ownership claimed over the language explains how their history was one of imposition on other communities. A proof of this difference is that while knowledge of Latin was a threat to proficiency of the vernaculars in Europe, this was not the case in South Asia. Knowledge of Sanskrit didn't affect the proficiency or development of the vernaculars, according to Pollock (2006, pp. 476–77).

The political implications of linguae francae are conveyed also by the names which they developed for the geographical domains that they occupied. Latin and English imposed their identity on the land which they conquered, unlike Sanskrit. Pollock observes, "In contrast to the West, with its political category *imperium romanum* and literary and cultural category *latinitas*, there was no self-generated descriptor for either the political or the cultural sphere that Sanskrit created and inhabited. The fact that Sanskrit never sought to conceptualize its own universality is indeed entirely consistent with its historical character as a cultural-political formation" (Pollock, 2006, p. 571). Similar to Latin, English named the lands it spread to as a part of the British Empire. What this contrast shows is that while Sanskrit spread to other communities like all other linguae francae, "those who participated in Sanskrit culture chose to do so, and mediated their creation everywhere it traveled and often at the very moment it arrived" (Pollock, 2006, p. 571). A similar comparison relates to the way the lingua franca in South Asia and Europe related to cultural practices such as religion. Latin and English became isomorphic with Christianity. However, Sanskrit was used by divergent South Asian religions for representing and propagating their beliefs: "Buddhists, Jains, Saivas, and Vaisnavas all wrote more or less similar poetry and engaged in identical political practices. Sanskrit cosmopolitanism was not about absorbing the periphery into the center but turning the periphery itself into a center" (Pollock, 2006, p. 572).

Literacy beyond South Asia

We also have emerging scholarship on translingual literacy practices from communities outside South Asia now. Ethnic rhetoricians and post-colonial literary scholars are recovering information on literacy practices in diverse local communities before they were suppressed by European colonial ideologies. While *manipravala* was mostly an alphabetic literacy, other traditions are more multimodal. I give some examples of such literacies below in order to understand their dynamics of production and reception.

Damian Baca (2009) has researched the multimodal and multilingual literacy practices of the *tlaquilolitzli* of the Oaxacan Federation in Mexico. This mode of textuality applied a combination of pictorial images, hieroglyphs, and abstract signs in order to exchange knowledge, as was typical of other ancient Mexican textual compositions. Presumably, reading involved an alignment of different types of symbol systems for meaning-making. Contrary to the Western ideology that only alphabetic literacy is suitable for higher order knowledge transmission, in the Oaxacan Federation non-alphabetic literacy worked effectively for such needs. Baca notes: "Local Mexican composition traditions were formally taught through the *Calmécac* system, a 'higher education network' with a remarkable influence on Mesoamerican societies. The *Calmécac* institutions supported the realization of an organized and operative legislature, civil courts, and other public forums; an exact science of time, mathematics, and astronomy; complex faith systems; advanced knowledge of herbal medicine; elaborate architecture, sculptures, and paintings. All of this was supported not with the global import of letters or books, but with unique pictographic record keeping systems" (Baca, 2009, p. 235). If one wonders how abstract concepts were conveyed in this literacy tradition, Baca informs us that one of the most commonly employed stylistic devices is the use of parallel expressions, repetitive and recurrent phrases, and the blending of two concrete terms to convey an abstraction. And yet, when the Spanish conquered the region, they put on fire many of these codices as they associated this literacy with ignorance and superstition.

The Oaxacan tradition is largely visual, though it uses different symbol systems. The literacy tradition of the Kashinawá (who inhabit the Amazonian state of Acre in north-western Brazil) is more multimodal. The *kene/dami* literacy tradition of the Kashinawá people features a complex integration of diverse symbol systems and modalities, that is, words, pictures, icons, color, and spatial arrangement. More importantly, literacy is a new medium for this oral community, leading to the invention of non-alphabetic symbols to capture grammatical distinctions available in their speech, thus merging orality with writing. In fascinating forms of contact zone literacy, recent texts even find ways of accommodating dominant Portuguese alphabets into their texts. De Souza (2002) articulates the complex grammar that enabled locals to put together the icons, multilingual resources, and diverse modalities for meaning.

The Kashinawá used two basic modes of visual representation on paper. The first is a highly codified set of abstract geometric patterns called *kene* which may appear in reduced size in the form of an "icon" in the corner of a page or as a frame occupying the margins of the page. *Kene* drawings may also appear as tattoos covering a human figure or an object on the page. The drawings may occur alone on the page or in multimodal combinations with the other kind of drawing (called *dami*), together with alphabetic text. The second visual mode of representation, *dami*, consists of figurative line drawings and may be used to represent animals, objects or human and supernatural beings. There is no attempt made to pre-establish a point of view for an observer of the drawings, so no perspective is imputed to the drawings. The *dami* drawings rarely appear alone and normally occur in sets of figures suggesting a narrative scene or sequence.

With the advent of writing among the Kashinawá, new cultural modes of representation have developed. The pre-literate oral verbal narratives are now transferred to paper. This enterprise, however, is not an innocuous and simple transference from one medium to the other. The previously oral representational modes interact with the new written modes of representation and the new materials available (such as the alphabet, colored pencils and paper), transforming the previous modes and producing a new multimodal written discourse. For instance, the high value attributed to the *kene* patterns means that their presence on the written page now functions as a marker of truth and legitimacy.

The oral resources of the Kashinawá language also mediate literacy. In the Kashinawá language, there are two verbal suffixes which function as markers of modal truth-value, and correspond to the use of *dami* and *kene* drawings in multimodal writing. According to de Souza (2002), the suffix –*bin* in a sentence indicates that the speaker is the source of the information in his speech. As this information has not been witnessed or legitimated by the social collectivity, any utterance marked with –*bin* acquires the aspect of subjectivity and low truth-value. On the other hand, the suffix –*kin* in a sentence indicates that the information has been legitimated by the collectivity and, therefore, has high truth-value. Mythical narratives are narrated with the suffix –*kin*. In multimodal writing, a parallel may be made between the use of the suffix –*bin* and *dami* drawings and the suffix –*kin* and *kene* patterns. The advent of writing and the introduction of the new representational modes of meaning-making on paper and with writing means that the previous meaning-making function of the oral suffixes –*kin* and -*bin* has been transformed into written language on paper with the multimodal use of the *kene* and *dami* drawings. Kashinawá culture, with its vision-seeking rituals of *ayahuasca*, and its wealth of mythical oral meaning-making modes, has led the community to place a high value on the visual mode of meaning-making. With the introduction of alphabetic writing, the Kashinawá feel that alphabetic writing on paper is insufficient and needs to be complemented by other visual modes of representation. The visual modes of *kene* and *dami*, rather than functioning as mere complements of the alphabetic text, are themselves complemented by the alphabetic text.

Such local traditions of literacy provide useful heuristics to understand the new texts emerging in late modernity, especially in the multimodal, polysemiotic, and hypertextual examples in cyberspace. To cope with these emergent "multiliteracies" (see Cope and Kalantzis, 2000) and redefine existing literacy paradigms, we can gain useful insights from local practices from precolonial times. We must also note that multiliteracies, much celebrated today, are not new or unknown in precolonial and premodern communities. There is a need to understand more the logic and rhetoric which local people adopted to encode and decode these texts, in order to complement contemporary engagements with multiliteracies.

Post-colonial language contact

Unlike the forms of language contact in everyday interactions and interpersonal relations in villages and markets (as we found in Siva's case), the colonial contact of languages involved greater power disparity. It was deeply political and institutional, having the power to thrust one group's language ideologies onto the other. The colonizing languages had the power to reproduce their monolingual ideologies and hierarchical social relations in local communities through their institutions (such as schools and civil administration). This is an impositional form of language contact. However, even in such contexts, processes of appropriation and creolization were at play, leading to translingual practices.

We now have examples of how local communities absorbed the newly entering languages into their traditional practices. While some forms of translingual practice were relatively spontaneous, others were conscious acts of appropriation and resistance. Their translingual practices defeated the colonizers' attempts to impose a monolingual acquisition of their own language. We have records of English education in Sri Lanka, where students were kept in boarding schools so that their learning of English (and presumably British culture and knowledge) would be protected from contact with their home culture and language (see Chelliah, 1922). Students were also fined on each occasion where the vernacular language was used. However, we see references to some "unruly" students who were dismissed from the school for escaping from the boarding houses at nights to attend Hindu temple festivals, maintaining secret miniature shrines for Hindu deities in their cupboards or desks, and surreptitiously practicing what were called "heathen" songs and dances (Chelliah, 1922, p. 37). Chelliah, a local Tamil teacher in one of these missionary schools, who was writing at a time when the British were still ruling Sri Lanka, suggests that students continued to maintain contact with vernacular practices despite their isolation. Translingual practices therefore were preserved, often surreptitiously, despite efforts by the British to keep the language from mixing and (from their perspective) from impurity. The fact that the mixing of languages did occur and that students retained their vernacular and translingual competencies at that time is also evident from oral history and narratives (as I recount in Canagarajah, 2000). We have trickster stories from this tradition according to which local students used codemeshing to convey different messages to the foreigners and their compatriots. They thus used their repertoires to hoodwink the colonial administrators and teachers. Translingual practices had a resistant implication at this time.

Local people also constructed texts in the *manipravala* tradition, mixing English and Tamil or Sinhala in their writing. Soon the British administration itself began to acknowledge this mixing of languages, relaxing their monolingualist policies. Manique Gunasekera (n.d.) notes that the colonial administration started publishing guidelines on the appropriate usage and spelling convention for local languages used in English texts. In 1869 the British administration published a *Glossary of Native and Foreign Words Occurring in Official Correspondence and Other Documents* (see B. Gunasekera, 1893). Since then, there have been periodically revised and updated glossaries to ensure consistent practice in the use of spelling and the meaning of Sinhalese and Tamil words in officialese in English. Through these glossaries, perhaps the British administration implicitly recognized the fact that translingual practice was an indigenous tradition.

Pratt (1991) gives another example of the politics of translingual practice from South America. She interprets how Guaman Pomo de Ayala, a Quechua noble in Peru, appropriated Spanish and wrote a text of mixed codes and visuals to subtly critique the ruthlessness and illogic of the Spanish rule. Though the text was not understood in the West at that time, the resistant messages of the text are not lost on those who interpret this text now. Certainly, the Quechua subjects knew what Pomo was writing. The codemeshed text articulates forms of resistance that the locals understood but the foreigners didn't. This could also be a part of the resistant implication of the text.

Guaman Pomo's text was a 1,200-page letter to King Philip III of Spain. It was dated in the year 1613, in the city of Cuzco in Peru. This is about forty years after the fall of the Inca empire to Spain, and shows a very early but linguistically advanced form of translingual practice. The Inca's was largely an oral civilization, supplemented by the numbered knots *quipus* used for bureaucratic record-keeping purposes. Interestingly, the community had an advanced administration without alphabetic literacy. Pomo's letter shows the intuitive translingual practices multilingual communities were able to undertake. Pomo adopts the Roman alphabet to write not only Spanish but Quechua, his native language that didn't have an alphabet. In addition to the 800 pages of alphabetic texts in Spanish and Quechua, there are about 400 pages of representational drawings combined with the spatial symbolism that represented Andean values in Pomo's text. In other words, Pomo is taking over resources from the representational system of the Spanish to form alphabets he didn't have. He adopts it to his own tradition of spatial symbolism to articulate a parodic view of the Spanish rule in their community. The mixing of Spanish and Quechua, the representational and the spatial, and the alphabetic and non-alphabetic constitute a fascinating form of translingual practice.

Consider one of the descriptions. Pomo imagines life in Spain after the conquest of the Andes: "In all Castille, there was a great commotion. All day and at night in their dreams the Spaniards were saying 'Yndias, yndias, oro, plata, oro, plata del Piru' (i.e, Indies, Indies, gold, silver, gold and silver, Indies, the Indies, Peru)" (quoted in Pratt, 1991, p. 35). Pomo is parodying the lust and materialism of the Spanish. What is translated in English above would have appeared in Quechua in the original. The speech of the Spanish would have been represented in Spanish. The utterances of the Spanish, in being embedded in Quechua, give a different framing for their views. This strategy brings out a critical perspective and introduces the author's parodic perspective. What are even more insightful are the representations of the interactions between the Spanish and the Incas in everyday conversation. In one of the drawings in Pomo's letter, the Inca says in Quechua, "You eat this gold?" and the Spaniard replies in Spanish, "We eat this gold." (quoted in Pratt, 1991, p. 34). This is an act of polyglot dialog, using receptive multilingualism, as introduced in Chapter 1. The example suggests that both the Spaniards and the Incas adopted this form of translingual conversational practice at that time. It is also interesting that in this form of hybrid literacy, the meshing of codes enables Pomo to bring out the voices of both parties, while also framing the interaction according to his resistant perspective.

Translingual practices in the West

It is important not to go away with the impression that only the East was the locus of translingual practices. Before modernity, when the ideologies of monolingualism, language purity and ownership were constructed and actively promoted (as discussed in Chapter 2), there were vibrant forms of translingual practices in the West. Despite the differences in dominant ideologies and dispositions between the East and the West, as I have described above, unacknowledged translingual practices have gone on before modernity and later, continuing into the present in the West. I will indicate a few sources for glimpses into translingual practices in the West in the past.

To consider the language of focus in this book, English has always been a creolized language, meshing with diverse other languages in its development. Monolingualist language ideologies have not allowed us to acknowledge its creole history. As I mentioned in Chapter 2, English was a set of mobile and fragmented semiotic resources, lacking unitary identity, in its very inception. It emerged from the tribal dialects of Angles, Jutes, and Saxons that migrated to England from the European mainland around 449 AD (see Fennell, 2001). It then combined with local language resources from Frisian and Celtic tribes, which were themselves already influenced by Latin colonization, to gain an identity as English. Furthermore, Latin influenced English even before the latter's formation in England. Latin was in contact with the Germanic dialects that migrated to England, contributing many loan words that continue in English. The Christianization of Britain since the sixth century AD brought with it other Latin influences into English. However, these forms of contact with elite Latin and rustic Celtic were not as profound as the later contact with Old Norse. With the eighth-century invasion by the Scandinavians and their settlement in large numbers in Britain, we see a closer contact between the languages. Old English and Old Norse were so structurally similar that linguists talk of a "linguistic fusion" (Fennell, 2001, p. 90), posing difficulty in finding which language influenced which, and where certain words and structures in Modern English derive from. Some credit Old Norse for the simplification of the English morphology (Fennell, 2001, p. 91). During the Middle English period, there was literary activity in Latin, French, and English, with English lagging behind the other two. Speakers of English, then, read a lot in the other two languages. Literary activity was also going on in Irish, Scots Gaelic, Welsh, and Cornish at the same time. Using one language for literacy and another for speech can be labeled bilingual diglossia (Fishman, 1967). There was similar bilingual diglossia in oral interactions too. French was the language of the Court and English the language of the commoners, in around the eleventh century. The former was the High Language and the latter the Low variety. Though Bailey and Maroldt (1977) have claimed that Middle English was a creole of French during the eleventh to the thirteenth centuries, one might see creole processes in previous periods also: for example, with Scandinavian in the tenth–eleventh centuries, and with Celtic in the fifth–sixth centuries. In fact, one might say that such creolization has been continuing all the time, invisible only to those wearing monolingual ideological glasses.

Till a consensus was developed about a standard language in around the sixteenth century, especially through the effects of the printing press, there were multiple competing dialects, compelling people to shuttle in and out of codes in speech and writing, and between regional dialects. There were four major dialects in Anglo-Saxon England, with their own regional identities: Kentish, West Saxon, Mercian, and Northumbrian. Each of them influenced literacy too, with texts in all four dialects. Even though the West Saxon dialect functioned as the dominant variety for Old English texts, the dominant spoken dialect was West Germanic. Thus there would have been a switching of dialects between speech and literacy. However, even West Germanic didn't play a major role in the development of Modern English. Modern Standard English is considered to be a construct of the Mercian speech of the eastern section of the Midland area. The diversity of dialects continues into the Middle English period with even greater vigor, even in literacy. Barbara Fennell notes, "The most fascinating aspect of these Middle English texts is that they document widespread variation in the language of the early Middle English period, unrivalled in any other period of the language before or since" (Fennell, 2001, p. 108). To contribute to the polyphony of the texts in terms of vocabulary and grammar, there was also no dominant scribal or spelling system. One can only imagine the contextual negotiations and translingual practices readers may have had to adopt for interpretation.

Many authors used both Latin and English that were code mixed and meshed in complex ways for their expressive purpose later, as was the case also of the *manipravala* style. We know of this practice through the polemical writings of those like Phillip Sydney who tried to combat this practice. Many writers continued to use both languages to varying degrees much later into history. Kellman (2000) includes many such writers in literature and the sciences as part of his "translingual imagination." For example, John Milton exemplifies this tradition in his poetry, both writing bilingually and drawing from Latin resources for his English writing. Even Newton is included as a "latent-translingual" in this tradition (Kellman, 2000, p. 60). There have been other European literate traditions that codemeshed. Pollock considers Occitan in the South of France around 1100 as similar to the *manipravala* tradition in South Asia. He treats Occitan as: "the creation of a courtly culture that defined itself by a new aesthetic and a linguistically unified—or at least supradialectal—Occitan and produced a new literature … Assessments of this Occitan poetry in recent scholarship suggest that it was an unqualified expression of the kind of cosmopolitan-vernacular impulse we have seen across southern Asia: it strove to combine a 'lyric drive' that was oral, vernacular, secular, and courtly, with a 'poetic drive,' or better, a literary drive, that had hitherto been literature, Latin, sacred, and church-schoolish" (p. 448).

English was gradually standardized through technological developments such as printing, the political imposition of rulers such as King Alfred, and the lexicographical efforts of scholars like Samuel Johnson. After Caxton set up the printing press in 1476, strong dialectal traits disappeared from written texts. It took another hundred years for spoken standard to coalesce around the London dialect. Even then, to provide values of standardization and prestige to the Received Pronunciation (RP), it took more conscious and sustained ideological work. Agha (2003) describes the enregisterment undertaken from the seventeenth–nineteenth centuries through institutions such as schools, textbooks, and newspapers to index RP as elite and desirable. What such sustained efforts suggest is that the diversity and hybridity did exist and had to be suppressed all along.

The scene in the USA was no less diverse. Trimbur describes the hybrid languages in currency in the USA during the formative period of the nation in the eighteenth century. While the founding fathers adopted a policy of expediency that subtly favored English, a vibrant linguistic culture formed around "a polyglot and multiethnic multitude that emerged through the very energies of mercantilism aboard ships and in port cities, in the slave castles of West Africa and on the New World plantations, and in pan-Indian resistance movements" (Trimbur, 2010, p. 27). Among them were African creole varieties of English. Parallel to the English varieties imported to the USA from England (specifically from East Anglia), West African Englishes which were formed in slave castles in the lower Guinea coast also thrived as an alternate tradition. They became the plantation creoles that were spoken in the USA and also in the Caribbean, South America, and West Africa. Their wide currency and lingua franca status motivate Trimbur to emphasize a non-Eurocentric explanation for the development of English in the USA. There were also other varieties, such as the Afro-Seminole creoles in Florida that emerged out of the union between the escaped slaves from Africa and the Native American tribes. They formed maroon communities that stayed out of reach of the US state and its language ideologies. There were also nautical pidgins, borne out of a merger between English, the Mediterranean lingua franca "sabir", and West African languages, that had a circum-Atlantic currency. As English Only ideologies become powerful in the USA, these forms of translingual practices are also being erased from the US "linguistic memory" (Trimbur, 2010, p. 38). Silverstein (1996) discusses the ways in which "plurilingual" practices are still being combatted by monolingual language ideologies in the media, political, and educational discourses in the USA.

Conclusion

The purpose of this chapter is to understand translingual practices not as new but as existing in diverse communities in the past and continuing underground despite the dominant monolingual ideologies. As we attempt to understand similar communicative practices in the context of late modern social and technological developments, it is important to recover the knowledge from past traditions. Apart from providing useful models and analogies to understand contemporary practices, these traditions also remind us of the knowledge and practices that multilnguals from post-colonial communities might be bringing to English in contemporary lingua franca encounters.

From this perspective, translingual practices may not be as difficult or esoteric as we might assume from the lens of contemporary monolingual ideologies. It is monolingual communication that might seem strange to many. We will turn now to considering how a perspective from translingual practices will motivate us to redefine English as a global language.

4

ENGLISH AS TRANSLINGUAL

As we saw in Chapter 3, English has always been a contact language. In recent contexts of post-colonialism and postmodern globalization, English has been undergoing further changes in relation to the diverse new languages and communities it has been coming into contact with. Many scholars are addressing the changes English is going through as it travels beyond its traditional homes and speakers. The models of World Englishes (WE), English as an International Language (EIL), and English as a Lingua Franca (ELF) are some of them. These models offer useful insights into how English has to be understood differently when it comes into contact with other languages and develops hybrid grammars. And yet, they are significantly different from the translingual approach developed in this book. It is important to understand the differences, as I proceed to define English as a form of translingual practice.

To begin with, these models define the emergent varieties largely in terms of form, constituting each into a separate system. They provide greater importance to grammar as giving coherence and identity to these varieties. These models also treat these varieties as having separate identities, which are located in unique speech communities. As a result, they run into many limitations. The most important of these is the proliferation of varieties of English, an unending compendium of regional, national, subnational, ethnic, and pidgin and creole varieties. I will demonstrate that orientating to the global spread of English as a translingual practice enables us to address the common processes underlying these diverse and emergent varieties. A focus on the *products* of these common underlying processes can be misleading. These models end up reifying each variety, limiting further changes, and preventing us from being open to studying further diversification. The focus on the product also takes away our attention from the processes of contact, mobility, and sedimentation that underlie these varieties. It also prevents us from understanding the dynamics of meaning-making practices, as we are made to focus on the superficial outward manifestations of the form.

To adopt terms coined by Halliday (2002) we can say that the dominant models of global Englishes focus more on *glossodiversity* and not much on *semiodiversity*. While the former approach focuses on the emergence of form and language varieties, the latter focuses on meaning changes. There are important processes in semiodiversity relating to global Englishes that require more analysis, as other scholars have also argued (Kramsch, 2006; Pennycook, 2010). In fact, semiodiversity can take place even without changes in form. We should not consider the diversity and appropriation of English in instances of form changes only. The same word or grammatical item can be made to index new values and meanings as it travels through diverse spatio-temporal contexts. I am not arguing that glossodiversity should be discounted. However, there is a danger in treating it as the primary resource for meaning and not focusing on the semiotic practices that engender new meanings. Furthermore, the dominant models treat the patterns and systems which they see at the level of form as being stable and originary. These patterns are ever-changing, and they do so because practice is primary. The norms at the level of glossodiversity, then, are always in a state of becoming. Moreover, these models recognize varieties when they reach a status of stability and regularity after much sedimentation. However, the practice-based perspective considers emergent forms at different levels of stabilization as still being meaningful. Since it is not form but practices that generate meaning, forms that are idiosyncratic can still contribute to semiodiversity. In fact, even violations of the system or norms can be meaningful and can contribute to semiodiversity. Though there are different levels of formal patterning at the level of glossodiversity (i.e., pidgins, creoles, dialects, genres, and discourses; native versus non-native varieties of English), and there is value in considering their relationship, we mustn't treat any of them as deficient or ignore the underlying practices that explain their emergence and meaning-making potential.

Furthermore, we must develop an orientation to English as having been already always diverse. It hasn't become translingual or hybrid only because of its flows outside its traditional homeland or native speaker communities. Native speaker communities also engage in translingual practices. Not surprisingly, the dominant models of global Englishes leave out native speakers and their communities from their analyses. The diversification of English seems to matter only in cases of its use by multilinguals or non-native communities. However, the position adopted in this book is that no community is homogeneous. While the "community" itself embeds a lot of diversity (not only in cultural terms, but also in terms of gender, class, region, and lifestyle choices), it is open to interactions with other communities all the time. I therefore consider translingual practice as the process whereby native speaker varieties have also been developing. A consideration of translingual practice enables us to see the practices that underlie all forms of glossodiversity.

There are also questions about communication beyond the varieties of each community that the dominant models are unable to explore effectively. How do diverse people represent their own identities, negotiate unequal power relationships, and still manage to use English to get their inter-community relationships accomplished? These models have to resort to positing a common variety beyond the local varieties to facilitate communication between communities. The translingual approach makes a neutral variety unnecessary. People adopt negotiation strategies to retain their difference and still communicate with each other. Therefore it provides a more satisfying explanation, in my view, on how complex personal, cultural, and ideological tensions are resolved in inter-community contact.

It is important to review the assumptions of the dominant models about the nature of language, community, competence, and meaning in order to understand their conception of English. I must acknowledge that it is difficult to generalize about these models, as a lot of rethinking and retheorizing is taking place among their proponents. Yet, making their differences clear and their theoretical assumptions explicit will help us to engage with the full implications of a practice-based translingual perspective.

World Englishes

The World Englishes (WE) model is among the earliest and most popular in addressing the ways in which the usage of English is changing in contact with other languages and communities. It demonstrated that the English language is not monolithic, but a changing complex of multiple varieties. It put forth the argument that the indigenization of English in diverse communities was leading to local varieties that have their own system and norms. In this sense, they are not broken Englishes or deficient, simply different from native speaker norms.

Kachru's (1986) original formulation of the "three circles model" is now well known. The circles are defined according to the historical spread and social functions of the varieties. The Inner Circle is called "norm providing" and constitutes the "owners" of this language, who largely use English as their first and often sole language for their social interactions. It is their norms that are treated as having spread to other communities. The Outer Circle constitutes post-colonial communities which have adopted English as a second language for intra-national uses. Because they have developed their own norms over time, in relation to their own languages and values, this circle is called "norm developing." Kachru's main contribution was in establishing the legitimacy of these post-colonial varieties of English. Indian English was valid for Indians, and Nigerian English for Nigerians, just as British English for the British. The Expanding Circle constitutes countries that didn't come under British colonization, but are using English as a foreign language for contact with other similar countries. Since they are not assumed to have internal uses of the language, they were labeled "norm dependent." The norms which they were supposed to adopt are those of the Inner Circle.

Despite its radical outcome of achieving acceptance for newly emerging varieties of English, WE doesn't go far enough in pluralizing English or reflecting the dynamic changes in communicative practices. The construction of this model in terms of nation-states ignores many currently existing and still evolving varieties of English. The move to posit a community to anchor each variety is perhaps a gesture in the direction of the monolingualist orientation. WE scholars are now acknowledging diverse varieties within the nation-state, such as: the subcultural and social varieties in the Outer Circle (i.e., Campus Kiswahili in Tanzania) and immigrant second language varieties in the Inner Circle (Chicano English in the USA). However, calling them "local varieties" as some scholars do (see Kirkpatrick, 2010, p. 32) is still an acknowledgement of the nation-state as the frame of reference. There are other varieties being identified at transnational levels, positing communities of other scale levels—Asian Englishes (Bolton, 2008), ASEAN English (that of the Association of South East Asian Nations—Kirkpatrick, 2010), and Chinese Englishes (Bolton, 2003; based on a transnational speech community of Chinese speakers). WE scholars are also unclear about the place of pidgins and creoles. These were not included in Kachru's original formulation. This omission is motivated by the "creole exceptionalism" (DeGraff, 2003) shared by the other models of global Englishes also. Pidgins and creoles are treated as inferior or deficient forms of communication, as they arise in unequal contact among less privileged communities. However, these forms participate in the same creative meaning-making processes of translingual contact. They are now included in a model that supersedes WE, and named "English Language Complex" by Mesthrie and Bhatt (2008). Though it is salutary that other varieties beyond and beneath the nation-state are being recognized, this proliferation of new varieties can be potentially unending. Based on the scale level one adopts, one might identify features that make up a new pattern of usage. Pennycook calls such obsession with identifying new varieties an "enumerative strategy" (Pennycook, 2010, p. 82) that will initiate an endless race to identify more and more varieties. A more productive undertaking is to identify the processes underlying the construction of all these varieties, that is, the translingual practice—as I have articulated above. It is better to treat contact and practices as more primary and varieties as always emergent and changing at diverse levels of localization.

The normative orientation of WE models also leads to some limitations. Though it pluralizes English, WE still anchors the emergent varieties and their functions in terms of one set of norms or another. The Outer Circle norms are this model's unique contribution. Kachru asserts that the English as spoken in Outer Circle communities is not deficient, but is systematic in its own way. To appreciate this fact, we have to stop comparing these post-colonial uses of English with native speaker norms. Though this point is extremely significant, the normed nature of local varieties excludes many domains and varieties of English within these countries. Blommaert (2005) shows many uses of English in rural and urban contexts in Tanzania (an Outer Circle country) that may not be treated as part of Tanzanian English. Others like Parakrama (1995), and Bhatia and Ritchie (2004) show examples for Sri Lanka and India, respectively, which also may not be included in standardized local varieties. They are often treated as "uneducated" varieties, revealing the bias against them (see Kandiah 1984 for more on educated and uneducated varieties of Sri Lankan English). These examples reveal that the uses of English that are too hybrid and transitory are not treated as part of WE. The varieties recognized by WE require a level of stability that leaves out other creative and emergent uses that are still meaningful and functional in local contexts. The legitimized WE models also tolerate limited mixing from other languages, treating excessive mixing as evidence of incompetence. From this perspective, the pluralization of WE doesn't go far enough. A more reasonable approach is to consider how people's processes of negotiating diverse languages for their purposes lead them to adopt strategies of meaning-making and co-construction of intersubjective norms similar to translingual practices.

The position on the norms relating to the Expanding Circle has also generated much rethinking. Empirical evidence (House, 2003; Jenkins, 2000) shows that multilingual speakers in the Expanding Circle don't adopt Inner Circle norms for their communication. They negotiate their differences in interpersonal relationships (whatever nationality they come from) by adopting effective pragmatic strategies for the co-construction of norms that facilitate communication. More importantly, *within* Expanding Circle countries, there are significant uses of English. This has led many scholars to argue that intra-community patterns and norms are developing here as well (see Erling 2002 for Germany, and Clemente and Higgins 2008 for Mexico). It is a testament to globalization's reach that no community is devoid of contact with English today.

Furthermore, WE treats Inner Circle varieties as uniform or monolithic when, in fact, there are diverse norms and uses within these countries. There are translingual practices within Inner Circle countries, as diverse ethnic and migrant groups negotiate English in relation to their own languages. For example, WE scholars are unsure how to relate to the longstanding forms of African American Vernacular English (AAVE). Debating the extent to which they are like a creole or a decreolized standard, Mesthrie and Bhatt (2008) drop AAVE from consideration in their treatment of WE. However, definitions of what is or isn't a "variety" shouldn't prevent us from acknowledging significant communicative practices. It is far better to acknowledge that translingual practice occurs within the Inner Circle communities also. No community is isolated from contact or bounded as to exclude other influences. Even "native speakers" are engaged in translingual practices as they use English in relation to the other languages which they come into contact with. Furthermore, language contact has been taking place in relation to Welsh, Irish, and Scots Gaelic, let alone other colonizing languages such as French and Latin, influencing English in important ways. We cannot leave the Inner Circle varieties outside the pluralization process, assuming a monolithic standard. In other words, Inner Circle Englishes are also localized varieties. The creative contact processes underlying the formation and use of the Inner Circle varieties are ignored by WE, assuming their norms and standards to be homogeneous and originary. Attitudes of ownership and purity may inhibit NES engagement with other languages and communities, but cannot leave their competence or norms unscathed from the results of such contact.

WE perceives the local varieties in other communities as emerging from one original variety belonging to native speakers and the Inner Circle. It thus perceives the spread as centrifugal. Note, however, that the formation of English was itself fluid and hybrid. It was formed out of a confluence of tribal dialects outside what people consider as the home of English, that is, the British Isles. It is possible to see the post-colonial diversification of English varieties as also radically localized. The local initiative of Outer and Expanding Circles in appropriating English resources and giving new indexicalities appears to receive less complexity because of the centrifugal orientation that gives more importance to the native speaker varieties in language spread. Pennycook (2010) gives more importance to local initiatives by considering English "already local," (p. 74) and not dependent on the influences or initiatives from the Inner Circle. From this perspective, there are local social practices, linguistic processes, and contact dynamics already underway in relation to diverse local languages, which English also participates in.

More importantly, the WE model leaves out a consideration of the contact between the circles, as it focuses on varieties within the three circles and nation-state boundaries. Whose norms apply when a member from the Expanding Circle talks to one from the Outer Circle? Whose norms apply when someone from the Outer Circle talks to a member from Inner Circle? Obviously, these interlocutors have to engage in situated practices of negotiation and the co-construction of meaning across local norms. In striving to establish the rule-governed nature of each nation-state's variety, WE has left the complexities of transnational contact unaddressed.

English as an international language

Another set of models relating to the globalization of English, which I will call English as an International Language (EIL), addresses better the relationship between the varieties in translocal contact. I include the slightly different models of McArthur (1987), Gorlach (1990), Crystal (2004), and Modiano (2004) under this orientation. This model also makes a significant departure from WE by accommodating all varieties of English into the same non-hierarchical plane. The distinctions within the circle are functional, not hierarchical. For scholars like Crystal (2004) and Graddol (1999), the justification for this egalitarian model is purely demographic. They show that the number of people who speak English as an additional language far exceeds those who use it as their sole or first language, that is, the traditional native speakers. They therefore argue that the time has come for speakers of all varieties to negotiate English on equal terms. Though it might be said that Inner Circle varieties enjoy more prestige in many institutional circles (e.g., schools, universities, and the media) even in multilingual communities, there are occasions in globalization when Inner Circle speakers find themselves in unprivileged situations, when they have to negotiate on equal terms with their interlocutors. But power is not dependent on the prestige of the language alone. In terms of scales such as economy, commerce, or industry, there are other communities in the Outer and Expanding Circle that wield more power these days. Besides, the nature of globalization in late modernity is such that economy, production, and even military intervention require more international collaboration and networking. In such contexts, English has to be negotiated and one's norms cannot be imposed on others. EIL models therefore place all the varieties on an equal footing.

EIL models also go beyond WE in accommodating varieties beyond and beneath the nation-state. There are slight differences in their treatment. Whereas McArthur

(1987) places regional varieties (East Asian or South Asian English), subnational varieties (Inuit, Quebec, and Athabascan English within Canadian English), and pidgins and creoles in the same circle, Gorlach (1990) differentiates them according to different layers for regional, national, and subnational varieties. Despite the advances in orienting to "English as a family of languages" (Crystal, 2004, p. 40), this egalitarian model is still marked by some of the limitations discussed in relation to WE. EIL simply adds to the number of varieties in English, participating in the "enumerative strategy of counting languages" that assumes discrete language systems (Pennycook, 2010, p. 82). It is also still norms-based, as it treats grammatical norms as the criterion for identifying self-contained varieties, often in an impressionistic manner.

More interesting is the way EIL addresses the question of communication in contact situations across these varieties. For this purpose, scholars posit a neutral transnational variety of English with its own norms. It is labeled differently in different models: "World Standard Spoken English" (WSSE; Crystal, 1997), "World Standard Auxiliary English" (McArthur, 1987), "English as an International Language" (Modiano 1999), and "International English" (Gorlach, 1990). These scholars see this as another variety into which speakers will switch, away from their own varieties, when they engage in translocal communication. Crystal predicts, "It may not be many years before an international standard will be the starting-point, with British, American, and other varieties all seen as optional localizations" (Crystal, 2004, p. 40). As Crystal's statement indicates, this common international standard is projected for the future. No empirical evidence is provided to show that it already exists. The more important point is that these scholars have to project another variety to solve the problem of global contact. They see the need for a shared uniform norm at a higher scale level so that people can engage in translocal communication and cosmopolitan relationships. As I will go on to show below, there is evidence that when people engage in inter-community relations they maintain their own varieties of English and adopt pragmatic strategies to co-construct intersubjective norms for meaning-making. Besides, this projection of a supra-norm for cosmopolitan relationships counteracts against the democratization initiated in other ways by EIL models. Is a neutral, that is, value-free model ever possible for transnational contact? Crystal (2004) acknowledges that WSSE would be heavily influenced by the dominant varieties of British and American English. Furthermore, what happens to local and specific identities when this neutral model is adopted? That is, do speakers hold their identities in abeyance for the sake of harmony? The need for people to adopt another variety (albeit neutral) over their own raises the same questions of power and hegemony that motivated people to localize and appropriate English in the first place.

English as a Lingua Franca

The English as a Lingua Franca (ELF) label has been adopted by diverse scholars, with considerable debate among them on the norms and identity of the language. My discussion in this section is restricted to the influential work of Jenkins, Seidlhofer and their collaborators. I treat other scholars like Firth, Gramkow Andersen, and

Meierkord as belonging to an alternative approach that I develop next. Though the ELF model of Jenkins and Seidlhofer also posits an emergent international norm that facilitates communication across communities, it doesn't claim neutrality for this norm. The model valorizes the creativity of non-native speakers by treating this norm as a co-construction from multilingual norms. This emergent norm is constructed in opposition to NES norms. Furthermore, while EIL scholars project the uniform norm almost prophetically, ELF scholars have been engaged in the laudable project of collecting empirical data to identify the lingua franca core (LFC). Their corpus-based studies have generated an identification of core features that are claimed to be critical for intelligibility across varieties, and non-core features that are not supposed to affect intelligibility. In the beginning, LFC features were treated as providing useful pedagogical implications. The recommendation was to teach the core features and ignore the non-core features, even if they violated native speaker norms. For ELF, contact purposes justified multilinguals using their own norms and not treating NES norms as their reference point. For conversations in which native speakers didn't participate, such a reference point was treated as unfair and irrelevant. However, almost in the manner in which Crystal envisioned WSSE, ELF posits a variety into which multilingual speakers can codeswitch for contact purposes. Seidlhofer argued in a state of the art essay: "The option of distinguishing ELF from ENL [i.e., English as National Language] is likely to be beneficial in that it leaves varieties of native English intact for all the functions that only a first language can perform and as a target for learning in circumstances where ENL is deemed appropriate, as well as providing the option of code-switching between ENL and ELF" (Seidlhofer, 2004, p. 229). ENL includes all national norms, whether British or Indian English. It is evident then that ELF is being treated as a variety that could be codified in terms of linguistic features. Seidlhofer goes on to express the desire to establish ELF as a "linguistic reality, named and captured in reference works alongside ENL and Outer Circle Englishes" (Seidlhofer, 2004, p. 215). She was confident at that time that there was a "descriptive basis for an eventual codification of ELF" (Seidlhofer, 2004, p. 215). This system-building work also motivated ELF researchers to focus more on phonology and ignore writing and pragmatics. Seidlhofer argued that pragmatics "does not comprise a closed set of features for study," and that it is "thus less constrained and thus less manageable in research" (Seidlhofer, 2004, p. 217).

The model, at least as posited in its formative period, is not immune from the questions raised against the neutral variety option of the EIL model. Scholars have asked questions about the identity and power relations implied by the LFC variety (Rubdy and Saraceni, 2006). Some scholars in the ELF tradition, such as House (2003), have projected that ELF will be a language for instrumental and not identity purposes, raising the possibility of neutrality in ELF. However, not only is it impossible to be neutral in language use, it is unnecessary to suppress identity for the sake of contact relations. More importantly, ELF is treated as a monolithic variety, similar to the EIL approach. It is a product that exists "out there." However, evidence from other researchers casts doubt on the existence of a stable variety or commonly shared norms in multilingual contact situations. What Christiane Meierkord finds instead is a mixture of features in contact encounters, that is, "overwhelming correspondence to the rules of L1 Englishes; transfer phenomena, developmental patterns and nativised forms; simplification, regularisation and levelling processes" (Meierkord, 2004, p. 128). This finding is consistent with Sampson and Zhao (2003) who study a group of international sailors in a ship. They find complex borrowing of lexemes and grammatical structures from each other, in addition to pidgin-like simplification processes. Based on findings such as these, Meierkord treats the language of contact situations as "a variety in constant flux, involving different constellations of speakers of diverse individual Englishes in every single interaction" (Meierkord, 2004, p. 115). In other words, there is no stable variety that marks contact zone communication. Such communication works because speakers are prepared to adopt strategies to co-construct norms *in situ*, and achieve intelligibility *through* (not despite) their local varieties and identities.

To the credit of ELF scholars, they have begun to address criticism of this nature and steadily redefine and expand their analyses. In recent years, ELF scholars have favorably cited works like Pennycook (2007) and Canagarajah (2007) on translingual practice, and given more emphasis to the exploration of pragmatic negotiations in contact situations (see Jenkins, *et al.*, 2011, p. 9). They recognize that the practices of interpersonal negotiation that enable people to achieve intelligibility and communicative success are as important as the shared grammatical norms. In recent years, ELF has gradually moved closer to the practice-based perspective adopted in this book (see Seidlhofer, 2009 for an example). Seidlhofer mentions, "In many speech events, boundaries between languages … seem to be perceived as fluid or irrelevant" (Seidlhofer, 2009, p. 242). Similarly, Jennifer Jenkins and her co-authors mention: "it becomes clear that ELF cannot be considered a 'variety' in any traditional sense of the term. Even the early language-focused ELF research had observed how ELF varied according to both speakers' other languages/cultures and the effect of contextual factors on accommodative behaviour. And since then, the contextual element has taken centre stage in ELF research and its role found to be rather more important than originally anticipated" (Jenkins, *et al.*, 2011, p. 9). It is implied that there is a change in the orientation of the ELF model on the relative importance of form and practice. It also appears that the mission to identify a neutral grammar or LFC is now abandoned.

Is ELF moving toward theorizing lingua franca English as a form of translingual practice? However, there are some inconsistencies in the position of ELF scholars. They have not fully transitioned to a practice-based perspective. It is important to do a close analysis of the ELF position in order to appreciate the implications of the translingual approach. To begin with, ELF scholars still retain an important place for grammatical norms, treating negotiation strategies as an add-on, perhaps of the same status as form. In the same article where Jenkins and her co-authors mention the practice-oriented shift, they still make a case for the continued importance of form in ELF research. Affirming that form serves "important purposes" (Jenkins, *et al.*, 2011, p. 9), Jenkins and her co-authors argue that: "The empirically proven existence of these features in the speech of skilled ELF communicators enables ELF researchers to counter any claim that ELF is merely a deficient form of native English" (Jenkins, et al., 2011, p. 9). It appears that they are focused on proving ELF's systematicity and logic based on form. Translingual practice focuses on accounting for communicative success based on negotiation strategies, treating form as emergent from these strategies.

Seidlhofer is similarly faced with a dilemma between form and practice as she adopts CoP as her theoretical framework for a practice-based perspective. She talks of the need to redefine the ELF community as follows: "A much more appropriate concept is that of *communities of practice* characterized by 'mutual engagement' in shared practices, taking part in some jointly negotiated 'enterprise', and making use of members' 'shared repertoire'" (Seidlhofer, 2009, p. 238). Though this is a laudable move, there are several limitations, partly resulting from the CoP model being used uncritically. Note that a shared repertoire is treated as already existing, not co-constructed. The repertoires are not presented as emerging from practices. Finally, pre-existing repertoires are not necessarily needed for communicative success. Negotiation strategies are able to ensure intelligibility and success in a practice-based orientation. Translingual practice focuses on accounting for communicative success based on negotiation strategies, and not purely or primarily on shared form, as I make clear in my critique of CoP in Chapter 2.

The need to posit a community to anchor ELF itself requires some discussion. Though foregrounding practice, ELF scholars still see a need for a community to give identity to ELF. Similar to Seidlhofer, Jenkins adds that ELF "suggests the idea of community as opposed to alienness ... and it emphasizes that people have something in common rather than their differences" (Jenkins, 2000, p. 11). Jenkins' rationale for this community orientation is that the competing model of EFL assumes that multilinguals are "foreign" speakers, thus framed as alien in relation to the community of native speakers. There is a need to posit a community in order to explain the alternate ELF norms and the possibility of intelligibility. However, translinguals are able to achieve communicative success in the contact zone without community. Community is a theoretical need ELF shares with other models of global Englishes, showing the influence of Herderian discourses that posit a community for language identity.

Seidlhofer moves closer to a practice-based perspective later in her essay. She states that: "Rather than limiting itself to the identification of particular linguistic features, this research has tended to take a much more processual, communicative view of ELF, of which linguistic features constitute but a part and are investigated not for their own sake but as indications of the various functions ELF fulfils in the interactions observed" (Seidlhofer, 2009, p. 241). It is laudable that linguistic features are not taken for their own sake. However, these features are not taken to emerge from practices either. They are indications of the functions they serve. There is still a traditional bifurcation of form and function here. The practice-based view perceives form as emerging from practices, not necessarily matching with practices, as if both exist independently. As we discussed in Chapter 2, Pennycook (2010) makes a distinction between *function* and *practice*. The former assumes that there is a preconstructed form that serves some functions, after the fact. The practice-based perspective perceives form and function as emerging from practice.

Jenkins is even more clear about the status of shared norms in ELF. Although she talks about "mutual negotiation" (Jenkins, 2009, p. 201) in other places, she gives more emphasis to form when she states:

> At its simplest, ELF involves both common ground and local variation. On the one hand, there is shared linguistic common ground among ELF speakers just as there is shared common ground among the many varieties of the English that are collectively referred to as "English as a native language" (ENL). ELF's common ground inevitably contains linguistic forms that it shares with ENL, but it also contains forms that differ from ENL and that have arisen through contact between ELF speakers, and through the influence of ELF speakers' first languages on their English ... The common ground in ELF is being identified in the speech of proficient speakers of English.
>
> *(Jenkins, 2009, p. 201)*

What we have to note is that there is a common ground hypothesized for contact situations. The common ground is defined in terms of form. The norms of the common ground belong to proficient speakers of English. The emphasis on proficient speakers shows the need to define the language norms in somewhat stable and systematic terms. As we will see below, there is other evidence suggesting that translinguals accomplish intelligibility without common linguistic norms. That is, they are able to succeed also with unshared local norms in contact zone communication. Moreover, those who are capable of adopting effective interactional strategies are able to accomplish communicative success without advanced competence in language norms. Therefore, communicative success in contact zone communication need not be defined in terms of a common ground of language norms. The significance of lingua franca communication is that communication succeeds even when difference is the norm.

Other revisions in the understanding of ELF are also significant in moving it closer to a translingual orientation. Though ELF was originally defined in relation to the neglected Expanding Circle interactions of the WE model, it has now broadened to include interactions across all three circles. During its inception, ELF left out NES from its analysis. In her 2006 state-of-the-art essay, for example, Jenkins says: "Indeed, in its purest form, ELF is defined as a contact language used only among non-mother tongue speakers" (Jenkins, 2006, p. 160). Now, there is a recognition that Inner Circle speakers too may participate in lingua franca encounters. Seidlhofer notes, "Obviously communication via ELF frequently happens in and across all three of Kachru's circles" (Seidlhofer, 2009, p. 236). Despite this change, Jenkins (2009) states that only 10 percent of "native speaker" interactions are included in their corpus. The important concern even now is that NES don't impose their norms on ELF communication. In a subtle way, however, the notion of "native speaker" still seems to influence ELF conceptualizations, limiting its relevance for contact zone interactions. The translingual orientation questions the use of NES in an essentialized manner as separated from multilinguals. I will show in the coming chapters that native speakers also have the capacity to negotiate English in contact situations through pragmatic strategies. The role of native speakers in contact zone communication is not unnatural and need not be excluded. Furthermore, NES may have other languages in their repertoire. There are also many multilinguals who boast of English as their most proficient language among a repertoire of other languages. Therefore, studying lingua franca English in terms of nativeness is misleading. All are involved in contact zone interactions in English, regardless of their native speakerhood. Linguae francae should be studied in terms of contact practices, not of non-native speaker status. It is for this reason that I adopt the label "Global Englishes" in this book, and not "Lingua Franca English."

There is also a move in ELF toward a "pluricentric approach" (Jenkins, 2009, p. 202) that resists the tendency to identify new and different varieties of English. Similarly, Seidlhofer speaks against talking about Englishes as "countable (proper) nouns implying separate bounded entities" (Seidlhofer, 2009, p. 242). A practice-based perspective would certainly identify the negotiation strategies underlying contact English and not focus on the sedimented forms to name new varieties of English. However, in a companion essay in the same volume of the journal *World Englishes* where Seidlhofer's article appears, Jenkins considers identifying further varieties of ELF based on language norms. She finds it likely that "researchers working on ELF in different parts of the world ... will identify different branches of ELF ... and different sub-varieties within these" (Jenkins, 2009, pp. 201–2). This approach would continue the enumerative approach on global Englishes, much in contradiction to the claims made for ELF in other places.

The inconsistencies of ELF partly result from the model's lack of philosophical clarity. The commendable empirical work that motivates its corpus research hasn't been matched by equally sophisticated theorizing. Clarity about the theoretical underpinnings of ELF would help the model move toward a more complex practice-based orientation. How does ELF explain language, meaning, and competence in contact situations? The closest ELF scholars come to discussing such concerns is in their brief mentions of CoP (as noted above). However, the applications of this model for ELF are not fully developed. As I indicated above, the connection between repertoires and practices, and their relative significance for community formation and maintenance, are controversial. Furthermore, the implications of the model for identity representation and power negotiations, though alluded to, are not fully explicated. Beyond discussions of multicompetence and the irrelevance of native speaker norms, ELF hasn't discussed the more subtle issues of power and difference in contact situations. How code choices and negotiation strategies of interlocutors facilitate and inform their identity and power negotiations will benefit from more explicit discussion. Bringing out the social theories and philosophical constructs underlying the model would steady ELF's progress.

Despite the current lack of clarity and the direction of the ELF model, we must acknowledge the contributions ELF has already made toward understanding English as a contact language. ELF scholars have established the fact that Expanding Circle speakers don't depend on Inner Circle norms for meaning-making. They have also shown that the Englishes spoken by multilingual speakers are not deficient. Despite their deviations from native speaker norms, multilinguals are able to achieve co-constructed intelligibility and meaning. Furthermore, they have argued for a form of competence, influenced by models of multicompetence (Cook, 1999), that is qualitatively different from those of native speaker orientations. In all these ways, ELF has moved the field closer to a consideration of English as a translingual practice.

English as translingual

My orientation to English as a contact language is influenced by the notion of translingual practice. In this model, I treat practices as primary, and grammatical norms as emergent. I hold that intelligibility and communicative success are not predicated on sharedness (deriving from grammar or community identity). I see the possibility of diversity and the retention of people's local identities in contact zone encounters, and don't assume that communication in these sites is neutral. Though I consider contact zone interactions as constrained by power differences, I see these inequalities as negotiable. For these reasons, I consider it important to focus more on strategies that enable such negotiation of power and difference for meaning and communication. This orientation helps me theorize how English is used across all three circles in contact situations, unlike the WE model that identifies varieties within specific communities.

I have previously adopted the label Lingua franca English or LFE (first used by Firth, 1996) to capture my focus on pragmatics rather than grammatical norms and distinguish it from the ELF approach (Canagarajah, 2007). While ELF gives the impression that there is another variety called English as a lingua franca, perhaps parallel to Englishes as community varieties in WE, my label gives emphasis to the contact relationship and treats English as a social process or mode of practice. Pennycook has added another argument to back up this different terminology, elevating my label to represent an alternate model. He states, "This distinction between English as a lingua franca and Lingua franca English is an important one, since the former tends towards an understanding of a pre-given language that is then used by different speakers, while the latter suggests that LFE emerges from the contexts of use" (Pennycook, 2010, p. 85). Though there is a risk that this label also objectifies this form of English and makes it a variety (and any labeling runs this risk anyway), Pennycook's distinction is useful in this chapter to distinguish a translingual orientation to English from the previous models of contact English.

What form does English take in situations of contact? English may find accommodation in the repertoire of a translingual, combining with one or more local languages. The person may not have any "advanced" proficiency in NES forms of English, and yet mix English words and grammatical structures into syntax from other languages. The English tokens may consist of borrowings, reduced forms (as in pidgins), and creative new constructions that might show the influence of other languages. The type of mixing will differ from speaker to speaker according to their level of proficiency in English and according to their language backgrounds. So, speakers of language A and language B may speak to each other in a form of English mixed with their own first languages, and marked by the influence of these languages. Without looking for a single uniform code, speakers will be able to negotiate their different Englishes for ✓ intelligibility and effective communication. In this sense, LFE is not an identifiable code or a systematized variety of English. It is a highly fluid and variable form of language practice. Meaning is an inter-subjective accomplishment. As interlocutors adopt negotiation strategies to align diverse semiotic resources, they will construct a hybrid form that meshes different languages for situated meaning.

This way of looking at the use of English is different from the models reviewed earlier. WE deals with highly systematized and stable varieties of English in post-colonial communities. Though borrowings from local languages may be included in WE, there must be a long tradition of using these borrowings to the point where they become stabilized as part of the local English variety. However, in LFE, English and local languages may be combined in idiosyncratic ways as it befits the speaker, context, and purpose. In this sense, while WE describes language varieties, LFE does not. LFE is a form of communicative practice, not a stable variety. Thus, while WE focuses on the variation at the level of form (i.e., glossodiversity), LFE focuses on semiodiversity (i.e., diversity at the level of meaning) with the implications for emergent forms. LFE treats the pluralization of meaning and meaning-making practices as primary, considering the diversification of form as a secondary outcome. There are many advantages to this approach. From a semiotic perspective, even the use of the same form or vocabulary item in a different context may take new indexicality. We are able to attend to these proliferations of meaning through a practice-based perspective. Also, such cases of meaning changes and negotiations are not limited to multilingual forms of English alone. Native speakers are also negotiating English in contact situations, with similar expansions and changes in the indexicalities of their English. WE, EIL, and ELF models leave out a consideration of such processes among Inner Circle speakers. More importantly, the translingual LFE approach addresses the processes underlying all such cases of language change and negotiation, whereas the other models focus on the products and forms that emerge out of these processes. While the products of these interactions are diverse and variable (and I will argue below that there is a place for a consideration of varieties and dialects), the underlying processes are of more explanatory value.

Annamalai describing the hybrid contact practices in India (without using the LFE label), makes some useful comparisons with pidgins and creoles to bring the significance of LFE to the fore. In some respects, LFE is similar to pidgins, without the pejorative implications attached to the latter. In referring to forms of contact English, Annamalai says, "It is similar to incipient pidgin in its indeterminacy. The words taken from the English language differ from speaker to speaker and even in the same speaker from time to time. Even the same sentence repeated after a few seconds may not have the same words from English" (Annamalai, 2001, p. 173). And yet, LFE should be separated from other contact varieties. While a pidgin is considered a functional language with a reduced grammar and semantic range, LFE is not so. It can have the full range of expression for all possible contexts. Though creole is considered more developed than pidgin, it is also different from LFE. LFE doesn't have an identity as a separate language, as creole does. LFE is a form of practice, not a language with a stabilized system or structure. Also, while creole has native speakers of its own, LFE doesn't.

Nor is LFE an interlanguage. LFE speakers are not moving toward someone else's target; they are constructing their own norms. It is therefore meaningless to measure the distance of LFE from the language of NES. Besides, we have to question the assumption in the interlanguage concept that there are gradations, linear progression, and an end point to be achieved in language learning. In LFE, each contact situation is a unique context, with a different mix of speakers and languages, raising its own challenges for negotiation. It may not be the case that one communicative act contributes to the other and so on, developing a cumulative line of progression toward an end point. Since the contexts are so variable and unpredictable, it is not possible to say that a target can be reached for perfect or competent translingual proficiency. Though translinguals do advance in their proficiency through practice-based learning, this development does not have to be marked by miscommunication or deficient usage, and should not be treated as such.

The translingual orientation gives complexity to processes like pidgins, creoles, and interlanguage. A form-based and monolingualist position has treated these forms of contact communication as deficient and incomplete. A practice-based point of view will reveal that these forms of communication are complex and functional. Similarly, a form-based and non-integrationist view of language has defined processes such as codeswitching and borrowing in dichotomous ways, despite their acknowledgement of hybridity. LFE shows how the meshing of codes can be more fluid and creative in these constructs. However, the LFE approach courts the danger of flattening all the sociolinguistic and multilingual distinctions. I must affirm that there are temporary and situated sedimentations of form. Translingual practices do give birth to varieties, registers, dialects, and discourses over time. However, a translingual approach would prompt us to treat these forms and norms as always in a state of becoming, open to reconstitution through ongoing socially situated practices. Also, these forms and norms shouldn't be treated as originary, giving birth to other forms and practices. Practices should be treated as primary. Granted these caveats, in contexts where there are relatively sedimented varieties with community ideologies backing those language labels, constructs such as codeswitching and borrowing may be relevant. We might be able to distinguish the sedimented language complex into which a marked item is switched or borrowed. Pidgins, creoles, and dialects may show different levels of sedimentation. Language ideologies enter into the picture to give these sedimented codes labels of deficiency (from the perspective of dominant groups) or ownership (from the perspective of marginalized groups). In other words, various situational norms and labels evolve from translingual English practices.

An illustration

I illustrate the explanatory value of the LFE approach by considering the following telephone conversation between Ahmad, an Egyptian cheese importer, and Hansen, a

Danish cheese exporter (from a transcript presented by Firth and Wagner, 2007 to develop a different argument). I provide a reinterpretation of this interaction to consider how these speakers negotiate English in a transnational conversation typical of contact zones. In many ways, this is a modest example of contact English. Since this is a telephone conversation, contextual resources for interpretation are reduced. Therefore, this analysis is less multimodal. Also, the speakers display considerable proficiency in English. Their sentences are fairly well formed and grammar doesn't cause major intelligibility problems. They don't mix their own languages explicitly into this conversation, though indirect influences might be there.

Let us focus on the meaning of the word "blowing":

1. Ahmad: we don't want the order after the cheese is uh:h blowing
2. Hansen: see, yes
3. Ahmad: so I don't know what I can we can do uh with the order now. (.) What do you think we should do with this is all blowing Mister Hansen (0.7)
4. Hansen: I am not uh (0.7) blowing uh what uh, what is this uh too big or what?
5. Ahmad: no the cheese is bad Mister Hansen (0.4) it is like (.) fermenting in the customs cool rooms
6. Hansen: ah it's gone off
7. Ahmad: yes, it's gone off

There is no evidence that "blowing" is from Egyptian English. The fact that Ahmad is hesitating before the utterance of the word on line 1 suggests that he made some effort in choosing it for this interaction. My students have suggested that the choice is based on a visual metaphor (i.e., the appearance of over-fermented cheese). Thus it could be a personal coinage and metaphorical in nature. Another suggestion has been that it might belong to a professional discourse in the cheese trade. An Anglo-Australian speaker has told me that he has heard the phrase "blown cheese" but not the progressive form of it (Rod Ellis, personal communication). However, since Hansen doesn't recognize it, we cannot say that the word is shared even in the cheese trade register. What is important from a translingual perspective is not sharedness or prior knowledge, but the way both interlocutors manage to co-construct meaning for an atypical item. They have to resort to diverse negotiation strategies for meaning-making. Meaning emerges from the interaction, rather than being assumed or given.

Before we analyze the strategies the speakers use to provide this word with a shared indexicality, we must appreciate the complications it creates for other models of contact English. To consider WE first, although Ahmad comes from a former British colony, it is not clear that an understanding of Egyptian English will help to resolve the communication problem here. There is no evidence that "blowing" is used with a local indexicality. The enigmatic word is a situational choice that lies outside stable and systematic use. In fact, Ahmad might be monitoring his use to avoid local resources here as he is talking to a non-local. "Blowing" is also not evidently part of the lingua franca core or WSSE. Thus, the word is not part of a universally shared norm as ELF or EIL models would postulate. Though this is a type of lingua franca interaction, between subjects from an Expanding Circle and an Outer Circle community, the speakers don't share the meaning of this word.

Some may explain that the word is a case of interlanguage and doesn't fall under the purview of existing models which theorize the stabilized usage of proficient speakers. They might thus argue that the word is idiosyncratic or erroneous in terms of their own models. However, the point to note is that the word is still functional. Both interlocutors end up giving this word its own indexicality and achieving their communicative objectives. Rather than being unusual in lingua franca communication, it is very typical of what takes place. Interlocutors negotiate their meanings situationally in relation to their needs. Translinguals do come up with forms and words that defy systematicity or stability all the time. They co-construct meanings and achieve inter-subjective understanding through negotiation strategies. The fact that norms and forms are unpredictable and heterogeneous I treat as typical of contact zone interactions. Rather than ruling out items that stand outside the shared norms as erroneous or idiosyncratic (in fidelity to systems), it is more important to consider how people do end up giving them meaning and achieve communicative success. Everyday communicative achievements in the contact zone shouldn't be puzzling if we focus on negotiation strategies and not forms, as the participants themselves seem to be doing here. Furthermore, this is a case of semiodiversity that is not captured by models orientating to glossodiversity. A word that is already available in the English language (i.e., "blowing") is being used in a new context, receiving new indexicality.

Some scholars may attribute the initial confusion to the local identities and values the interlocutors bring to the interaction. The very indirect way in which Ahmad frames his complaint (in #1) could be based on the face-saving strategies of non-Western communities. Rather than saying outright that he wishes to cancel the order, Ahmad frames his utterance in terms of a preference. The phrase "we don't want" may indicate a collective preference rather than a legalistic canceling of the order. His follow-up comment (#3) is even more indirect as Ahmad first frames the displeasure as a form of personal dilemma or confusion, and later as a consultation on what to do. The failure in Hansen's uptake is probably due to this indirect framing of utterances. It is on line 5 that Ahmad says very directly that the cheese has gone bad. There are also power differences that might complicate comprehension. It is possible that the indirect framing of utterances is due to Ahmad's deferential attitude toward Hansen. We also see that while Ahmad uses the less direct "we" and addresses his interlocutor as "Mister Hansen," the latter sounds more direct and authoritative. He uses "I" freely, proffers his own gloss for Ahmad's unintelligible word (in #4), and doesn't address Ahmad by any title or name. Though these traces of power and culture have a bearing on unintelligibility, I will show below that they are open to renegotiation. There are other factors in the context that motivate both interlocutors to negotiate these factors situationally, beyond the stereotypical differences.

Let us then ask how a word that cannot be legitimized according to WE, EIL, or ELF models turns out to be meaningful. Note first that both interlocutors are very supportive and collaborative in resolving the unintelligible word. On line 2, Hansen initially signals uptake (i.e., "see, yes"), though it is clear later that he didn't understand the critical word "blowing." This could be an accommodation strategy on his part (contrary to the presumed directness of Westerners) to be supportive in this conversation. This is a strategy translinguals adopt to go along with the flow of the conversation rather than disrupt it. It is motivated by the collaborative disposition researchers find to be common among translinguals. Firth (1996) calls this the "let-it-pass" principle. It is not adopted merely to be nice to the interlocutor. As the conversation progresses, the listener will get more clues to resolve the meaning of the unintelligible item (especially since the word will recur if it is critical for the communicative objectives). If Hansen had been judgemental or impatient, he could have conveyed negative attitudes that could have affected the negotiation.

On line 3, we see that Ahmad is clearly monitoring uptake as he repeats his query in a slightly more direct manner. Hansen's response on line 2 was not the right uptake, as he didn't respond to the illocutionary force of Ahmad's utterance. He didn't address the problem of spoilt cheese. Ahmad is again sensitive to the pause on line 3, after his first rephrasing of the problem. He is collaborative and supportive in providing another rephrasing, ending with a question that clearly requires an answer and not another vague uptake. All this shows that Ahmad is sensitive to contextualization cues such as silences and pauses, and uses them strategically for communication.

The longer pause after line 3 suggests that Hansen is now thinking more carefully as he has at least understood the need to make a decision about the order. What is interesting is that he is again supportive and collaborative, and offers a gloss to the word ("big" in #4) as he makes a request for clarification. Clarification strategies such as this are very common in contact zone interactions to achieve meaning (Kaur, 2009). Ahmad corrects him in #5 with a rephrasing with the word "bad." The short pause suggests that the gloss is probably too broad. It fails to gain uptake. So Ahmad offers another gloss with "fermenting" on the same line. Glosses by interlocutors are also well-known lingua franca strategies for meaning negotiation (Kirkpatrick, 2010, p. 141). One might say that even "fermenting" is not very helpful, as it is probably "over-fermenting" that Ahmad meant. At this point, Hansen offers another gloss for "blowing" (i.e., "gone off" in #6) and that gains uptake from Ahmad, as they now resolve the meaning of that word.

That "gone off" is a British expression and approximates British English might complicate the interpretation. However, the nature of the interaction makes clear that both interlocutors are not striving to adopt an NES norm, but only to make sense to each other in their own terms. Furthermore, "gone off" is only a gloss for "blowing" and not the co-constructed new word. The researchers (Firth and Wagner, 2007) mention that in a subsequent conversation these two subjects use "blowing" and not "gone off" as their shared indexical. This confirms the "make it normal" strategy identified by Firth (1996). That is, an unconventional word "blowing" gets normalized as a shared word, rather than being replaced by a British norm (even if we grant that both are aware of the pedigree of "gone off"). We may even say that the gloss doesn't fully capture the meaning of "blowing" as it is used by both participants. It is the whole trajectory of their negotiation, including alignment with multimodal resources in the context, that provides them an emic understanding of the meaning of the word.

We must realize that meaning negotiation is helped by resources beyond language or words. We have to be wary of giving too much importance to words alone for their meaning-making capacity. The models we have considered above (WE, EIL, and ELF) are constructed in the Structuralist tradition, treating language as a self-contained system. However, people are able to make meaning by violating the system (or prescriptively defined grammatical structures), because meaning emerges in alignment with other ecological resources. Note the role of features such as the topic of the conversation, the geographical context, and the immediate situation relating to the cheese import which probably help the interlocutors clarify the word. Note also other features such as the hesitation phenomena and silences on the telephone conversation for the way they communicate levels of uptake and need for clarification. If the fairly delocalized conversation on the telephone had not reduced ecological resources in the transcript, we would have seen how situational features of the ecology in face-to-face conversation provide even greater resources for intelligibility—as I will demonstrate in the chapters to follow. Matsumoto (2012) demonstrates how LFE interlocutors creatively use gestures to complement the negotiation of non-intelligible items, and sometimes to substitute for needed words.

My mention of collaborative negotiations shouldn't give the implication that the contact zone is egalitarian. As I mentioned earlier, there are power differences in this interaction. What is interesting is that they are renegotiated as the conversation proceeds. There are factors in the conversation that help both parties negotiate their statuses and identity positions differently. Though Ahmad is somewhat deferential at times, he is probably also aware that as the buyer he has the power to turn back the shipment, affecting Hansen's revenue. Even better, both people have different interests in this conversation, and they should take care not to harm their mutual interests through the conversation. It is probably this awareness that motivates Hansen to adopt more supportive and collaborative strategies himself, despite Ahmad's deference. Note also that Ahmad becomes increasingly more direct as the conversation proceeds. He can directly say that "the cheese is bad" on line 5. We mustn't take the presumed face-saving and indirect strategies of non-Western cultures too far. We must situate them in the context of the communication to see how they are used strategically at different points. Similarly, a one-sided exercise of power by either party may not have enabled them to achieve this kind of communicative success so effectively. Power is mutually negotiated to facilitate successful communication and satisfactory outcomes for both parties.

While the example shows that norms neither govern nor guarantee meaning-making, we cannot deny that certain patterned features of English help both interlocutors succeed in this conversation. Consider the fairly similar syntax structure both use, considerably similar to NES norms. Also, though "blowing" seems idiosyncratic, there are other words that they share. The issue, however, is that no airtight system exists to guarantee meaning. The "system" is porous to resources from other languages, ecological factors, diverse semiotic resources, and the personalized uses influenced by identity and cultural reasons. Furthermore, the system is always relocalized (Pennycook, 2010) with the language resources gaining new meaning and values all the time in each occasion of use. Words and grammatical forms are always gaining new indexicality in new contexts. The "system" is thus always in a state of becoming. Moreover, the example shows that although there are items of sedimented patterns guiding this conversation (such as the syntax and other shared words), one new and unshared word is sometimes enough to upset the functionality of the "system." Though the other shared items help in achieving communicative success, the new word has to be negotiated in context for the whole interaction to succeed. Note also that the negotiation of the idiosyncratic word doesn't lead to accommodating the predefined norms, as some versions of CA and SLA would analyze (for a critique, see Firth and Wagner, 1997), but to the co-construction of a new indexical. These are the reasons why a focus on norms and sharedness doesn't go far enough. We have to focus on the semiodiversity occasioned by the surprising new uses of words and co-constructed indexicalities. From this perspective, the pluralization and diversification of English cannot be controlled. "English" is never at a point of stability or stasis. The stable and shared grammatical system is a convenient postulation to help analysis. A more realistic approach is to focus on the practices of meaning-making that people use to achieve intelligibility in the unpredictable communicative conditions and changing norms of the contact zone.

Conclusion

A translingual perspective thus treats diversity as the norm in the study of English. It challenges the assumption of other models of global Englishes that sharedness and uniformity of norms at different levels of generality are required for communicative success. In contact zones, sharedness cannot be guaranteed. To explain how unshared words or grammatical structures gain situated meaning, the model of translingual English attends to the local contexts and practices of negotiation with the fullest ecological resources. My model focuses on practices rather than form to explain communicative success. While this chapter has made a case for adopting this orientation and demonstrated the possibilities in explaining contact zone communication, we have to now proceed to describing the strategies that facilitate meaning negotiation. This area of work is still relatively undeveloped, and the following chapters will take this inquiry further.

5

TRANSLINGUAL NEGOTIATION STRATEGIES

To carry forward the argument from the last chapter that English as a contact language works through the strategies people adopt to negotiate their differences, we need to know more about the strategies in such encounters. Though these strategies are not the same for everyone and for all situations, they are adopted by everyone for communicative success. Both NES and multilingual speakers have competence in these strategies, and treat them as resources for successful communication. These strategies constitute a "grammar of practices," so to speak. This grammar will give insights into the competence people bring to contact zone communication—one I label *performative competence* in Chapter 9. Unfortunately, this area of consideration hasn't developed adequately as scholars have been looking at grammatical competence as more primary in communication, under the influence of the monolingual paradigm. In this chapter, we focus on the range of strategies that translinguals use in lingua franca conversations to co-construct meaning. The few studies on pragmatics in contact English are reviewed and classified under an overarching model that provides a better explanatory framework. Finally, I analyze a conversation among multilingual students to illustrate the way such practices and strategies work to shape communication in interactions where there is no uniformly shared or "advanced" proficiency in grammatical norms.

Approaches to meaning negotiation in translingual English

Two schools in particular have helped in the exploration of negotiation strategies in lingua franca interactions. They are conversation analysis (CA) and pragmatics. In recent years, scholars of lingua franca English have adopted these approaches insightfully to promote an understanding of the creative communicative practices of multilingual speakers in English. In CA-based studies, the work of Firth (1990, 1996, 2009), Gramkow Andersen (1993, 2001), and Meierkord (2004) have been influential. In pragmatics, House (2002, 2003) and David Li (2002) have provided useful insights.

While I refer to their findings in the discussion below, I want to focus on some of the basic assumptions of both research approaches here to develop a more integrated analytical orientation for my data presented below. The translingual approach requires slight shifts to suit the theoretical orientation it brings with it. I will discuss the limitations in the current approaches before I move on to develop a more integrated model for translingual purposes.

The usefulness of CA is that it cultivates an emic perspective on conversational interactions. It encourages us to consider how the conversation is structured and meaning is shaped from the participants' own perspectives. In this manner, the biases of the researcher, especially relating to the deficiencies of multilingual speakers, are not allowed to affect the analysis. CA also encourages us to look at meaning-making and communicative success as a collaborative activity where the interlocutors take equal responsibility and display agency. CA provides analytical tools for a moment-by-moment micro-analysis of sequential talk to consider how the moves by interlocutors are patterned, strategic, and dynamic. Constructs such as repair, rephrasing, confirmation check, and clarification strategies help us discover how interlocutors achieve intelligibility (see Kaur, 2009; Pitzl, 2010). Some have adopted the principles of CA to challenge the biased orientations of second language acquisition (SLA) which treats grammatical deviations by multilinguals as deficient (see Firth and Wagner, 1997). They have shown that mulitlinguals may construct meaning even in cases where they deviate from NES grammatical norms. Firth and Wagner (1997) have also demonstrated powerfully through their own analysis of transcripts studied by SLA specialists that what were considered as deviations and communication breakdown actually were renegotiated by multilinguals through creative strategies to form their own meanings. The ability to tap into the meanings which interlocutors themselves co-construct challenges analysts' biases about the meanings and forms they consider normative.

Despite these advantages, there are certain other elements of CA that limit its analyses. Because of the emic perspective and the micro-analysis of sequential talk, CA treats contexts and identities in a quite restricted sense. The context is considered significant only to the extent that it is invoked in the talk. Even then, elements of the broader structure (such as power, culture, identity, and ecology) are not addressed with adequate complexity in the patterns and structures developed through its analysis. Moerman (1988) has argued that CA focuses too heavily on structures in talk while ignoring culture. These microstructures of conversation (i.e., adjacency pairs and IRF routines) have a self-contained order that leaves out a lot of information about the larger contextual details. There is also a sense that the conversational rules discovered by CA are basic and universal to all human communication. Admittedly, CA has to function at a deep-structural sense to arrive at such universal and microcontextual rules. Eventually, these patterns appear to favor a sense of sharedness at the level of practices and negotiation strategies, facing the danger that they might consider deviations motivated by cultural or identity differences as deficient. Similarly, though the model addresses meaning-making, it is more interested in discovering the structures that govern the talk rather than the subtleties of semiodiversity. In this sense, it is somewhat form-based. Or, at least, it turns interactional practices into sequential structures, limiting its focus on issues of semiodiversity.

Pragmatics, on the other hand, focuses on speech acts and gives more attention to information and meaning in interactions. In treating the way such speech acts are shaped by social and cultural backgrounds, it also gives more importance to semiodiversity. It has thrown light onto features such as contextualization cues and discourse strategies, and helped us understand how interlocutors negotiate meaning (see House, 2003; Li, 2002). In this way, pragmatics also gives greater attention to performance and shows that they have rules of their own and play a critical role in communication. However, this sensitivity to macro-contextual features is achieved at a price. The findings relating to pragmatic strategies of multilinguals in contact situations have been presented in lists (see Kirkpatrick, 2010, p. 143) that don't show the way these strategies are interactional, dynamic, and co-constructed. The approach is a bit too detached to tap into the insider meaning negotiation of multilinguals. Furthermore, in adopting an etic perspective, pragmatics is sometimes comparative and judgmental. It assumes the right to define pragmatic failure and provide recipes for success. As a result, the model is also somewhat problem-focused in its approach. It assumes normativity in judging failure and in making inter-community comparisons. Also, the notion of culture adopted by pragmatics has to be broadened considerably to accommodate culture as mediated, hybrid, and changing (as I show in the analysis of the conversation in Chapter 4). In fact, cultural difference can be a resource, not a problem, for meaning-making. Similarly, the cultures that people bring with them don't necessarily condition them to behave in particular ways. Interlocutors have the agency to move beyond their "native" cultures to reconstruct third cultures or new spaces for the negotiation of meaning. House (2003) for example posits a shared community and culture for lingua franca English users to adopt effective pragmatic strategies. The position of translingual English is that people can start from their preferred cultural values and identities and still engage in collaborative meaning-making. Culture doesn't have to be filtered away or finessed to construct shared meaning. People have the capacity to represent cultural differences and negotiate shared understanding.

Despite their differences, both CA and pragmatics have the similarity of being influenced by norm-oriented perspectives. At a very basic level, these models project a sharedness of norms and values to account for the success of communication. It is important for interlocutors to orient to this commonality (of conversational structure, pragmatic strategies, or cultural values) to make meaning. However, translingual English is open to difference being negotiable and serving as a resource for communicative success. Furthermore, we have to attend to the ways in which macro-level context and identity differences are factored into micro-level meaning-making processes. These are not extras, but central to meaning construction. For this purpose, the resources of CA and pragmatics have to be brought together, as was observed by Levinson (1983) some time ago. Furthermore, the translingual orientation won't filter the negotiation of meaning to derive a core structure that shapes meaning. We should attend to the trajectory of talk to consider how meaning is shaped. In this kind of analysis, apparent deviations or misunderstandings need not be dysfunctional.

They are productive and generative. More importantly, understanding and mis-understanding are part of a continuum where, through negotiation strategies, misunderstandings evolve into new understandings. As such, we have to focus more closely on such cases of momentary breakdown and give them more significance for the way they call forth the creative strategies of translinguals to construct meaning. Furthermore, rather than deriving core structures, translingual research calls for a sensitivity to procedures and processes. It compels us to treat variation, unpredict-ability, and deviation as the norm. What is more important is an inquiry into how translinguals deal with surprising moves and meanings with creative and adaptive strategies and succeed in meaning-making. In this sense, translingual research calls for a perspective that does not structure practice into new stable and abstract norms. We must also consider talk as multimodal. The ecology of contexts, participants, and texts should be taken into consideration in defining meaning. The notion of communica-tion and meaning adopted in this chapter to understand translingual practice is broader and more dynamic than the available models allow in our field.

Negotiation strategies

Some researchers of contact English have thrown useful light on the strategies trans-linguals adopt to negotiate meaning in the contact zones. Though not all these scholars adopt the practice-based orientation of the translingual model, it is useful to build from the strategies they identify. In this section I draw from these research insights and my own to develop a more holistic orientation to the strategies used to negotiate English in the contact zone. The ethnographies I have conducted with multilingual students and migrant professionals (to be discussed in this chapter and the following ones) have enabled me to formulate these strategies. It is useful to intro-duce the macro-level strategies first, before I analyze texts and talk in the contact zone to demonstrate how these strategies are enacted.

I divide these negotiation strategies into four components: *envoicing, recontextualization, interactional,* and *entextualization.* I consider them to be macro-level strategies, as each of them contains more specific strategies situated in the interaction. My formulation reflects the central constructs in any act of communication, that is, personal, con-textual, social, and textual dimensions respectively. Their relationship to each other in communication can be explained as follows: envoicing strategies shape the extent and nature of hybridity, as a consideration of voice plays a critical role in appropriating mobile semiotic resources in one's texts and talk; recontextualization strategies frame the text/talk and alter the footing to prepare the ground for appropriate negotiation; interactional strategies are adopted to negotiate and manage meaning-making activity; and entextualization strategies configure codes in the temporal and spatial dimension of the text/talk to facilitate and respond to these negotiations. These four strategies do not make up air-tight compartments. They are interconnected and inform one another. For example, recontextualization strategies are connected to envoicing, as they are ways of framing one's semiotic choices for successful uptake. Entextualization is relevant to all the others, as speakers/writers orchestrate their semiotic resources to embed their voice, and cue the listener/reader on the appropriate footing to encourage interaction. Though these strategies are common for speaking and writing, I will show that their realization will be different based on the resources available in the different modalities of communication.

I proceed to define each of these macro-strategies and describe their communicative significance in more detail:

Envoicing: This strategy refers to modes of encoding one's identity and location in texts and talk. In English at the contact zone, speakers desire to be understood with all their social and cultural particularity. In effect, voice is not an extra for communication. It is everything in communication. As Bakhtin (1986) theorizes it, to speak is to envoice—or populate language resources with one's own intentions and histories. From this perspective, it is difficult to separate meaning negotiation from identity representation. Furthermore, since language is performative, speakers/writers could be communicating complex rhetorical meanings through their choices, far exceeding their formal proficiency in a language. Translinguals achieve performative acts such as establishing different levels of relationships with different individuals and social groups, not to mention accomplishing diverse material and symbolic outcomes.

However, envoicing strategies have been left out of ELF studies, as scholars have adopted a narrow view of meaning as information transfer. "Negotiation of meaning," in many of these studies, is analyzed largely in terms of semantic content (see Kaur, 2009; Pitzl, 2010). This is part of the narrow context ELF scholars inherit from schools like CA. More importantly, certain ELF scholars have argued against the significance of identity in lingua franca interactions. As discussed in Chapter 4, House (2003, p. 559) treats ELF as a "language for communication," rather than a "language for identification." Such scholars assume that multilingual speakers will use English for utilitarian purposes with a pragmatic attitude, and not develop a cultural affinity with the language or represent their identities through English.

Translinguals have to make complex decisions about envoicing in their communication. What mix of language resources to mesh, and where and when, involves strategic choices. These decisions are especially complicated in contact zones, as language users have to be mindful of the language resources their interlocutors bring with them, and the affordances in the context for intelligibility and communicative success. I will demonstrate the practices of translinguals that enable them to negotiate their voices in text and talk.

Recontextualization: In order to gain uptake of their envoicing strategies, interlocutors have to attend to recontextualization. They have to frame their talk in ways conducive to uptake and achieve the appropriate footing for meaning negotiation. In situations of language contact, there might be ambiguity and confusion as to which frame or footing applies in an interaction. When speakers from diverse cultural and social backgrounds use English for the negotiation of meaning, there are questions as to whose frame and which footing applies. These options have to be appropriately cued so that meaning is successfully negotiated. Often, these decisions have to be continually renegotiated as the conversation or literacy event evolves. This doesn't mean making the other party always accept one's own preferred footing. As I will show below, recontextualization amounts to having both sides be comfortable with their differences. Interlocutors may communicate with the knowledge that they will both use different cultural frames or language norms, and both have to be prepared to achieve intelligibility across these differences. In other words, they will frame the event as one in which both interlocutors' differing norms have to be acknowledged and an egalitarian footing adopted.

This strategy is not unique to LFE interactions (see Silverstein and Urban, 1996). A certain amount of recontextualization work always takes place in talk in any context, even between native speakers of a language. Interlocutors have to frame their talk in relation to the relevant contexts that apply to their talk, and the communicative norms and conventions that bear upon that particular interaction. When Goffman originally defined the two key constructs in recontextualization, frames and footing, he didn't necessarily have lingua franca encounters in mind. Goffman defined footing as: "the alignment we take up to ourselves and the others present as expressed in the way we manage the production or reception of an utterance" (Goffman, 1981, p. 128). Footing is shaped to some extent by the way the talk is framed. Each frame assumes different types of footing that shape the stance of the interlocutors to negotiate their communication.

In much of ELF research, the perspective on context is narrow. Often, a macro-level consideration of recontextualization is left out of these studies. For example, Pitzl (2010) has focused on clarifying the place of context in ELF research that explores pragmatic strategies. She argues for focusing on micro-context rather than macro-context in her data, influenced by the CA approach she adopts. Pitzl also invokes Widdowson (1997) to argue that areas of macro-context are not relevant in lingua franca encounters, as these interactions are guided by institutionalized registers in clearly defined communities of practice, whose frames and footing are predefined and shared. However, I am open to norm differences even in specialized varieties. Furthermore, I hold that the extent to which macro-context can be embedded in talk is variable. The presence and relevance of context is an interpretive dimension that may not be explicitly available in talk. Moreover, contextualization cues are not limited to words, but gestures, body posture, and other semiotic resources in the context. The macro-context may be negotiated *through* such diverse semiotic resources.

The significance of recontextualization in LFE is brought out well by Planken. Comparing the discourse of professionals and novices, in sales encounters between Norwegians and Swedes, she finds that professionals are more successful as they focus on framing their talk and establishing the proper footing before they begin their sales negotiations. Through "safe talk," they develop rapport and prepare interlocutors for differences in norms and conventions (Planken, 2005, p. 397). In many cases, the topic of the "safe talk" relates to "interculturalness" (Planken, 2005, p. 397). These are reflexive comments on their own cultures, peculiarities, and differences. Planken goes on to say, "It would seem that by pointing out and acknowledging cultural differences, participants try to create a temporary in-group of (fellow) non-natives, whose common ground is the fact that they differ culturally" (Planken, 2005, p. 397).

Comments about their non-nativeness enabled them to build a solidarity that facilitated effective negotiation when gaps or mistakes occurred. Thus the interlocutors created a third space, that is, "a no-man's-land" (Planken, 2005, p. 397), activating flexible norms and practices that facilitated their own voices and norms. It is useful to note here that the space constructed for talk is not one with *shared* norms. It is, paradoxically, a space where differences can be displayed freely and negotiated actively. In other words, this is a collaboratively constructed space for aceptance of differences, not a sharedness. We might say that this is a space where people agree to disagree! As Planken herself articulates this paradox, for these Norwegian and Swedish professionals, their "common ground is the fact that they differ culturally" (Planken, 2005, p. 397). It is also important to realize that this negotiation involves work related to macro-contexts, such as people's cultures of communication. Though the interlocutors share a community of practice, as marketing professionals, this doesn't solve all their challenges in framing and footing. They have to undertake recontextualization strategies to negotiate context in all its complexity. The reason why novices fail is that they don't engage in such recontextualization work. Though Planken's study presents recontextualization strategy as a preparatory work before actual sales negotiations begin, I will show other examples from my oral and written data on how recontextualization continues at various points *during* the communication.

Interactional: I define this as a social activity of co-constructing meaning by adopting reciprocal and collaborative strategies. The enactment of these strategies is also dynamic. Participants do not necessarily use the same strategies. They are reciprocal in the sense that interlocutors adopt strategies that complement and/or resist those of the other for negotiation of meaning or rhetorical and social objectives. These are largely strategies of *alignment*, which we defined earlier as ways in which interlocutors match the language resources they bring with people, situations, objects, and communicative ecologies for meaning-making.

Research on ELF pragmatics has contributed to understanding interactional strategies. The studies by Pitzl (2010) and Kaur (2009) provide powerful insights into the negotiation of meaning to deal with miscommunication and shared understanding, respectively. These two studies can be treated as companion pieces, as they study the two sides of the same coin in meaning-construction (i.e., understanding and lack of understanding). Influenced by CA approaches, both provide insights into the creative and strategic moves multilinguals adopt in their conversations. What we find is that multilinguals can adopt very complex strategies that belie their formal competence to accomplish the successful negotiation of meaning. These strategies are anticipatory and reactive, both self-initiated and other-initiated. There is also a range of explicit and indirect cues that can be used for these purposes (see Pitzl and Kaur for examples). Kirkpatrick also provides a list of strategies grouped according to speakers and listeners. For example, listener-initiated strategies include: lexical anticipation, lexical suggestion, lexical correction, don't give up, request repetition, request clarification, let it pass, listen to the message, participant paraphrase, and participant prompt. Speaker-initiated strategies include spell out the word, repeat the phrase, be explicit, paraphrase, and avoid local/idiomatic references (Kirkpatrick, 2010, p. 141).

However, there are also important differences in my approach. What such lists miss is that these strategies are very dynamic. Interlocutors make instantaneous and strategic decisions on how to reciprocate the moves of the other. Furthermore, in the temporal context, there are reasons why speakers may use one strategy or the other. We must therefore go beyond the study of isolated acts and strategies in localized contexts to consider the spatiotemporal trajectory in which these strategies are deployed. For example, we will find that there are different meanings and rationales behind the use of the same strategy in different locations. My analysis of entextualization will provide a temporal orientation to these strategies. Furthermore, we must note that however insightful these strategies might be, scholars sometimes give the impression that a particular move represents only one strategy at a time. An advantage in outlining a diversity of strategies that focus on different dimensions of communication is that each move may signify different types and levels of meaning. As I will show below, what we might consider as a confirmation-seeking strategy (i.e., "This is too expensive, isn't it?") could also be a rhetorical question to seek affirmation.

More importantly, I look at these strategies not only in terms of meaning negotiation but in terms of rhetorical and social considerations as well. For example, these strategies help to negotiate identities and power (i.e., social dimension). They help to convey performative meanings, negotiate disagreements, or influence people's opinions (i.e., rhetorical dimension). Therefore, while ELF scholars study these strategies as part of meaning negotiation (with meaning treated narrowly as information-transfer), I consider these strategies more holistically for the different dimensions of their functionality. From this perspective, when I use phrases like meaning negotiation or meaning construction, I use "meaning" in the expanded sense to accommodate rhetorical and social meanings as well.

There is also an assumption in ELF research that all these strategies are shared by multilinguals. Kaur argues: "Even NNS's [non-native speakers] must, and do, subscribe to a set of 'common' procedures and methods to produce and understand talk in ELF. For if this were not the case, communication in ELF would never take place" (Kaur, 2009, p. 36). In effect, although multilinguals might not share language norms, it is their sharedness of interactional strategies that explains communicative success for ELF. We must be careful not to exaggerate sharedness even at the level of strategies. The notion of alignment allows for the possibility that interlocutors can negotiate different strategies in the context of other affordances in the communicative ecology for success. It is not sharedness but reciprocity that is key. Interlocutors should come up with strategies that respond to the moves of the interlocutor to negotiate meanings. The Indian linguist Khubchandani highlights the "mutuality of focus," and the "reciprocity of language skills" (Khubchandani, 1997, p. 49) rather than sharedness in his description of translingual communication in South Asia.

Furthermore, we must be careful not to explain all these strategies in terms of convergence strategies of speech accommodation theory (see Giles, 1984). This seems to be the rationale adopted by Kaur (2009) and Pitzl (2010) to explain the different strategies their interlocutors take to manage talk (see also Seidlhofer, 2004). However, interlocutors are not always or only interested in agreement and harmony. Though they do demonstrate solidarity to collaborate in meaning negotiation, they are also interested in accentuating their differences for voice (as I will show from my data later). In this case, these strategies can also be used for disagreement or resistance. We mustn't mistake these apparent disagreements, conflicts, and unresolved differences as dysfunctional for communication, however. These could be very intentional, and they have to be communicated well to succeed. We must note that the contact zone is power-ridden and interlocutors sometimes use a range of divergence strategies for effective negotiation of voice and interests. It is possible to be supportive in conversational procedures and resistant in the message.

Some scholars have pointed to more culture-based rhetorical strategies, going beyond the more structuralist and micro-level CA constructs which are dominant in ELF research. House demonstrates how students of English coming from different countries to study in Germany bring the pragmatic strategies valued in their own communities to facilitate communication with outsiders. Paradoxically, these are culture-specific pragmatic strategies that complement intercultural communication. This is also an example of how practices that are non-shared can still help achieve intelligibility. For example, House finds that "Asian participants employ topic management strategies in a striking way, recycling a specific topic regardless of where and how the discourse had developed at any particular point" (House, 2003, p. 567). This discourse of "parallel monologues" facilitates interlocutors from other cultures, as it helps them focus on each move as if it were a fresh topic. A second strategy is an echoing of the previous speaker's statement, which House calls "represents" (House, 2003, p. 568), done with the purpose of affirming contributions according to the politeness conventions of Asian cultures. This strategy also serves to remind interlocutors of the threads of the discourse and to facilitate communication. A third strategy is a "strong demonstration of solidarity and consensus-orientation" (House, 2003, p. 569), which is also influenced by Asian cultural patterns of group orientation. In all these cases, while the local cultural ways of interacting are alive in English, they paradoxically serve to negotiate difference and ensure intelligibility at the contact zone. The twin *"let-it-pass"* and *make it normal* strategies that Firth (1996) brings out in his path-breaking research on LFE also belong to this orientation.

Entextualization: This macro-strategy addresses the spatiotemporal production processes of text and talk for voice and intelligibility. It reveals how speakers and writers monitor and manage their productive processes by exploiting the spatiotemporal dimensions of the text. It will also orientate us to the trajectory of meaning-encoding practices in contact zone encounters. Of course, these textual decisions are made in relation to considerations of voice and context mentioned above. However, there is value in focusing on translinguals' control over the resources of the text. Apart from demonstrating their agency, their choices will also reveal more about their unfolding rhetorical and social intentions in communication. Such an analysis is more convenient in written communication as we have the advantage of studying successive drafts of writers for their intentions. As writers edit, omit, and revise their lexical, grammatical, and syntactic choices, we can infer their intentions and purposes. Similar strategies are adopted in talk, but realized differently, as fitting the face-to-face modality (see Silverstein and Urban, 1996). Revisions and changes often occur in real time, as would become evident in a turn-by-turn analysis of talk. There is evidence that speakers monitor their speech and deploy tokens and expressions gradually to entextualize their intentions with greater care, control, and creativity. However, these strategies are important not only for what they reveal about language use, but they are also performative. They help translinguals accomplish many other functions, that is: they may prepare interlocutors for unconventional choices; they may test the uptake of interlocutors; and they may elicit particular responses from interlocutors.

Some scholars of LFE have provided useful insights into entextualization strategies. Translinguals use discourse strategies (at the textual or syntactic level) to accommodate local variants. Focusing on syntactic variation, Meierkord (2004) finds that individuals retain the characteristics of their own English varieties, facilitating communication through entextualization strategies such as segmentation and regularization. Though Meierkord finds mostly less competent "expanding circle" speakers producing localized forms, they manage to communicate effectively thanks to skillful entextualization strategies. Of the two strategies she discovers, *simplification* strategies involve procedures such as segmentation. Utterances are shortened into clausal or phrasal segments which form the basic informational units. The second, *regularization*, involves foregrounding of forms that are explicit. Topicalization is one such strategy of regularization. This involves the movement of focused information to the front of the utterance.

An enactment

I illustrate the role of these negotiation strategies in a conversational interaction below. I take another look at a transcript which Paul Roberts and I have analyzed from a different perspective elsewhere (see Roberts and Canagarajah, 2009).[1] The conversational interaction involves five multilingual undergraduate students in the UK. The group members were all students at the University of Hertfordshire, between 19 and 23 years of age. They were all enrolled as "international students" and had been in the UK for three months at the time of the recording. The students were asked to participate in a group activity, requiring them to plan the forthcoming visit to the university of an international dignitary and to make proposals for spending the budget for the visit. The simulated activity enabled us to control the exact mix of subjects in each group, so that we might compare the performance of the groups with different variables. We compared the mixed student conversation to a set of nine conversations where the participants were in conversation with their co-nationals. The conversations were recorded, transcribed, and then tagged for key variables.

As we consider the features that contribute to the success of this communication, we must first realize the difficult challenge these students are faced with. They have been given a limited budget to organize the diverse needs and features of this visit by a dignitary. Not only do they have to handle the event under the budget provided, but they have to do so in a way that their own interests are not compromised. Since they each take responsibility for a particular component of this event (i.e., decorations, security, entertainment, refreshments, and publicity), they are somewhat invested in the negotiations. They want the best possible outcome for the task which they have individually undertaken, without harming group solidarity. There are thus material and emotional investments in this conversation. The conversation can be tense at times as each student tries to argue for more resources for his or her undertaking. The interaction calls for a lot of diplomacy. Individuals have to adjust the budget without letting the others get the impression that they are being slighted. And they have to do all this in a language that is not necessarily their preferred code or in which they are deemed not to have advanced proficiency. The personal investments in this interaction engender a very involved speech sample with complex strategies of negotiation. In other words, it is not only their utterances that they monitor in order to negotiate their non-shared semiotic resources, but they are also monitoring their positions on the project. They are very strategic in the way they negotiate their objectives with others. Not only are they able to modify their own positions (i.e., reduce the amount of money they claim), but they also make concessions to others (i.e., increase the amount awarded to them). Furthermore, not only are they able to lobby for their own needs, but they are able to do so without losing face with others or making their interlocutors feel exploited or imposed upon. Implicit in this encounter is a delicate negotiation of power, involving differences in gender, culture, and language ownership. In some ways, the interaction resembles an exercise on democratic deliberation in cosmopolitan relations.

The participants in the interaction are:

1. Hedda: a Norwegian female who started learning English at school at the age of five. Like many Norwegians, she is able to understand Danish.
2. Javier: a male from Equatorial Guinea who started learning English at school at the age of 11. He also speaks Spanish and Fang.
3. Hao: a Chinese male who started learning English at school at the age of 11. He also speaks his home language (unidentified since he referred to it as "only a dialect") and Standard Chinese.
4. Sofia: a German female who started learning English at school at the age of nine.
5. Milne: an Anglo-American male who started learning Spanish at school at the age of 13.

None of the participants described herself/himself as bilingual except Javier, who considered himself bilingual in Spanish and Fang. Though subjects 1–4 didn't claim advanced proficiency in English (or bilingual status in that language), we will find that they employed effective negotiation strategies to achieve intelligibility and accomplish their problem-solving activity successfully. I will show that the native speaker, Milne, is also quite proficient in these negotiation strategies, confirming the translingual perspective that everyone has the aptitude for these strategies. However, we must note that Milne's status is considerably mediated by other variables. He is in the UK, where he too is an international student. He has to negotiate his variety with the locally dominant British. More importantly, he is a minority in this contact situation, and sees the need to negotiate with the other multilinguals. To some extent, he too is a multilingual by virtue of his proficiency in Spanish.

Diversity in form

Before we look at the negotiation strategies adopted by the students, it is good to analyze their proficiency in form. The findings show that the students don't bring uniform resources in form. Though the multilingual students deviated from NES norms, each had their own ways of deviating from them. We might say they had their own idiolects, confirming the tendency of translinguals in contact zones to retain their own norms as they negotiate for meaning. The choices may also be motivated by voice considerations. Despite this diversity at the level of form, we will note that there is no serious communication breakdown in this interaction. This finding thus shifts the focus to their negotiation strategies that enable them to resolve their differences in form.

To illustrate their idiolects, consider first their differences in phrasing. Sofia talks about the VIP having "security of his own" while Javier refers to a "security at your own:"

29 Sofia: Because maybe the important person have, has a security of his own. [...]
34 Sofia: You don't think that the VIP, important person uhm not has security of
39   his own?
40 Javier: Yeah, they may have but you, you need to feel safe even if you have
41   security at your own, yeah?

However, both of them understand each other, and don't ask for clarifications or corrections. The same is true of other participants who follow the conversation despite these lexical and idiomatic differences. The students also have their own styles of collocating words. Hao collocates "raise" with "banquet." Sofia collocates "too" with "less."

82 Hao: My plan was kind of to raise a banquet or something
196 Sofia: two
197   thousand, is too less for me. Two thousand is too less.

We also see differences in the lexical choice of the participants. Hao uses "quid" to mean "pounds sterling," and "sweet" to mean something approximating "good":

240 Hao: Let's hold it in a warehouse or something. To pay four thousand quid
241   to clean this up-
279   Yeah, it's sweet xxx sweet all the light

To consider grammatical items next, participants seem to have different rules for the use and position of "just":

86 Hao: You don't want your
87   just important guest to just stay around

94 Javier: Two thousand, three thousand is a
95   lot of money for just food yeah?
146 Sofia: But maybe he will stay just for one hour
234 Hao: Yeah, just clean
293 Milne: Shall we switch from a movie and maybe just try and make a
294   booklet (.) with photos (.) and maybe writing about the story?
296 Javier: You mean just for newspaper?

Despite their different rules for this usage, the participants don't experience problems in intelligibility. It is possible that they are adopting the "let-it-pass" principle or intuiting the meaning in context. There are other idiosyncratic uses. Javier uses "isn't it" as an unmodified question tag; no one else does. Milne uses "that" to introduce relative clauses; no one else does. Javier makes extensive use of "going to" to express future predictions, Milne a little, the others not at all. Sofia and Hedda use "will" for future predictions, the others do not.

There are also instances of unmarked verbs in the third person singular present. These instances are confined to two out of the five participants, Javier and Sofia. Their use is unstable, however, with the simplified form competing sometimes with the standard one. Here is Javier's use:

31 Javier: Yeah, that's what this University need its own security
33 Javier: own security in case there might be a student or somebody don't like
50 Javier: even if the person haves his own security and he come to visit
94 Javier: Depend how many people.
230 Javier: And security need to be too
284 Javier: the security don't need

Here is Sofia's use:

297 Sofia: Because maybe the important person have, has a security of his own.
307 Sofia: Is it sure that he @he need one@?
387 Sofia: You don't think that the VIP, important person uhm not has security of
397   his own?

The native speaker, Milne, always uses "s" to mark third person singular verbs, a characteristic he shares with both Hao and Hedda. However, these three seem to have figured out the rule of Javier and Sofia. The transcript doesn't show any problems in intelligibility due to this grammatical difference.

The subjects also draw on their own repertoire of words, and make their own choices regarding how often they choose to use those words. The corpus analysis shows that of the 15 most frequent non-grammar words used by the four multilingual speakers, only "two" and "thousand" are shared by the whole group. "Need" and "important" are shared among four out of five, and "yeah" and "think" are shared by three. In other words, there is no widely shared word stock among this group of students. Comparatively, there are more words shared in the groups with homogeneous nationals.

We also find that the subjects in the mixed group interaction use certain forms and strategies which they don't use in their in-group communication. This suggests that they are adopting strategies specially intended for contact purposes. The native speaker in the interaction, Milne, is doing the same. For example, he uses more back-channeling cues with his compatriots than with the international students. He also frames his statements in declarative statements and not in open-ended questions, as he does with the international students. He is switching to a different discourse when he is with multilingual students. This suggests that contact zone communication displays more careful monitoring and sensitivity to the negotiation of differences.

What we find from this description of the overall analysis of the formal patterns in this conversation is that there is a lot of diversity among the speakers. Though there are many features they share, the subjects don't come to the conversation with norms that are completely or uniformly shared. Also, the usage of the multilingual speakers deviates from the grammar of NES (represented here by Milne). Yet, the deviations (and the mix of idiosyncratic features and standardized native speaker norms) don't hinder intelligibility or communicative success. As Kaur (2009) observes, and as is confirmed by other ELF scholars like Seidlhofer (2004) and House (2003), there is a "near absence of communication breakdown" in such lingua franca interactions (Kaur, 2009, p. 235). These observations make an analysis of negotiation strategies more important. We have to analyze how these students managed to accomplish their task so successfully even when their characteristic language forms and conventions were different.

Meaning-making practices

Envoicing

We must first note that the differences in form that we observed above can be part of envoicing. They serve to individuate the speakers. The preferred choice of form and conventions of the participants are designed to distinguish them. Speakers may accentuate their differences from others by moving away from uniform uses and shared norms. Such strategies provide each of them an identity and voice. This shows that achieving intelligibility and success in communication doesn't involve a sacrifice of people's peculiarities. We don't have enough evidence from this data set to say that these strategies are cultural. However, we mustn't treat culture in an essentialized manner and consider all features in a speaker's repertoire as deriving from his or her culture. Various performative reasons might influence someone to adopt a particular voice in a particular situation. Envoicing is part of a complex patterning of features for situated social and rhetorical acts.

In addition to the grammatical peculiarities, there are also rhetorical tendencies that serve envoicing purposes. It is useful to compare Hao with Sofia in this regard. Hao adopts an exaggerated and tongue-in-cheek manner of expressing himself. This manner of speaking is also designed to code disagreements effectively and persuade his peers in a non-threatening way. For example, Hao faces a difficult predicament as he is compelled to convey to Javier and Sofia that they have both used up the full budget of £10,000 for their own projects, leaving nothing for others. Consider his strategies of persuasion below:

68	Hao:	OK, my idea is kind of spend two between two and three thousand
69		dollars on food and drinking. Because I think OK you're two to
70		spent (.) I mean ten thousand pounds-
[...]		
77	Javier:	So we have to reduce the price.
78	Hedda:	Yeah
79	Hao:	I think the job is done
80	ALL:	@@@
81	Javier:	(.) So you are going to have-
82	Hao:	My plan was kind of to raise a banquet or something but you spent
83		all the money so it just-
84	Javier:	Well that this is our, our idea, yeah, where we think-
85	Hao:	No matter how, how secure the security are or as how beautiful the
86		place is, you still needs to some food or drink. You don't want your
87		just important guest to just stay around and spend all day and thirsty
88		very hungry. You don't want that.

Hao first vaguely hints that they have spent all the money when he makes his pitch for refreshments on line 68. When his point seems to have been conveyed (and Javier and Hedda see the need to reduce the price), Hao says something intriguing on line 79 (i.e., "I think the job is done"). He seems to be saying that if Sofia and Javier can only reduce their expenses the task can be successfully accomplished. I interpret this statement as an attempt to be humorous and to emphasize the importance of working within the budget. The fact that the others laugh suggests uptake as a joke. Similarly, when Hao says on line 82–83 that he wanted to plan a banquet "but you spent all the money," this too seems an exaggerated way of putting the idea across. The others haven't spent the money yet. Hao exaggerates similarly in his next utterance when he argues that the guest will be famished if they don't provide enough refreshments. This way of putting his point—in a sarcastic, exaggerated, and comical way—is very distinctive of Hao's style. No one else speaks like him.

Beyond serving identity purposes, these envoicing strategies also have a persuasive dimension. In all of the utterances above, Hao is trying to win over his interlocutors to his way of looking at things. Therefore, these utterances serve a significant role in interactional strategies as well. The increasingly more direct way in which he tackles the issue as the conversation progresses also suggests an entextualization strategy. After his vague hint to others to request their expenses on line 68, he becomes more direct. On lines 82–83, he accuses Sofia and Javier of spending all the money. On lines 87–88 he is even more forceful when he paints a hypothetical picture to convey the ridiculousness of the situation. He is thus careful in framing his criticism so that the collaborative nature of this interaction is not spoilt. The interlocutors are prepared gradually to understand his criticism. He thus eases the others into his point of view. The humor is not only part of his voice, it also helps add some levity and reduce the tension in this negotiation process. It helps mitigate the challenges to others on their unreasonable expenses. It thus helps save face for the others. More importantly, his humor is persuasive. It nudges others subtly to see the reasonableness of Hao's position.

In contrast to Hao's assertiveness, Sofia adopts deferentiality as her envoicing strategy. However, in its own way, her deferentiality also has a persuasive dimension. Thus, paradoxically, it functions as a winning interactional strategy. Sofia manages to negotiate with the other males, including an NES, to eventually gain the most amount of money for her project. In this sense, there are statuses of gender and language ownership that her strategies are calculated to renegotiate. Part of her deferential attitude is her recurrent laughter. We will consider how this envoicing strategy also works as a negotiation strategy, helping in diverse ways to reduce tensions, sweet coat challenges and disagreements, save face, and mitigate assertiveness. It is also designed to convey lack of understanding at times, a strategy of repair that other scholars in CA and ELF have also observed (Schegloff, 2000; Kirkpatrick, 2010; Pitzl, 2010; Kaur, 2009).

It is important to note that Sofia's use of laughter in contact situations is somewhat distinctive. She uses less of that in her in-group communication with fellow Germans. With her multilingual colleagues, there are 12 occasions of laughter in 49 turns. In her conversation with her fellow German students, there are five occasions of laughter in the 105 turns she takes. From another perspective, altogether Sofia laughs 12 times while delivering 332 words in the multilingual interaction (1 in 27.6). In the conversation among Germans, she laughs five times among 2,356 words (1 in 471). This comparison suggests that laughter plays a distinctive role in contact zone communication.

Consider the frequent occasions of laughter (@ in the transcript) in the stretch of conversation below:

11 Sofia: Five thousand for me and five thousand for you.
12 Javier: Yeah. (.)
13 Sofia: Why not? (@@@)
14 H/J: @@@.
15 Javier: So, what do you think about that?
16 Sofia: @If the area is not too big, that we, then we don't need@ (.) uh (.) so
17   much money-
18 Javier: Uhm. Uhm.
19 Sofia: to decorate and clean the places.
20 Javier: Yeah. I mean decorate and clean is important but the security staff is
21   important too.
22 Sofia: Yes, it's important.
23 Javier: Because they have to feel safe, isn't it?
24 Sofia: @@@

25	Javier:	in the University.
26	Sofia:	Yes. But which important person is it?
27	Javier/Sofia:	@@@
28	Javier:	(.) isn't it, so-
29	Sofia:	Because maybe the important person have, has a security of his own.
30		Is it sure that he @he need one@?
31	Javier:	Yeah, that's what this University need its own security because they
32		want to bring and for just look around but the University need their
33		own security in case there might be a student or somebody don't like
34	Sofia:	@@@.

Initially, Javier shows some disapproval when Sofia claims half of the budget for her responsibility of cleaning the hall for the event. On line 13, she challenges Javier's opposition. Her laughter here mitigates her challenge. As Javier hesitates to give in, she makes a modified request for a reduced amount. This concession is also preceded by laughter, possibly to save her own face this time. Then, when Javier claims an equal amount of money for security (on line 23) in defiance, Sofia laughs in response. I find from similar occasions elsewhere in the transcript that this laughter enables her to buy time for a better response. It also subtly indicates a lack of uptake on her part, and a refusal to go along with Javier's proposal. The lack of uptake here, then, is not a communication breakdown, but an intentional divergence strategy. Despite subtly coding a reservation of opinion, the laughter additionally helps maintain comity and preserve group solidarity.

On line 29 Sofia challenges Javier and suggests that they may not need to spend money on security because the VIP will bring his own. Here she seems to use laughter to soften her challenge to Javier. It may also soften her divergent stance. However, we must note the fairly direct expression of her challenges in some of her statements, as for example on line 29, indicating that her laughter shouldn't be misconstrued as weakness or accommodation. It masks her insistence on the amount she needs for her purposes. Eventually, Sofia does end up getting the most amount of money among all five participants—£3500. The outcome suggests the way her envoicing turns out to be strategic for negotiation purposes.

We find that laughter serves diverse purposes in voice and negotiation. ELF and CA scholars have largely seen laughter in relation to repair. For example, Pitzl observes: "In ELF situations all participants are equally likely to employ laughter simultaneously as a 'symptom' of 'non-understanding' and as a face-saving device" (Pitzl, 2010, p. 41). Schegloff also notes, "There appears to be a deep relationship between laughter and repair" (Schegloff, 2000, p. 219). Sofia does laugh when she fails to understand something, as in line 34. However, the other examples above show that what is construed as misunderstanding can at times be strategic. It can indicate a lack of uptake to favor a different position by the respondent. We have also noted that laughter is multifunctional. In addition to the different persuasive strategies noted above, we should finally observe the possibility of a performative strategy. Through the deferential laughter, Sofia might be "performing" gender. She might be giving the impression of being passive. However, this identity is strategic and persuasive, as it masks her quiet assertiveness and insistence on getting the resources needed for her objectives.

In general, Hao and Sofia adopt different envoicing strategies. If Sofia is deferential, Hao is more aggressive, and both adopt them strategically to achieve their purposes. Sofia deals with power differences and shapes the conditions in her favor. Hao softens his persuasion with humor, so as to not affect comity with others in the group. Such strategic assertions of their voices and values lead to effective negotiations, whereby individual interests are accomplished without affecting group solidarity.

Recontextualization

The variations in language repertoires and rhetorical strategies don't create problems in intelligibility because the interlocutors adopt a framing for the conversational activity and a footing that facilitates effective negotiation of their differences. The framing of the talk is relatively unproblematic in this encounter. The task that was given to them and the responsibilities assigned to each in organizing the dignitary's visit, together with their knowledge of their multilingual identities and international student status, provide a shared framing for this interaction. The presence of majority multilingual participants in this encounter also frames this interaction as a contact zone activity. The context above is well understood by all and gives them a shared framing for the discourse. For this reason, we don't see too much work on reframing taking place in this interaction. Furthermore, framing in face-to-face conversational activities is different from writing. Authors have to make more effort to frame the text suitably for varying contexts of reception and negotiation, where the text can be potentially read by unknown readers in unanticipated contexts. However, in face-to-face conversation, the framing of the talk is more directly negotiated.

This is not to say that people don't occasionally break the frame. Milne, for example, adopts a more authoritative and one-sided native speaker orientation to speaking at some points. When he uses an idiom, Sofia has to explicitly ask for explanation and subtly remind him of the multilingual framing of this encounter. In fact, "unilateral idiomacy" often violates multilingual norms and creates communication problems (see Seidlhofer, 2001, p. 16). We will consider how Milne and Sofia manage this potentially tense frame-breaking later below, in relation to their interactional and entexualization strategies.

Though there is a macro-level context that is shared by everyone and rarely explicitly entextualized in the conversation, there are of course negotiations of footing that take place occasionally. As each speaker gets carried away with their own responsibility and divides the resources in their favor, they have to be reminded by the others that they have to compromise. The footing has to be negotiated to favor the sharing of the resources fairly and equitably. This is not just an ethical responsibility, but also a practical need, as the budget cannot be increased indefinitely.

Consider the example below. As Sofia and Hao argue in favor of their own expenses, Javier has to explicitly remind them to negotiate fairly:

92   Javier: Yeah security staff I can reduce, to reduce the security price.
93   Negotiate, so we can have a couple of thousand to spend on food,
94   isn't it? Depend how many people. Two thousand, three thousand is a
95   lot of money for just food yeah?

Note that his reminder to "negotiate" (line 93) may be treated as a metapragmatic cue to change their footing. Javier initiates the change of footing himself by reducing the budget for his undertaking of security (line 92). In a sense, he is practicing what he is preaching. He goes on to ask Hao to reduce the amount he is requesting for food. Note that his "yeah?" (line 95) in the end is both a confirmation check and a persuasive strategy. This is not only to see if the others have understood the meaning, but also to see if they are with him in his approach. In the latter sense, this is a rhetorical question. Thus, the phrase functions both in meaning and social negotiation.

However, in the heat of the negotiations, they all often forget the need to compromise. Milne's entry into the conversation is striking. As Sofia and Javier divide the whole amount of money among themselves, forgetting to consider if money might be left for other aspects of the organization, Milne recontextualizes the talk by reminding them of the framing of the interaction. He initiates a change of footing, whereby they can modify their claims and accommodate the interests of the others:

154   Milne: I think we need to consider the reason that the very important person is
155   coming, and that's to attend a conference and do a presentation event
156   and that that needs to be I think at the bottom of the budget what we
157   spend. And the conference and presentation, uh, together with the
158   microphones and speakers and everything, and everything that you
159   need to have at something like that is going to cost two thousand
160   dollars, or two thousand pounds, I mean-
161   All: @@@
162   Milne: So we uh, we have to have the presentation event; that's why he's
163   coming and maybe we can cut costs on it, less than two thousand, but,
164   to start, we've got to have that, at the bottom.
165   Javier: Yeah. I think that's a very important thing because the visit is for the
166   conference, yeah. Then the-
167   Hao: So a compromise.

The fact that the others laugh (line 161) shows the uptake. They realize perhaps that they got carried away and they show a willingness to change their footing. There is a more explicit uptake by both Javier (line 165) and Hao (line 167). Hao's mention of "compromise" might be considered to be another metapragmatic cue to recontextualize the footing. After this, the others renegotiate the figures more equitably. These reminders on footing play no small role in contributing to the manner in which all the participants successfully meet their objectives within their budget in the end.

Interactional strategies

We will now move on to consider interactional strategies. As indicated earlier, I like to consider not only meaning negotiation but identity negotiation in the interactional strategies of the participants. To first focus on the negotiation of meaning, what we find is that there are very few instances of misunderstanding or non-understanding, despite the differences in the forms used. This also means that there are comparatively fewer instances of repair required. The sharing of the multilingual framing of this talk and appropriate footing no doubt contributes to the openness to negotiate on all sides. Because of this effective recontextualization, it is possible that everyone is also monitoring their talk carefully to facilitate uptake by others.

The transcript shows that features of what we might consider deviations from NES grammatical norms don't cause misunderstandings or non-intelligibility. It is noteworthy that the participants don't even make an issue of these deviations. Consider the following exchange:

```
1    Sofia:   My idea is to spend the money for clean and decorate all the areas
2             the VIP will visit
3    Javier:  Yes. How much that going to cost?
4    Sofia:   I think about ten, five to ten thousand
5    Javier:  Uh, I think it's important to xxx do arrangement for the security
6             because this is a visit important. xxx the person, so you need more
7             security in case there's an accident xxx might happen by the
8             University. So I think we should spend more money on the security
9             staff. That might cost around five thousand, so it can combine it
10            between what you're talking and (.)
11   Sofia:   Five thousand for me and five thousand for you.
```

Sofia's proposal doesn't elicit a complaint about its ungrammaticality ("to spend the money for clean and decorate all the areas"). Javier's rejoinder indicates uptake and intelligibility—which is itself coded in another ungrammaticality ("How much that going to cost?"). Sofia's appropriate response, specifying the amounts she needs (line 4), indicates that she too hasn't faced any problems in understanding Javier. We have to therefore consider the possibility that intelligibility is not dependent on form alone. There are other contextual factors such as the topic, the task, and the familiarity of interlocutors that can help them deal with their language differences. Through alignment of these features, the participants are able to construct meaning for language resources that are idiosyncratic. In some cases of non-intelligibility, the participants seem to be using the "let-it-pass" principle to ignore problematic features and focus on the meaning in context. They are successful in achieving intelligibility through other contextual cues. In the interactions in the following chapters, I will bring up the diverse contextual cues to explain how talk gets negotiated. ELF scholars have generally treated non-verbal cues as irrelevant for such negotiations. Pitzl, for example, resorts to explaining "non-linguistic means for clarifying matters" (Pitzl, 2010, p. 92) only in one case of fragile talk in her data. However, alignment of diverse ecological resources is an interactional strategy used by translinguals for meaning construction all the time.

To address how interactional strategies go beyond meaning negotiation to other strategic social and rhetorical outcomes, consider how the "let-it-pass" principle is used in some cases. It is adopted where meaning is negotiated in subsequent turns in ways that are rhetorically advantageous for participants. The ambiguity of certain utterances provides scope for renegotiation in subsequent turns. Repair or clarification is not necessarily the most preferred option in some cases of misunderstanding. Consider Hao's strategy below:

```
231  Hao:    It's very (.) very important person. I don't think decorating too much
232          is very necessary.
233  Javier: No is necessary, yeah.
234  Hao:    Yeah, just clean
```

Javier's response on line 233 is unclear. Is he saying "It is not necessary," or "No, it's necessary"? Hao doesn't disambiguate this utterance. He lets it pass. However, he imposes his own meaning strategically to shape the conversation in his favor when he takes his turn. He interprets Javier's response to mean that cleaning is necessary, but that decorating is not. While in some cases the "let-it-pass" principle may leave things unresolved, in others (such as this) it allows respondents to renegotiate these utterances in their favor.

It is also important to find out why interlocutors may not always let unintelligible items pass. They sometimes stop the conversation abruptly to ask for clarification. Pitzl notes, "Concerning the environments or situations, in which non-understandings were most often negotiated in the data, two environments were noticeable: questions and 'fragile' activities. ... Both of these environments require a certain degree of precision and clarity: if a participant utters a question, s/he wants to obtain a certain piece of information; a 'fragile' activity is usually concerned with a delicate subject" (Pitzl, 2010, p. 132). We will consider situations where my subjects don't adopt the "let-it-pass" strategy below.

There is a potential for breakdown as Javier and Sofia debate the relative significance of their different projects (i.e., decoration versus security). Sofia asks if Javier's requested expenses for security can be reduced if the dignitary brings his own security. However, Javier attempts to explain why the university still needs to provide security:

```
31  Javier:  Yeah, that's what this University need its own security because they
32           want to bring and for just look around but the University need their
33           own security in case there might be a student or somebody don't like
34  Sofia:   @@@.
35  Javier:  You don't know, isn't it?
36  Sofia:   Mmm
37  Javier:  Uh, so-
```

38	Sofia:	You don't think that the VIP, important person uhm not has security of
39		his own?
40	Javier:	Yeah, they may have but you, you need to feel safe even if you have
41		security at your own, yeah? Or the University needs to have the own
42		security for make sure everything's all right, in case the important
43		person is (.) group, something like that (.) the University is going
44		to be-
45	Sofia:	@Slowly please@
46	Javier:	is going to be-
47	Sofia:	I can't understand
48	Javier:	Yeah. It's going to be the University who going to get the blame. If the security is not very good
49	Sofia:	Uh-uh
50	Javier:	even if the person haves his own security and he come to visit this
51		University, is University's obligation to keep the person safe. Now I
52		think uh-
53	Sofia:	OK.

It appears that Sofia is having some problem understanding Javier's explanation. Her laughter on line 34 and vague back channeling cues on line 36 are signs of "minimal feedback" (Pitzl, 2010, p. 38) and indicate her lack of uptake. On line 38 she persists in asking if the university should provide security, and this "reprise of non-understood part" (Pitzl, 2010, p. 38) indicates that she hasn't understood Javier's explanation. As Javier attempts an impassioned explanation in run-on sentences, Sofia is forced to ask him to speak slowly (line 45) and then declare her lack of understanding through explicit metalinguistic cues (line 47). Note however that this direct intervention is preceded by her face-saving (for both herself and the interlocutor) laughter. The non-use of "let-it-pass" is explained by the fact that this information is crucial at this time in the conversation as they have to make decisions on how much of their resources they have to expend on the competing projects. It qualifies as a "fragile activity" in Pitzl's terms. From an entextualization (and temporal) perspective, we also have to acknowledge that Sofia has attempted an indirect means of getting help before resorting to a direct request. In Javier's favor, it must be noted that he does adopt a few confirmation checks on line 35 ("isn't it?") and on line 41 ("yeah?") which however don't help much. Note that Javier's utterances from line 48 onwards are shorter in construction. They also result in a couple of rephrasings (see lines 48 and 50). They reflect Meierkord's (2004) findings of regularization and segmentation, illustrating how entextualization strategies can help in repair. The revised strategies of Javier gain uptake, as is evident on line 53.

In other cases, the potential mis- or non-understanding is renegotiated for a better outcome. In these cases, it is difficult to say if what researchers consider to be the original meaning makes a difference. The renegotiated meaning is satisfactory for the participants, leaving them with even better results. Consider how Hedda's proposal about making a movie about the VIP's visit is negotiated. Though the

interaction is marked by a lot of misunderstanding and misintepretation, the
co-constructed new meaning results in a satisfactory outcome for everyone. When
Hedda originally introduces the idea, it is not clear if she is thinking of a movie or a
video for recording the VIP's visit:

109 Hedda: And also we need to film the event so we can sell the movie
110   afterwards, maybe earn some money on the movie

The others are prepared to go along with that idea even though they think the
£5000 she requests is too expensive. Therefore, Javier modifies that project to reduce
the expense:

128 Javier: You can make a home movie just by Camcorder, (.) student, just
129   record it. Won't cost that much, isn't it?
130 Sofia: Yes
131 Hedda: Yeah but that will look so unprofessional
132 Hao: By the way I don't think this is very important
133 Hedda: That, yeah and then the very important person will be @so disappointed@

The notion of making a home movie with a camcorder simplifies the project. Note
Javier's "isn't it?" (line 129) which is a confirmation request as well as persuasion
toward his suggestion. Note also the downtoner in Hao's "by the way" to mitigate
his challenge to Hedda's insistence on her original plan. That Hedda is still resistant
suggests that she is indeed thinking of a movie. In both cases where she repeats her
original plan, however, she uses diverse strategies to save face and mitigate the resistance. She begins both cases of dissent with "yeah" (lines 131 and 133) resembling
House's (2003, p. 568) notion of "represents." She also laughs on line 133, a strategy
we see Sofia using in other places.

It soon appears as if Hao is thinking of this project differently. He understands the
movie as something screened for the VIP's entertainment:

134 Hao: I don't think they want to see the movie after
135 ALL: @@@
136 Javier: Uh xxx The budget like five thousand, five thousand, five hundred?
137 Hao: Because it was, there was, in my, in my plan a kind of mu.mu.musical
138   eve – entertaiment-
139 Javier: Yeah yeah yeah
140 Hao: involved instead the movie, you can just cut movie a little bit and-
141 Javier: Yeah
142 Hao: add some music
143 Hedda: You can do that
144 All: @@@
145 Hao: Oh no no no Maybe some of us can dance, instead of movie.

In Hao's incomplete sentence, "after" indicates that he is thinking of this as an event at the end of the visit to entertain the VIP. He wants to propose a musical entertainment instead (lines 137 and 140). In order to reduce the budget, he improves on that and then proposes that the students provide the entertainment by themselves by putting up a music and dance show. Initially, they all laugh at his suggestion on line 135, which usually marks a lack of uptake and/or of understanding. There is also an element of uncertainty about what Hao really means. However, they are prepared to adopt the "let-it-pass" strategy and keep Hao's suggestion on the table.

It appears, as the conversation progresses, that they are maintaining all three suggestions (making a movie, producing a home video, and screening a movie or producing a musical event for entertainment) in parallel. Milne, for example, reopens Hedda's suggestion later:

269	Milne:	Is it worth making a movie if we only put a thousand pounds into it?
270	Hao:	Yeah. Will be. It will be.
271	Sofia:	No, we said students can do it. @@@
272	Javier:	Yeah I think the students can do it.
273	Hedda:	Then it's (.) it is embarrassing.
274	Hao:	Or you do the music.
275	Sofia, Hedda:	@@@

Hao still continues with his understanding that the others are talking about the need for an entertainment when he proposes music on line 274. Here the group lets the proposal about the movie and music stay, although they are not the same. The participants are not bothered by the apparent inconsistency. They are relaxed about making a clarification about which proposal they are talking about. However, in the end, Milne proposes a better alternative to Hedda's original proposal of making a documentary of the VIP's visit for publicity purposes:

293	Milne:	Shall we switch from a movie and maybe just try and make a
294		booklet xxx with photos xxx and maybe writing about the story?
295	All:	@@@
296	Javier:	You mean just for newspaper?
297	Milne:	Maybe do a newspaper story.
298	Javier:	Yeah, newspaper story.
299	Hao:	Yes whatever xxx
300	Javier:	Can reduce the budget.
301	Sofia:	Journalists do it all. xxx to write the article for the newspaper. Journalists
302		do it.
303	Hao:	Journalists?
304	Milne:	Yeah we xxx
305	Hedda:	Then we have to hire a journalist.
306	Hao:	Yeah.
307	Javier:	Yeah we can get a local journalist. It won't cost that much. (.) just

308   local.
309 Hao: I don't think you need–
310 Hedda: But it all depends on–
311 Milne: If the person's very important
312   the journalist will want to write–
313 Hao: Yes
314 Hedda: Yeah, that's true
315 All: hm hm [Agreement].

There is a difference in understanding in the above interaction too. Milne's idea of a booklet with photos (as a variation of Hedda's project of documenting the visit through a movie) gets understood as a story for the newspaper by Javier. However, once again, the group is tolerant about this "mistake." Milne lets it pass. As they go on thinking about this possibility, they come to the realization that they can gain many other benefits through the news story, that is, publicity, documentation, and a reduced budget as journalists cover the story for free. What we find is that the group's relaxed attitude to "mistakes" or ambiguities leads to a better renegotiated outcome. Even Hedda is in agreement with this option. It is made normal (Firth, 1996) in the end, without any concern about this being a misunderstanding of Hedda's original proposal or Milne's subsequent proposal.

We must appreciate how multilingual negotiations lead to co-constructed meanings here. If speakers or interlocutors had relied on ideas being understood similarly and resisted any reinterpretation, they may not have ended with the better outcome. The "languaging" of their different options leads them to think more about them and construct a better outcome. As Kaur observes: "Understanding and non-understanding [should not be] regarded as discrete states but rather as varying levels of interactional achievement that are continuously updated as the talk unfolds" (Kaur, 2009, p. 40). Furthermore, we have to consider that a focus on errors in localized situations may prevent us from co-constructed meanings in the longer sequence. Traditional SLA scholars would have been obsessed with the many misunderstandings in this interaction, which they would have attributed to the "non-native" status of these participants (see Firth and Wagner, 1997 for a critique). Even some CA analysts would have emphasized the need for good repair strategies to resolve the ambiguities and mis-understandings. However, the trajectory of the talk shows a co-constructed meaning that elicits the agreement of everyone, both at the level of meaning and of decision. The outcome shows the value of negotiated outcomes in lingua franca interactions.

We will now consider interactional strategies that help the interlocutors achieve conflict resolution. The participants have diverse strategies for negotiating disagreement. When Sofia divides the allotted £10,000 between herself and Javier, it of course evokes some hesitation from Javier:

11 Sofia: Five thousand for me and five thousand for you.
12 Javier: Yeah (.)
13 Sofia: Why not? (@@@)
14 H/J: @@@.

It appears that Sofia doesn't understand the reason for Javier's hesitation (indicated by the pause). When she challenges Javier for an explanation, she also laughs a bit. This laughter is an attempt to mitigate the challenge. It saves face for Javier and tempers any harshness in the challenge. As we saw earlier, Sofia adopts this laughter at other points in the conversation for diverse other functions in negotiation.

What these occasions of disagreement show is that multilingual communication is not fully or always collaborative and harmonious as ELF scholars have characterized it (see Seidlhofer, 2004, p. 218). We have to qualify this notion. Though multilinguals are committed to negotiating meanings and collaborating in meaning construction, this doesn't preclude acts of disagreement and resistance in conversational goals. Note how Javier negotiates the difficult process of getting Sofia to lower her expenses for cleaning and decorating the venue for the event:

15   Javier: So, what do you think about that?
16   Sofia: @If the area is not too big, that we, then we don't need@ xxx uh xxx so
17   much money-
18   Javier: Uhm. Uhm.
19   Sofia: to decorate and clean the places.
20   Javier: Yeah. I mean decorate and clean is important but the security staff is
21   important too.
22   Sofia: Yes, it's important..
23   Javier: Because they have to feel safe, isn't it?

Javier sees that Sofia is conceding that she needs to reduce the expenses for the decorations, but only on the condition that the space is small. Partly to encourage her on this line of thinking, and partly to persuade her to reduce further, he says on line 20: "Yeah. I mean decorate and clean is important but the security staff is important too." He first affirms that Sofia's project is important before insisting on the importance of security (which is his own undertaking). This "display of solidarity" (House, 2003, p. 569) is a way for Javier to help Sofia save face and show comity even as he disagrees with her. Many other disagreements are framed this way, through a display of solidarity, so that interlocutors are assured of the challenger's respect at the same time.

However, Javier is also subtly persuading Sofia toward his position as the conversation proceeds. The many rhetorical questions in the interaction indicate this strategy. In some ways, these questions can function as a confirmation check for the meaning. They can also be a persuasion strategy. They can help interlocutors indicate their position in mitigated and non-threatening ways. Note Javier's rhetorical question on line 23. Incidentally, it also reframes Sofia's ambiguous statement on line 22 in his favor. Sofia's statement could either mean that decoration is important or that security is important. What she means by "it's" is not clear. However, Javier's rhetorical question assumes that she is accepting that security is important. Letting the ambiguity pass, Javier offers an interpretation to his advantage.

Subjects are also careful in coding their challenges. They adopt many strategies to do so. Consider the following where Sofia challenges Javier's request for more money for security:

23	Javier:	Because they have to feel safe, isn't it?
24	Sofia:	@@@
25	Javier:	in the University.
26	Sofia:	Yes. But Which important person is it?
27	Javier/Sofia:	@@@ they didn't know
28	Javier:	(.) isn't it, so–
29	Sofia:	Because maybe the important person have, has a security of his own.
30		Is it sure that he @he need one@?

As it becomes evident later (line 29), Sofia wants to challenge Javier's proposal by suggesting that the VIP will come with his own security personnel. However, the first time she poses this possibility (line 26), it is framed as a simple information-seeking question. Note also the minimal uptake on line 24, where she simply laughs. Then she makes a declarative statement on line 29, but couches this again in laughter as she recognizes that it is a potential challenge to Javier's position. We will find that a few turns later, as Javier refuses to give up his claim, Sofia frames this question a bit more forcefully through a rhetorical question:

38	Sofia:	You don't think that the VIP, important person uhm not has security of
39		his own?

She is very direct in her challenge and refutation here.

Such examples show that the moves of translinguals cannot be all treated as strategies of indirection or collaboration. They can be more direct at times. In the case above, Sofia can afford to be more direct in her challenge for a variety of reasons, that is: she has prepared Javier for her challenge through her previous questions; she has indicated her desire to be considerate of his feelings by adopting many mitigating strategies earlier; if Javier hasn't caught on to her challenge, she may have to adopt more direct strategies to convey her point. The sequence of increasing directness is also an example of entextualization (as I will discuss later). Sofia is monitoring her thoughts and utterances carefully through successive turns to frame her challenge with a lot of sensitivity and diplomacy. In this regard, compare her statements on line 30 and line 38 for their increased force. She first asks: "Is it sure that he @he need one@?" (line 30). This framing is milder than the more challenging "You don't think that … " on line 38. Note also the laughter that is interspersed to mitigate the challenge even further on line 30. While Pitzl (2010), Schegloff (2000), and others analyze laughter in terms of meaning negotiation (i.e., signaling a lack of uptake), we see in this instance that laughter can also help in the representation of dissent and power negotiations.

How power relationships are negotiated between the interlocutors in the above encounter needs elaboration. In this case, gender stereotypes are also questioned.

Sofia adopts a mix of indirect/passive and more direct/resistant strategies as the interaction proceeds. More interesting is the way she negotiates this mix of strategies with sensitivity. Though she might be "performing" the gendered role of passivity in the beginning, she proceeds to be more direct later. This also shows that we shouldn't use values such as passive/aggressive and direct/indirect as binaries. Sofia uses both of them strategically in different contexts, as our temporal analysis above shows. Such a combination of styles of indirection and directness also make us qualify our comments on the role of downtoners, saving face, and indirectness as a voicing strategy based on gender and language ownership. What we find by the end of this discussion is that Sofia succeeds in getting the highest allocation in the budget. She ends up with £3500 whereas the others all got less than her. It appears that she employed a combination of direct and indirect strategies to work in her favor. Particularly interesting is the way she uses these strategies to negotiate power. Though three others in the group are males, and Milne is a native speaker, she negotiates these differences well to gain an upper hand in the interaction. The conversation ends with Sofia taking possession of her share of the money and signing off with her characteristic mitigating laughter.

This outcome provides an interesting perspective on power in contact zone interactions. Though the space is not free of power differences, it is open to inequalities being renegotiated or at least temporarily modified to suit one's interests. Language and rhetorical strategies play a big role in enabling these negotiations. We also observe how the place of the native speaker in lingua franca interactions is negotiated. Though Milne is very confident, directive, and authoritative in his talk, he is careful to negotiate the interaction in relation to the strategies employed by the other students. As we will see below, he monitors his language use in deference to the norms of the other interlocutors, and also finds that the outcome is not necessarily in his favor.

Entextualization

Among the two major cases of lack of understanding that disrupt the conversation (in addition to the one above where Sofia asks Javier to speak slowly) is the one when Milne uses the idiomatic phrase "bottom line." The instance in question is the following:

195 Hedda: (.) we can have two thousand on everybody, two, two four six eight
196 Sofia: two
197   thousand, is too less for me. Two thousand is too less. I can't decorate
198   the area with two thousand pounds. It is impossible.
199 Milne: Let's say we need decorations and we need it cleaned up. What's your
200   bottom line?
201 Sofia: What's my what?
202 Milne: What is the bottom line. What, what's the-
203 Hao: bottom line, yes
204 Milne: least you can do it for? The least
205   it can be done for?

206 Sofia: The lowest, uh–
207 Milne: Yeah
208 Sofia: price? Four thousand.

Sofia has to disrupt the conversation in this case to ask for clarification (line 201). She doesn't adopt the "let-it-pass" principle as there is a serious decision to be made following a tense negotiation on ways to reduce the budget. She had herself come to a firm position at the end of the negotiation, putting her foot down and saying that she couldn't do her project for less than £2000 (on lines 197–98). This is therefore a "fragile situation" (Pitzl, 2010, p. 132). Note also the directness and firmness with which she insists on her position, qualifying her gendered stance of comity, indirection, and passiveness earlier.

In response to Sofia's request for clarification, Milne immediately provides a rephrasing: "least you can do it for" (line 204). However, Sofia adopts her own phrasing: "the lowest price" (line 206). Milne indicates an uptake of this formulation. This shows Milne's openness to negotiation and the co-construction of new terms, thus adopting an equal footing with his interlocutors, despite being a native speaker. He is able to adopt the orientation of translinguals and engage in negotiated meaning-making. If he had forgotten the framing and footing for this interaction, Sofia's question reminds him and helps recontextualize the interaction for him.

What is more important is that Milne does monitor his speech well; he entextualizes his word choices with sensitivity to the different norms and competencies of the interlocutors, and is sensitive to the multilingual and contact zone framing of this talk. This becomes evident if we take a broader temporal view of the trajectory of this negotiation. We will realize that Milne didn't use his idiom without some level of monitoring as he began the interaction. The transcript shows that Milne had been wary of using this idiom earlier when the phrase "bottom line" was badly needed. He had used this idiom cautiously. He instead used the word "bottom" twice earlier, as we see below:

154 Milne: I think we need to consider the reason that the very important person is
155   coming, and that's to attend a conference and do a presentation event
156   and that that needs to be I think at the **bottom** of the budget what we
157   spend. And the conference and presentation, uh, together with the
158   microphones and speakers and everything, and everything that you
159   need to have at something like that is going to cost two thousand
160   dollars, or two thousand pounds, I mean–
161 All: @@@
162 Milne: So we uh, we have to have the presentation event; that's why he's
163   coming and maybe we can cut costs on it, less than two thousand, but,
164   to start, we've got to have that, at the **bottom**.
165 Javier: Yeah. I think that's a very important thing because the visit is for the
166   conference, yeah. Then the–

In fact, "bottom of the budget" might be considered by some to be unidiomatic. Milne is attempting a new usage of "bottom," in deference to the needs of multilinguals, at the risk of deviating from typical usage. The awkwardness of the phrase also suggests that he seems to be explicitly avoiding the idiom and striving for a more literal expression. Note that the second usage of "bottom" is understood by Javier, as he notes that it points to "a very important thing" (line 165). Javier intuits cleverly that the word has to do with priorities. Javier's example shows how even fresh language uses are interpreted for meaning in the context of other ecological resources. It is clear on line 203 that Hao also understood the idiom, perhaps aided by Milne's gradual introduction of it earlier. Therefore, it is evident that Milne had monitored his speech, shown sensitivity to language diversity, and used the idiom carefully. The fact that he had adopted a slightly modified and simplified version of the idiom about forty lines earlier, and twice at that, shows his entextualization strategies. Perhaps he had adopted this strategy to prepare his listeners to the idiom, check their uptake, and introduce its meaning gradually to them. Perhaps Milne was emboldened by the uptake of Javier to assume that the others would also understand the idiom, and used it the third time around. In addition to this monitored meaning negotiation, the fact that Milne is able to achieve intelligibility with multilinguals according to their norms of usage also confirms the position of this book that NES don't lack the aptitude for translingual practices.

There are many other strategies of entextualization we have seen above in the interaction. Note that Sofia's and Javier's strategy of coding their dissent through indirect and mitigated forms before adopting more direct strategies is an effective form of entextualization. Through this strategy, they prepare the interlocutor for their perspectives and adopt subtle means to save face before they consider alternate approaches. These entextualization strategies also show that interlocutors have an orientation to language and texts as evolving in time and space. They show monitoring strategies that suggest care in the use of language and sensitivity to the norms and conventions of others.

Conclusion

What we see in the analysis above is how language resources take on new meaning as speakers use them in context in alignment with diverse ecological resources for their own purposes. The words and grammatical items they use, although they deviate from conventional NES norms and display considerable variation, are functional and serve powerful social and rhetorical purposes. While the processes by which new meanings are created are largely invisible, as they are assumed by the participants most of the time, we do see the trajectory of meaning in certain language resources. We see how "movie" means video and how "story" in a booklet comes to mean a "news story." Similarly, we see how "bottom" indexes "bottom line" for some participants. These are ways in which familiar words take on a new indexicality. They are also examples of semiodiversity.

How are the interlocutors able to make meaning with these mobile and shifting resources? My position is that they are able to do this through their negotiation strategies. Unlike other models of global Englishes which treat practices as supplementary to predefined language norms, I treat practices as fundamental and generative. The shifting and hybrid language resources, with their relative and changing norms, cannot guarantee communicative success. In an effort to formulate a grammar of practices, I have identified four macro-strategies that help negotiate contact zone communication, that is, envoicing, recontextualization, interactional, and entextualization strategies. This formulation suggests a multi-dimensional approach to communicative strategies. We need to take into consideration how voice considerations, context (with its fullest ecological and material resources), interpersonal relations, and the spatiotemporal dimension of the text/talk are creatively used by subjects for communicative success. In this manner, I also move away from studies that treat lingua franca communication as merely instrumental for information transfer, with a focus on the primacy of the word to convey disembodied meanings. Furthermore, in adopting these negotiation strategies, participants accomplish different functions. They accomplish semantic, rhetorical, and social meanings. We cannot keep these meanings separated either. The negotiation of semantic meaning is often tied to negotiation of power relationships. Unlike other contact English studies then, I keep these components together in my analysis.

Aren't such strategies of meaning negotiation similar to what traditional scholarship has demonstrated? Not really. In studies in SLA and CA, such negotiations have been analyzed to show how interlocutors correct their deviations from a purported norm in order to make sense. What we find in the translingual negotiations is the use of these strategies to create new values and meanings for existing words or the construction of new indexicals. Rather than treating a predefined norm as the frame of reference, these interlocutors negotiate meanings to co-construct situated new norms. Rather than relying on an unavailable shared norm, they achieve sharedness through their negotiation strategies.

How do we account for the competence of translinguals to negotiate effectively for intelligibility and communicative success in contact zones? How do they develop these strategies? Kaur argues that these strategies "mirror the competence they demonstrate when interacting in their native language" (Kaur, 2009, p. 237). She argues this way because these strategies appear so natural and intuitive to these speakers. However, the strategies we observe above are attuned for contact purposes among people of diverse language backgrounds, without the ability to rely on shared norms or neutral values. I will provide evidence from other migrant and multilingual subjects in the coming chapters to demonstrate that translinguals develop this competence from their socialization in multilingual contexts. However, in contrast to ELF approaches, I see these negotiation strategies as not unique to multilinguals. This approach explains how NES such as Milne can also display such practices when the communicative occasion demands them. From this point of view, though other ELF scholars have observed that NES/multilingual interactions are riddled with communicative problems, this doesn't have to be the case. Kaur for example, notes: "misunderstandings are particularly pronounced between native and nonnative speakers of a language" (Kaur, 2009, p. 43). Other scholars such as House (2003,

p. 567) agree. But my studies show that this doesn't have to be the case. I will develop a perspective on translingual competence as transcending birthright (whether native or non-native, monolingual or multilingual) in Chapter 9. Labeling this *performative competence*, I will show how these strategies are developed among translinguals for contact zone communication.

6
PLURALIZING ACADEMIC WRITING

While translingual practices in conversation are increasingly being studied, written English communication is treated as normative. Even those who accept localization and voice in conversations argue against such practices in writing. Many assume that there is a universal norm for written language that is widely shared—one that American composition scholars call standard written English (SWE) for English literacy, which they treat as standing beyond local language differences (Elbow, 2002). The assumption is that SWE doesn't belong to any one community. This orientation to the neutrality of writing is bolstered by the notion that written language is not native to anybody. All writers, including native speakers, have to learn writing in formal educational contexts. Furthermore, the need for a universal norm for writing is supported by the widespread understanding of literacy as constituting self-standing texts. According to the model of *autonomous literacy* (Street, 1984), texts should contain meanings that can be extricated conveniently by detached readers, especially as literacy doesn't permit the types of face-to-face negotiations of conversations. The assumptions relating to the stability of written language and detached/unnegotiated texts have also kept ELF scholars from studying or pluralizing international written discourse in English (see Seidlhofer, 2004, p. 215). In a recent state-of-the-art essay on ELF, Jenkins and her co-authors observe, "There are still some major gaps, particularly relating to the written language" (Jenkins, *et al.*, 2011, p. 281).

However, multilinguals are increasingly questioning the attitude to written language as being standardized and neutral. They argue that SWE is based largely on the norms of Inner Circle communities and distant from the norms of multilingual communities (Canagarajah, 2006a). As English is also treated as a lingua franca for written communication in academic domains, multilingual scholars have questioned the way NES norms are taken for granted in academic communication and publishing (see Ammon, 2007). They are also not prepared to treat writing for professional purposes or academic contexts as devoid of values or voice, even though no one is native to it.

No act of communication is free of values. The universality of SWE or written language is also treated increasingly as a language ideology, similar to the orientation of texts as being self-standing and devoid of meaning negotiations. SWE cannot be treated as a monolith, masking the diversity that is already there in written discourse. Now there are increasing efforts by multilingual scholars to bring their voices and values into written texts and pluralize academic writing.

However, teachers fear that deviating from SWE is costly for multilingual scholars and students. Bringing one's own values and voices into high-stakes writing will lead to failure and stigmatization. It is my contention that *codemeshing* enables us to address the process of pluralizing written discourse with sensitivity to the dual claims of voice and norms. Codemeshing offers a middle position between the extremes of disregard for dominant norms and the suppression of the authorial voice. Some senior multi-lingual scholars have already adopted the strategy of codemeshing to resist established norms and to subtly pluralize writing so as to make spaces for diverse Englishes and languages. Below, I offer a close analysis of a research article in a refereed journal by African American scholar Geneva Smitherman to show how she adopts the strategies identified in Chapter 5 to mesh forms of African American Vernacular English (AAVE) into SWE. Before doing that, we have to consider the arguments against the pluralization of written language to appreciate the challenges involved in this enterprise.

Positions against pluralizing writing

There are many reasons why scholars adopt a hands-off policy on writing. I will group their positions into five areas: the modality, register, pragmatist, liberal, and temporal schools of argument.

Modality Argument: Scholars of this persuasion believe that speaking and writing are of different modalities, with a diversity of norms which are manageable in conversation but not in writing. The resources available in both modalities are cited for this difference. Consider Steven Barbour's (2002) position. After making a powerful case for accepting diverse varieties of English in European oral academic communication, Barbour goes on to argue that multilingual authors have to use the established varieties of British or American English for writing. He argues that since the rich paralinguistic cues of speaking are not available for interpreting written texts, multilingual authors should get the help of editors and translators to eliminate the localisms in their English. The lack of gestures, tone, and situational resources might be construed as reducing the resources for meaning in writing. Also, the lack of a face-to-face inter-action between readers and writers in most writing activities is treated as limiting the possibilities for meaning negotiation. However, literacy has always involved diverse ecological resources for interpretation. In addition to some of the affordances of oral communication, such as accentedness and multimodal resources, writing has other affordances unique to literacy. We should take into account resources such as space and fonts, in addition to the materiality of the text, its portability, and relative per-manence that provides affordances for negotiating meaning. I will argue in the next chapter for a model of literacy that actively negotiates and co-constructs meaning, not unlike the negotiation of speech in contact zones.

Register Argument: Another group of scholars adopt a descriptive orientation to written discourse and treat the differences between speaking and writing as one of distinct registers. Many of the scholars in this school adopt an apolitical orientation, typical of descriptive approaches. They treat the register differences in writing and speaking, or academic writing and other modes of academic communication, as neutral of values. Scholars in corpus-oriented studies (Biber, 2006; Hyland, 2003) and researchers of English for Academic Purposes (Swales, 1990; Reid, 1989) are focused on describing written academic register for the purpose of teaching it to students. A senior scholar in the text linguistics tradition once argued with me that comparing the Englishes of multilingual communities to academic norms was misguided as the former were social dialects and academic English was a register. His point was that registers of specific domains were common to all social groups. Scholars in this tradition treat registers of specialized communication (i.e., in professional, technical, and academic domains) as distinct from social or national dialects and of limited relevance to issues of identity, values, or ownership. However, all languages are value-laden. There is also differential access to these registers for different social groups. A long tradition of sociolinguistic work shows how the home language of certain social groups is closer to the language of their school and professions (see Heath, 1983; Bernstein, 1971; Bourdieu and Passeron, 1977). These privileged social groups have an advantage in the academic and professional domains for this reason. The connection also serves to reproduce social inequalities, maintaining the power of those whose language resembles that valued in privileged domains. The difference of language preference in these domains is often explained in biased terms, with the language of lower social groups treated as deficient for privileged domains.

Pragmatist Position: Some scholars adopt a variation of the above position in that they acknowledge the power differences in the language of academic writing, but don't argue for change. They recognize that academic English is closer to the norms of dominant communities and alien to language-minority students. However, they treat the norms of academic written English as a fact of social life, perhaps based on power differences that are too difficult to change. Therefore, they focus their efforts on providing access to this language of power to minority students. Ironically, many well-known minority scholars themselves adopt this position. African American scholars Baugh (1983) and Delpit (1995), for example, are among those who consider it their pedagogical mission to provide access to written language for minority students rather than changing the norms. In some ways, this position pits the claims of *access* against *voice*, that is: Should minority students focus on mastering the dominant conventions or using their preferred codes for identity? This poses a dilemma for well-intentioned teachers. However, I will show that the choice doesn't have to be either/or. I develop codemeshing that allows us to address both at the same time. While recognizing the dominant written norms and developing an awareness of them, it is possible to enable less privileged social groups to represent their voices in academic writing.

Liberal Approach: Some scholars in the field of composition do make a space for voice, but in a restricted sense. These scholars argue for ways in which the values and discourses of minority students/scholars need to be represented in academic writing. However, the changes they envision are at the level of discourse rather than grammar (see, for example, Schroeder *et al.*, 2002; Fox, 1994), that is, they consider the ways in which alternate values can be accommodated at the extra-sentential level (i.e., tone, organization, paragraph development, style, etc.). Perhaps they share the view of the previously mentioned schools that changes at the level of grammar are too radical as SWE is simply the established norm. However, voice has implications for form. The separation of grammar and discourse is untenable. One may have to resist or appropriate dominant grammatical norms, even develop new indexicals, to represent one's voice in academic discourse. For thinkers like Bakhtin (1986), to use language is to populate the resources with one's intentions, with resultant changes in form.

Temporal Argument: A final school of scholars do acknowledge the need to pluralize the grammatical norms of academic writing. However, they believe that this is a historical process that should be left to time. American compositionist, Peter Elbow, who is otherwise very sympathetic to making a space for the English varieties of ethnically and socially marginalized students, urges teachers to adopt a two-pronged approach to tackling the power of academic writing, that is, "to work for the long-range goal of changing the culture of literacy, and the short-range goal of helping students now" (Elbow, 2002, p. 126). This way, he would help students to acquire SWE in order to become competent in the dominant culture of literacy, and succeed in education and society. However, by keeping other varieties alive in the composition classroom and helping students develop written competence in them in low-stakes activities (i.e., journal writing, informal assignments) he would work toward the long-term goal of full acceptance for all dialects. Elbow's position is based on the assumption that "Literacy as a culture or institution almost always implies just one dialect as the only proper one for writing: the 'grapholect'" (Elbow, 2002, p. 128). Unlike speech that can accommodate diverse norms in the same interaction (as in codeswitching and mixing), Elbow believes that writing accommodates only one grapholect at a time (i.e., the formal/"standard" variety, or SWE in English). However, this assumption doesn't hold true for many non-Western communities, as it should be evident in their traditions of literacy (i.e., manipravala, *kene/dami*, tlaquilolitzli) that I reviewed in Chapter 3. More importantly, the text is becoming diversified again in the context of digital communication and new technology. The World Wide Web, for example, enables us to feature not just different languages, but also different symbol systems (icons, images) and different modalities of communication (video, audio, photographs) within the same text. Therefore, the text is able to accommodate more than one grapholect.

The positions of these different schools lead to fairly predictable pedagogical options. They are all open to the fact that the languages of minority communities have their own norms and values, and have to be preserved. They simply think that they don't belong in academic writing, or at least not now. They all adopt a position similar to Elbow in promoting a dualistic approach to literacy. Elbow would go as far as letting minority students use their own varieties for their early drafts, but teaching them copy-editing skills and/or getting help from copy editors so that their final product conforms to the expectations in the academy. Others make similar dichotomies in other domains, that is: community variety for home and SWE for school; community variety for informal classroom interactions and SWE for formal writing; or community variety for low-stakes writing and SWE for high-stakes or graded assignments. Similar to Elbow, almost all scholars reviewed above further consider how the community varieties can be used to help to transition minority students to SWE. They hope to accomplish this by showing the differences between the varieties, developing positive attitudes toward community varieties which help students lose their inhibitions against SWE, and developing their fluency in both varieties for literacy purposes.

Despite the well-intentioned approaches of these scholars, one might interpret them as adopting a model of diglossia. Home languages are treated as a lower form and SWE is treated as a higher variety. All these approaches have rightly been called *codeswitching* models (Young, 2004; Canagarajah, 2006a). Not to be confused with codeswitching in sociolinguistics, critical writing scholars adopt this term as a metaphor to refer to the distinction of language norms in diglossic terms, with different spaces or functions assigned to SWE and vernaculars. Though there is a liberal orientation to this model (in acknowledging that at least the language of minority communities has its validity and its own space), critical scholars point out that the codeswitching approach still maintains power differences and doesn't go far in envisioning change. For example, teaching students that their community/home languages have their place outside formal written contexts in academic settings conveys to them that their languages are inferior or not acceptable in elite, formal, or high-stakes contexts.

There is evidence to suggest that this bifurcated approach to language norms doesn't satisfy minority students and writers. Young (2004), an African-American scholar, argues that this separation of codes suppresses his voice. He considers it racist to be forced to segregate the languages of his repertoire and asked to write without relevance to all his identities. In implementing the codeswitching approach in my teaching, I have found that minority students are reluctant to hold back their Englishes. They find the separation of codes artificial. In my ethnography of both African-American and ESOL students, I have discovered the strategies students covertly adopt to bring their Englishes into formal academic writing (Canagarajah, 1997a, 1997b). For these students, to use the academic language without any personal engagement, even for temporary utilitarian and pragmatic reasons, is to mimic not speak. It means "acting white" for my African-American students, and "putting a show" for Sri Lankan Tamil students. It appeared that my students were looking for a way to appropriate dominant codes and/or mesh their preferred codes with SWE for voice.

The possibility of codemeshing

In the context of the dilemmas reviewed above, codemeshing suggests a way forward. It offers a possibility of bringing the different codes within the same text rather than keeping them apart. In my ethnographic studies I found that my students were trying to do exactly that, in however faltering and limited ways, especially since I didn't have the pedagogical rationale to scaffold their attempts. They tried to use features of their own Englishes within a text that was otherwise in SWE. In other words, their essays turned out to be a hybrid text that accommodated both SWE and AAVE (see Canagarajah, 1997a for examples). One might call the process one of *lamination* (Bakhtin, 1986). That is, in the overall context of a text in one language (SWE), the authors embed another language variety (AAVE or Sri Lankan English). To adopt Blommaert's (2005, p. 237) terminology, we can also call this a case of "layered simultaneity." Such a process of codemeshing is a model for multilinguals to merge diverse codes for voice, as a realization of translingual practice.

Let me explain how this approach resolves the dilemmas in writing pedagogy for progressive teachers and multilingual students and scholars. This is a pragmatic resolution that is sensitive to the competing claims in this debate, that is, the importance of challenging the inequalities of languages and yet mastering the dominant codes for social and educational success. The scholars reviewed above are right to say that it is costly to deviate from the established norms of academic writing. Idealistic resistance to SWE will only lead to authors of such texts being treated as unproficient in the norms of written discourse and penalized accordingly. As writing is strictly gatekept in many contexts, we go against the established norms at our own peril. However, codemeshing affords authors a way to satisfy both demands, that is, norms and voice. They are not using their own English varieties wholesale, but using it only in a qualified manner. In using SWE, they are able to signal to readers their proficiency in the elite genres and norms. However, in bringing their own languages in measured ways for significant rhetorical and performative reasons, they are representing their identities and pluralizing the text.

The power of codemeshing is that it enables us to acknowledge the reality of established codes in formal literate institutionalized contexts, while also making spaces within the text for alternative discourses. This is a strategy of resisting from within. In doing this, translinguals will satisfy the expectation of their audience for the current and conventional expectations for writing (i.e., the use of native speaker varieties of English and discourse conventions), while also satisfying their own need for a voice through their preferred codes and conventions. Through this strategy, minority students and scholars have a good chance of vying for the educational and social rewards associated with the mastery of the dominant codes, while doing so on their own terms. They can succeed in the mainstream discourses without sacrificing their criticality and voice. This strategy is transformative. While Elbow waits for history to initiate norm changes, with codemeshing we find translinguals already exercising their agency to initiate changes. While Elbow delays the pluralization of texts, with codemeshing we see the inclusion of other codes in current practice. With such hybrid texts, academic writing is already getting pluralized. Seeing the inclusion of their own language norms in elite and formal institutional texts, minority students and scholars will gain more ownership and voice in academic writing.

However, why not go the full length and make a case for encoding the whole text in a marginalized code if our intent is pluralizing writing? Codemeshing is motivated by pragmatic sociolinguistic considerations. If all speech events are language games, the rules of the game that all the players currently share need to be acknowledged. This is important even if the current rules favor one group more than the other, and may have come into force as a result of that group's dominant status. If we suddenly bring in new rules, we could be disqualified from that game. At the most charitable, this will be construed as a different game altogether and we can be asked to play that game elsewhere. This is not necessarily a favorable outcome for minority scholars in academic communication. I don't want my text written in Sri Lankan English ruled as non-academic or treated as addressing only Sri Lankan readers. I don't want my use of Sri Lankan English to make my text a different genre of communication for a different audience. By inserting the oppositional codes gradually into the existing conventions, I deal with the same audience and genre of communication but in my own terms. To be really effective, I need to work from within the existing rules to transform the game. Besides, I need to socialize the players into the revised rules of the game. The qualified use of alternate codes into the dominant discourse will serve to both play the game and also change its rules.

Or to use a more technical metaphor—the metaphor of indexicality from the school of language ideology—we might say that it takes time and effort to develop new indexicalities. Minority codes that didn't previously enjoy academic uses or values have to gain that kind of uptake from readers. Authors have to use alternate codes in creative ways, adopting the negotiation strategies introduced in the last chapter, to build this academic indexicality. Through a collective social process of repeated use and sedimentation, it is possible that alternate codes will develop academic indexicality over time. There are linguistic and ideological processes involved in this activity of *enregisterment* (Agha, 2003), whereby a set of codes develop an identity with specific resonance, values, and implications. Codemeshing helps translinguals earn this new indexicality gradually within the dominant norms and conventions. We will study how a minority scholar strives to develop academic indexicality for vernacular codes in the example below.

An illustration

Geneva Smitherman's 1999 publication "CCCC's Role in the Struggle for Language Rights" is a good example of a minority scholar employing a range of vernacular dialects to represent her voice and identity in formal academic writing. Interestingly, the article takes stock of the pedagogical advances made since the 1972 "Students' Right to their Own Language" (SRTOL) statement by the American professional organization Convention of College Composition and Communication (CCCC). Though its radical implications have not been fully realized, the statement is far ahead of its time in making a space for minority students in writing instruction. As Smitherman was herself part of the committee that formulated and passed that statement, she is obviously in sympathy with students' right to their languages in academic writing.

In reviewing the implementation of this statement in her article, Smitherman probably feels compelled to practice what she preaches. Codemeshing is the strategy she adopts to make a place for AAVE in her academic writing.

I analyze the instances where Smitherman introduces AAVE in an essay that is primarily in SWE. I aim to bring out the strategies she adopts to gain uptake for her new codes and accomplish her rhetorical objectives. This is primarily a textual analysis. My attempts to interview Smitherman about her strategies were not successful. She wrote to me that her strategies were intuitive. She understood the need to "do some kind of conscious, meta-linguistic, outta body or whatever to figure out just how and when I do this code switching"[1] (personal communication, 10 February 2004). However, she felt that she was not the best person to do this analysis. She also didn't have previous versions of her draft of this article to help me study her composing process.

That Smitherman hadn't done a "conscious, meta-linguistic, outta body" analysis is understandable. Though many advanced multilingual scholars have adopted code-meshing strategies for voice from their writing experience intuitively, it is possible that they haven't developed a reflective and studied orientation to this strategy because such practices had been proscribed in formal contexts. Ironically, it is left to outside analysts to study this practice and explain to the authors themselves their own strategies. For subsequent messages, where I sought confirmation of my reading and asked for member check on my interpretation, Smitherman didn't comment much. It is possible that she wanted me to analyze freely a practice in which she didn't have a meta knowledge. I have received a similar response from a Sri Lankan scholar whose codemeshing I have also studied and reported elsewhere (see Canagarajah, 2006b). The predicament shows the difficulty in doing this kind of research. It also shows the importance of explicating the intuitive strategies adopted by multilingual authors, so that teachers and researchers can present them to students as models.

In my analysis below, I focus on the decisions Smitherman seems to have made on where, when, and how to mesh AAVE with SWE. This focus raises questions such as the following: How has Smitherman made codemeshing rhetorically persuasive and contextually appropriate to facilitate uptake? What strategies does she adopt to seek new indexicality for her unconventional codes? How does she laminate heterogeneous codes to achieve an internal coherence for her text?

For the most part of the paper, Smitherman uses the established codes and the conventions of scholarly publication. The article is objective and analytical, with citations, footnotes, and scholarly evidence, in addition to SWE. The essay is also very balanced in representing the alternate positions to the ones she herself holds on SRTOL. The instances of AAVE use are few, but are carefully deployed to construct her desired voice for this article. AAVE is not used much in the opening of the paper where she provides the background and reviews the scholarly developments leading to SRTOL. Her writing thus earns academic credibility among readers before she begins using AAVE. Curiously, most of the cases of AAVE begin to appear in the middle section of the article where Smitherman narrates the debate that accompanied the formulation of the resolution. While invoking the dominant framing for

Research Articles (RA) then, Smitherman adopts another framing for the AAVE norms. As I will show later, AAVE use doesn't stop at the level of grammatical norms. These items also index another discourse, featuring a more personal, passionate, and informal ethos. The double framing of the text helps Smitherman strategically. Readers still situate her essay in the academic frame and read it as a scholarly text while also recognizing the community ethos invoked by AAVE. They may thus treat AAVE as not motivated by deficiency. This process of lamination, then, is a strategy of recontextualization, as defined in Chapter 5.

Such a recontextualization strategy is different from Smitherman's practice about twenty-five years earlier (see "Soul 'n' Style," Smitherman, 1974) when she wrote the complete article (starting from the title) in AAVE. It is important to ask why Smitherman gave up this practice of writing an article completely in AAVE after that attempt. When I read the 1974 article, I took it initially as a parody. It was hilarious to see AAVE replacing SWE in a serious academic article. It appeared to me that Smitherman was satirizing the academic prose. However, if Smitherman's purpose in the article was to convey serious scholarly concerns, it was not well achieved. The prose that deviated so radically from the established conventions, almost without any relevance to the RA genre, probably distracted readers from her serious purposes. The unitary framing of this article in street speech provided a context that was not appropriate for academic uptake. Her AAVE items probably indexed different values and meaning in that context for many readers. It received a different uptake from that of an academic article.

Codemeshing, on the other hand, serves as a better strategy for accomplishing her serious purposes while also representing her voice. In her SRTOL piece in 1999, therefore, Smitherman takes pains to indicate to readers that she is framing this article within dominant academic conventions and conveys her authority in this genre before she deviates for voice. By laminating both frames (i.e., academic and community) into the current text, and recontextualizing the academic text according to alternate norms, Smitherman has it both ways. The meshing is treated more seriously and serves to add value to her academic writing, rather than index deficiency or rhetorical ineptness.

It is significant that in most uses of AAVE in her article, Smitherman doesn't employ quotation marks to flag them or gloss them as distinct or strange (the two exceptions are discussed later). Using quotation marks would have distanced the author from AAVE, invoking the traditional biases of deficiency or inappropriateness. Without them, most readers would now process these switches without pausing to consider them unnatural. This acceptability also results from the fact that some elements of AAVE have become mainstreamed (i.e., words such as "signifyin," "whole nother level," and "blessed out" discussed below). Through repeated use in mainstream contexts, these words now index meanings that are fairly well known and accepted in wider contexts of communication. We are losing the ability to classify such items as categorically "non-standard" or non-academic. Perhaps these words have become sedimented to take on alternative meanings. This process shows the benefits of codemeshing. As readers confront marginalized codes meshed in privileged texts, these codes are beginning to gain meaning and acceptability, appearing "natural" in such contexts. This is an example of the way gradual but bold uses of the vernacular lead to their becoming naturalized and widely shared over time, gaining new indexicalities.

Consider the first occasion of AAVE use: "In his scathing critique, with its signifyin title, 'Darkness is King,' Lloyd took Knickerbocker to task ... " (Smitherman, 1999, p. 350). To understand the signifying function, we must note that Knickerbocker's paper, which derides ungrammatical expressions in student writing, is entitled "The Freshman is King." An in-group motif from folklore (see Abrahams, 1985), "signifiyin" has now received near global currency. After Henry Louis Gates' (1990) *Signifying Monkey* and other publications like Smitherman's (1990) own book, *Talkin and Testifyin*, this reference to instigating has become familiar to non-AAVE speakers like me. Though this is a mere lexical switch, what might be considered a single cultural borrowing, it indexes a whole vernacular speech event. Even such single vocabulary items in an essay dominantly in SWE serve envoicing purposes. They change the ethos of the text, invoking an alternate set of values and language norms.

Note also the lexical items italicized in the following statements:

> At the time, my Womanist consciousness was just developing, and so I was not very vocal in this hours-long debate, for which I was soundly *blessed out* by one of the women when we took a bathroom break ... The debate was finally resolved when Elisabeth McPherson, genius that *my girl* was, proposed that we cast the wording in the third person plural.
>
> *(Smitherman, 1999, p. 361; emphasis mine)*

> As I listened to their arguments, all I could think about was the *dissin* and *doggin* I had endured during the "Students' Right" years, and I kept saying "no way".
>
> *(Smitherman, 1999, p. 368; emphasis mine)*

These too are in-group expressions that have gained new indexicality in wider society now. They belong to the urban vernacular, distinct from the more marked rural (Southern) speech we will see later. These lexical items index certain special attitudes and feelings. That the author refers to being "blessed out" suggests that she is taking this as an in-group chastisement that should be embraced and treated as inoffensive. The next usage, "my girl," indicates the close relationship between the interlocutors, evoking in-group solidarity. The other two nouns "dissin and doggin" reflect the tone and attitude toward the insulting speech of the out-group members. The context invoked in all these uses provides rhetorical justification for these switches. The switches index the type of relationships and feelings referred to. The meshes gain uptake as there is a subtle recontextualization going on in the local context of the text. Though the overall framing is that of an academic article, there is a more local framing behind these AAVE items. They occur in the context of interpersonal relationships between in-group members in an academic committee meeting (relating to the deliberation of SRTOL). There is thus a local framing of a narrative, in the macro frame of an academic article. This is another case of lamination. The local frame recontextualizes the text and persuades readers (or makes it easy for them) to accept the vernacular items in an academic article.

Another category of AAVE use is in the stylistic choice of emotive, repetitive, and rhythmic expressions valued in oral communication. Such collocation violates the established formal register in academic prose. Such language may be considered too informal for academic writing, but it certainly serves to index the desired voice of the author. Consider the satirical humor in the following:

> Not content with *knocking* Knickerbocker *upside the head*, Lloyd also *slammed* the journal and the organization ...
>
> *(Smitherman, 1999, p. 350; emphasis mine).*

> As an organizational position, the "Students' Right" resolution represented a critical mechanism for CCCC to address its own internal contradictions at the same time as *marching, fist-raising, loud-talking* protesters, spearheaded by the Black Liberation Movement, *marred* the social landscape of "America the beautiful"
>
> *(Smitherman, 1999, pp. 357–58; emphasis mine).*

The rhyme (knocking Knickerbocker) and rhythm (marching, fist-raising, loud-talking) evoke a register that is more oral and non-academic. There is also the hyperbole in some word choices here that may be considered very unacademic (i.e., slammed, marred). Though the lexical items in themselves are not "non-standard," it is the collocation and the context that give them a special resonance. All of these lexical choices index the voice of a speaker from a relatively more high-involvement oral culture, and potentially jar against the conventions of a low-involvement academic genre (Tannen, 1982). However, the words evoke the author's identification with the acts described and index the attitudes presented. Also, the language is rhetorically appropriate for acts and attitudes that are oppositional to the dominant values of the academy. The lamination of dual frames helps these unconventional codes gain uptake. There is an additional performative dimension to the meshing here. The conflicting frames (academic and political) bring out the resistant dimension of SRTOL even more.

In some cases, the author doesn't have to use her own words but makes her cited authorities evoke a divergent discourse to accomplish her purposes. She, however, recontextualizes the quotations from her sources. For example, she writes, "Lloyd even goes so far as to say that linguistics 'is a promised land for the English teacher'" (Smitherman, 1999, p. 352). The phrase "promised land" has special resonance for the African American community. Apart from being biblical and showing the importance of the Bible in vernacular culture, we know that the metaphor of a promised land has enjoyed currency in Black consciousness ever since Claude Brown's (1966) book of that title. Through this allusion, Smitherman is also appropriating the field of linguistics for the oppositional causes of enlightened instructors who wish to challenge the popular biases of the dominant community. The phrase "promised land" indexes new associations. The same recontextualization strategy is used again when Smitherman cites a verse from the Bible: "But we also knew that without 'vision, the people perish'" (Smitherman, 1999, p. 358). She embeds these phrases from a non-academic text (Bible) in a new context (academic) to index moral values oppositional to dominant discourses. In using quotation marks in both cases above, Smitherman is indicating that these are other people's words, though she doesn't provide a citation. The quoted texts gain new indexicality through their lamination in dual contexts (non-academic and academic). By inserting one text into another with a different rhetorical context, Smitherman is generating oppositional meanings, alternate ethos, and a strategic voice in her article.

In the second part of the above quotation, Smitherman quickly shifts to the most direct grammatical violation of SWE in this article: "Besides, as I commented to a fellow comrade (a psychologist, who was one of the founders of the Association of Black Psychologists), *what else was we gon do while we was waitin* for the Revolution to come?" (Smitherman, 1999, p. 358; emphasis mine). Smitherman embeds these features of AAVE grammar in a clear dramatic context which provides a different frame for deviations from SWE. In the case above, it is clear that the usage reflects the language of the persona who uttered that statement and the in-group solidarity enjoyed with the interlocutor in that speech event. In using AAVE grammar, the author is being true to the context and the interlocutors. Thus, the rhetorical context disarms criticism. Once again, the lamination of dual frames in the text—invoking an informal sub-frame for the narrative context in the larger frame of academic norms for the research article—is strategic for gaining acceptance for the meshing.

We find a similar narrative context—and an alternate framing—in the examples that follow. Discussing the divergent responses to SRTOL, she writes "A few simply said that CCCC *had done lost they cotton-pickin mind*. ... [Then, after discussing more favorable responses, she continues:] A few simply asked CCCC *why it took yall* so long. ... Such ideas elicited strong reactions among CCCC professionals (irrespective of whether they supported the resolution or not) and moved the intellectual production of knowledge in the field *to a whole nother level*" (Smitherman, 1999, pp. 362–63; emphasis mine). The meshing does give evidence of the "strong reactions" elicited by the proposal. The mention of "cotton-pickin" makes the stupidity one notch worse. "A whole nother level" indicates that the production of knowledge was not just moved to the next level but to a different dimension. These statements alternate with more scholarly views from others, presented in staid prose, showing that the author is switching codes with remarkable control over her repertoire of Englishes. The voices of the author and her African-American colleagues being represented in AAVE are rhetorically appropriate, and serve envoicing purposes. In addition to the switches between SWE and AAVE, we must note that there are different dialects of AAVE orchestrated here. While the examples in the previous paragraph are largely from the urban vernacular, the ones in the latest example are largely rural and southern. We must remember that AAVE is not monolithic. There are diverse dialects within AAVE. There is thus an orchestration of diverse voices in the article. They serve to make the text polyphonous.

However, different spaces in the text permit different layering, footing, and framing for purposes of recontextualization. The Acknowledgements section in the article gives space for alternate discourses. Though it is part of the academic text, it is also framed as a space for more personal discourse. Smitherman gives "a shout out" to one of her undergraduate student assistants (Smitherman, 1999, p. 374). This language is motivated by the youthful persona addressed. A more senior scholar would not appreciate this manner of acknowledgement. For the only other person thanked in this section, the author writes "I would like to express my gratitude and special thanks to –, for his most capable assistance and archival work" (Smitherman, 1999, p. 374). The more formal language suits the senior scholar addressed in this statement (indicated by the title, "Dr." in a later version of this article—Smitherman, 2003, p. 36). Apart from the different interlocutors, there is additional reason why the switch to vernacular is rhetorically appropriate here. In certain low-stakes environments in the text, the vernacular is generally treated as unobjectionable. There is considerable latitude in using non-standard elements in such peripheral sections of the RA. These sections are framed differently and call for a different footing. Other low-stakes sections are dedications, titles, and conclusions (Thaiss and Zawacki, 2002). In the more conservative pages of the *TESOL Quarterly*, Smitherman uses AAVE prominently in the safe space of the title ("Dat Teacher be Hollin at Us" Smitherman, 1998, p. 139). Except for glossed uses of "homiez" and "capping," this is the only place where she uses AAVE authorially in this article—clearly a strategic choice. What such examples show is that the text (and the academic text in this case) already has spaces framed differently which call for a different footing. The academic text is not a monolithic product. Smitherman is skillfully exploiting the different spaces of the academic text with different framing/footing to insert her voice and alternate norms. They perform no small function in pluralizing the text.

Ironically, in the only case where Smitherman flags a non-standard expression, she does so not to mark the unusual usage behind the peculiar item, but to evoke the widely shared usage of a well-known expression. She says "(I report with pride that I was the first to introduce 'cussing' into committee discourse, to the relief of one of my male comrades.)" (Smitherman, 1999, p. 361). While she makes AAVE items seem natural in other cases, she makes the expression in this case appear unnatural. Perhaps this is a performative act to indicate how the conventional discourse for committee meetings was disturbed by her "cussing." She is drawing attention to this word for a performative reason. Similarly, the only case where she provides a gloss is to introduce an item that is recent and probably an in-group expression among a subcultural group—Black teenagers: "In the 1998 celebration of African American History Month, a television commercial for Mickey D's [gloss: Ebonics for McDonald's] featured a White father and his young son browsing through a gallery with paintings of African American heroes and she-roes" (Smitherman, 1999, p. 366). The gloss for "Mickey D's" indicates that it is perhaps new to the older generation of AAVE speakers. It needs more clues to its indexicality, and the context is not adequate to help in its interpretation. ("She-roes" doesn't warrant a gloss as its meaning is clear from the context.) The latter examples show that Smitherman is variating the

AAVE used—not only between regions, that is, urban and rural, but also between age groups, that is, adult and teen talk. This variation also contributes to the polyphony of the text.

It must be noted that all these instances of AAVE don't amount to much in an article running to about 30 pages. But they are sufficient to change the ethos of the text. More importantly, they demonstrate what Smitherman argues for in this article. Referring to the strategy behind SRTOL, she says: "It has been said that politics is the art of compromise. And compromise we did. After the lengthy debates and verbal duels, we finally produced a document that we all felt we could live with" (Smitherman, 1999, p. 362). This text is again a compromise—something we can all live with—till more spaces are available for other Englishes and more diverse language resources can index academic values. To give further insight into this strategy, she later says in conclusion: "The documented spirit of resistance in the 'Students' Right' and National Language Policy is an important symbol that change is possible—*even within the system*" (Smitherman, 1999, p. 373; emphasis added). These are interesting meta-pragmatic cues that reflexively comment on Smitherman's own strategy in this article. This is the rationale for her codemeshing in this essay. The careful deployment of vernacular items within an SWE text is an example of a strategy of resistance from within. However, change is already underway in Smitherman's text. The few instances of meshed codes pluralize the text and move academic writing to a whole nother level.

This strategy of resistance from within is different from the uncompromising strategy in her 1974 article where she composed without regard to SWE norms. We must also realize that Smitherman's entextualization of AAVE items is carefully chosen for the audience and the textual context. As mentioned earlier, in her article in *TESOL Quarterly (TQ)*, Smitherman uses AAVE prominently in the safe space of the title only. As this is a more conservative journal when it comes to style, largely associated with the positivistic research tradition, Smitherman doesn't engage in the kind of meshing we see in the *CCC* article. In other words, the extent and nature of meshing is decided in relation to the publishing/writing context. *CCC*, being a composition journal which largely publishes essayistic pieces, is more friendly to codemeshing than *TQ*, which publishes more empirical and data-driven articles.

That Smitherman is very cautious in her entextualization is also evident in her response to my email on her writing process. She said "I can tell you this much, I write first drafts in LWC and compose at the computer usually, from notes. Then in the editing stage I introduce the AAL forms" (personal communication, 10 Febraury 2004). It emerges that Smitherman first writes in SWE or the "language of wider communication" (LWC; her preferred term) and then inserts AAVE in the final draft. The writing process suggests that codemeshing is a conscious strategy for Smitherman. There is nothing spontaneous or unplanned about this practice. The strategies which I have identified above are probably the ones that (albeit intuitively) motivated her to insert AAVE items in a text which she first composes in SWE. The lesson here is that we have to convey to multilingual scholars and students that they have to entextualize their preferred codes strategically. Where and how they wish to encode their voices in academic texts is a matter of strategic, conscious, and creative decision. Critical for uptake is the recontextualization strategies Smitherman adopts to laminate alternate codes into dominant norms.

Implications for the politics of publishing

It is worth emphasizing that Smitherman's essay was published in a top-tier peer-reviewed journal. I would like to explore the wider implications of codemeshed writing for pluralizing academic publishing. Since RA is the most valued genre in academic writing (see Swales, 1990), I would like to consider if translingual practices have a place in international academic communication. Because of its power, the norms governing the RA genre are also very tight and rigid. The fact that this genre is strictly gatekept enables publishers to enforce these norms and conventions. It is well-known that academic publishing is unfairly structured to favor those from Inner Circle communities (see Canagarajah, 2002a). There are a host of historical, material, and geopolitical reasons that account for the power of developed and English-dominant communities in this genre of writing. The upshot of all this is that native speaker norms (in the form of SWE) are emphasized in RAs. In order to get their research findings published, multilingual authors have been prepared to go to any length to get editing help and services to conform to the dominant conventions and language norms of RAs. Publications such as the *Modern Language Journal* officially recommend multilingual authors to send their papers to outsourced copy-editing services before submitting their articles. Even well-meaning scholars who understand the inequalities in publishing and the need for a voice for multilingual authors haven't dared question the power of SWE norms. Many of these scholars aim to help multilingual scholars conform with supplementary resources and the editing help of "literacy brokers" rather than creatively complicate the dominant norms (see, for example, such recommendations by Lillis and Curry 2010 in their book on the inequalities in academic publishing).

It appears to me that codemeshing may provide a way for multilingual scholars to show their competence in academic norms while also appropriating them for their purposes. In addition to Smitherman, a few other scholars have adopted this strategy for achieving a voice in academic contexts. I have narrated the example of Sri Lankan scholars who have managed to get published by meshing discourses in their favor (see Canagarajah, 2002a for examples). In book publications there is greater latitude for multilingual authors to encode their voices. Minority scholars like bell hooks (1989), Gloria Anzaldúa (1987), and Victor Villanueva have practiced codemeshed forms of writing in their scholarly books, with Villanueva (2011) introducing slightly more qualified uses of codemeshing in journal articles.

I have codemeshed in some of my research articles. The reason I have not codemeshed to the same extent in all my writing is because we have to consider the context and entextualization possibilities carefully before doing so, as I have argued through Smitherman's practice above. In an article in *CCC* where I analyzed Smitherman's writing strategies and advocated codemeshing (Canagarajah, 2006a), I used some Sri Lankan English in the essay. The article went on to win an award for the best article in the journal for that year and was also anthologized in a major collection of composition articles (see Miller, 2009). Rather than being stigmatized, the use of Sri Lankan English seems to have enhanced the article's significance. There are many reasons why I felt comfortable codemeshing in that article. Codemeshing would be expected in an article where I proposed this as an option. The journal *CCC* had published some creative articles that showed considerable deviation from the norms. For example, it had published articles which used AAVE, including that of Smitherman's own essay. Based on all these considerations, I assumed that the journal would go a few extra steps in publishing an article that used Sri Lankan English. Still, I had to alert the copy editors that Sri Lankan English items were used on purpose and I wanted them retained, before they treated them as errors and edited them out. I also flagged them to the editor in my cover letter so that she would interpret any possible derogatory comments of the reviewers in the appropriate manner. In my manuscript itself, I adopted some recontextualization strategies, learnt from Smitherman. I subtly conveyed that my Sri Lankan items were part of a different framing, calling for a different footing from the reader. I placed them in narrative and intertextual contexts where it was clear that these items were framed differently. My correspondence with the editor and copy-editors was also acts of recontextualization. I was indicating to them that my essay is framed differently and, thus, calls for a different reading.

Is this book codemeshed? There are certainly diverse semiotic resources from the data I am citing from my multilingual research subjects. They contribute to a polyphonous text. Authorially, I also adopt certain uses of Sri Lankan English in some places. The narrative on Siva's communicative strategies in Chapter 3 is codemeshed, with Tamil words that readers have to interpret in context as they are not given translations. In writing that, I wanted to simulate for the readers the negotiation process that trans-linguals would undertake. More importantly, I assume that semiodiversity and voice derive from my ethos and the fresh contexts in which I am using SWE, inbuing similarity with difference (Pennycook, 2010). Reviewers of this book have commented a bit critically on the "passionate" or "informal" writing in some places which requires tightening. However, I have left them intact as I consider these effects as deriving from my preferred practices in Tamil writing.

Recently, editors of some collected articles in books have edited for intelligibility rather than accuracy. In the place of native speaker norms then, these books feature diverse approximations of SWE. The ELF scholar from Finland, Anna Mauranen, explains the justification for her editing practice, in a recent book *English as a Lingua Franca: Studies and Findings* she co-edited, as follows:

> Some of the papers in this book have been written by native speakers of English, others not, but all have been written by expert users of English. No policy of having the L2 authors' texts checked by native speakers for linguistic correctness has been applied, because this was regarded as an irrelevant practice in a book presenting international scholarship. Whether English has been the first or an additional language to the writers, they have been addressing an international audience, not primarily ENL (English Native Language) communities. Their

contributions thus reflect the kind of language use they discuss: effective English as an international lingua franca.

(Mauranen, 2009, p. 6)

Similarly, the ELF scholar Jennifer Jenkins mentioned in a conversation recently that she and her co-editor focused on intelligibility and overlooked the issues of idiomatic peculiarities in the articles which they published in a book featuring multilingual authors (personal communication, September 2010). The book referred to is *Global Englishes in Asian Contexts* (Murata and Jenkins, 2009). Since these books are about lingua franca English, there is a rhetorical justification—and need—for using diverse norms in such publications.

What has helped these recent publishing efforts in pluralizing the language norms in academic publishing is that there is a questioning of the norms and conventions of academic writing in the context of the backlash against modernist values in scholarly inquiry. Scholars now understand the limitations of positivistic approaches that inform the dominant norms of academic writing. The post-Enlightenment approaches to inquiry, which favor an acknowledgement of the values that motivate research, an adoption of holistic and diverse approaches, and an awareness of the contexts and contingencies that shape findings, are more open to diversity in writing approaches (see Canagarajah, 1996). This opening can be exploited by multilingual scholars for representing their voices and values in writing.

While there are favorable models and conditions for codemeshing in academic publishing, multilingual authors have to keep certain negotiation strategies in focus as they decide how much to codemesh, where, and when. There are important entextualization and envoicing decisions to be made as one considers codemeshing in RAs. The following are some:

- There are differences among academic fields on the extent to which they might tolerate language diversity. In general, fields in the natural sciences are more resistant to issues of voice than humanities. There is anecdotal evidence that scientific journal editors are not tolerant of grammatical deviations, may insult the authors about their non-nativeness, and reject their articles outright for stylistic peculiarities.
- There are differences in tolerance for codemeshing within the same field. In general, certain avant garde journals are more open to language diversity than mainstream journals, which are still steeped in empirical and positivistic traditions. However, for the same reason, the former journals may not have much academic cachet. It is also important to consider the publishing history of a journal before submitting an article that meshes codes. If certain journals have published creative genres in the past, one can be confident that they will be friendly to a pluralization of norms. One can even reference such articles in one's work to make a case for codemeshing in the same journal. An article I published on the need to accommodate more diversity in *TQ* (Canagarajah, 1996) has now been referenced by other scholars to publish their own experimental writing in the same journal (see Norton and Early, 2011 for example).

- The subject of the article can also indicate if and how much codemeshing would be tolerated. As in Smitherman's case, an article on language diversity naturally calls for some experimentation with one's medium. Similarly, in my essay, where I analyze Smitherman's codemeshing, my own authorial meshing was warranted. In other words, codemeshing may appear more "natural," or can be made natural, with some rhetorical sensitivity to the content of the article.
- Authors also have to exploit certain spaces within the text which may tolerate more meshing. As mentioned earlier, there are "low-stakes" environments in the text that accommodate meshing. Acknowledgements, epigraphs, and titles are such spaces (see also Thaiss and Zawacki, 2002 for interview data from a discipline-based faculty who confirm this openness). However, the beginnings of articles are too early to codemesh (as Elbow, 1999 too observes). Authors usually prepare the readers for the codemeshing and build their own scholarly authority as insiders to the academic discourse before they begin to mesh.

Critics of codemeshing in RA have asked me if I was willing to publish such articles when I served as the editor of *TQ* from 2005 to 2009. My position has always been that I will accept codemeshed essays if they were rhetorically justified, strategic, and displayed a critical and creative design. What will help me decide if those choices can be permitted in a published article is whether they are appropriate in that text and context. Did the author think through the use of his or her choice? Did the usage enhance communication and voice? Was the choice rhetorically well motivated? Did the author take into consideration the dominant discourses and readership of the journal to choose the extent to which he/she can introduce variant language and discourse? Whether and how much to codemesh is a rhetorical decision. My main concern has mostly been with the author's recontextualization, envoicing, and entextualization strategies that would make the choices negotiable and persuasive.

Conclusion

Examples such as Smitherman's and other experimental pieces by experienced scholars can be treated as useful models to encourage students and novice scholars to codemesh in their academic articles. It is important for students to know that there are successful multilingual scholars who are representing their voices and norms in academic writing. Note that my proposal demands more, not less, from minority students. It demands proficiency in established varieties, expert use of local variants, and the rhetorical strategies of meshing. In other words, this strategy requires not only awareness of the established and local norms, but the competence to bring them together strategically for voice and for one's objectives. Codemeshing calls for complex linguistic and rhetorical competence. It is not a practice of deficiency.

However, it is appropriate to ask if students must master SWE before they can mesh their preferred codes in academic writing. I am open to the possibility that increasing awareness of SWE norms can go hand in hand with meshing of one's vernacular. I have seen the very practice of codemeshing developing the metalinguistic competence of students. As they shuttle between languages, they develop a keen sensitivity to the differences and similarities of language resources. In fact, codemeshers often develop a more critical awareness of SWE and its potential as they shuttle between diverse norms. Furthermore, we have to ask if codemeshing is possible only for advanced writers, like the scholars I have mentioned above. What my description in Chapter 3 suggests is that multilingual students come from communities which have enjoyed multimodal and multilingual literacies for centuries. Codemeshing may therefore come easily to them. They could be experts in codemeshing, though new to SWE norms. We don't have to consider them deficient in any way.

We must, however, emphasize that codemeshing is not a strategy guaranteed for success. As in all cases of communicative activity, there are risks involved. Seeking new indexicality for unconventional codes is a strategic activity. Enregisterment is a complex process. Not everyone can always be persuaded for successful uptake. Smitherman's practice suggests what it takes to gain uptake for new indexicals. Strategies such as recontextualization and entextualization can help minority students and scholars agentively develop new meanings and values for their codes as they pluralize dominant norms and literacies. We gain a perspective into the *process* of enregisterment and appreciate the role of human agency in Smitherman's practice. Such a perspective on indexicality complements the more impersonal historical model described by Agha (2003) and the geopolitical model of Blommaert (2010).

7

NEGOTIATING TRANSLINGUAL LITERACY

Smitherman's writing practice might seem extreme to some readers. Among other things, they might feel that it is difficult to interpret texts that don't employ a shared code. They might find themselves helpless against the diversity of codes that inhabit a codemeshed text, many of which they might not be familiar with. Veteran composition instructor, Pat Bizzell (2010), has recently asked: "How does one read a codemeshed text?" The essays written by her multilingual students pose unsettling questions for traditional notions of literacy: How do we interpret a codemeshed text when it uses languages we may not be familiar with? How do we assess deviations from SWE? How do we judge the rhetorical effectiveness of texts which challenge traditional notions of coherence? If Bizzell seeks new orientations to literacy, Vanessa Sohan wonders about a new orientation to literacy pedagogy when she asks: "How can we as teacher-scholars change the way we respond to (read-write-think about) and teach the words of 'others' so as to work against the grain of dominant discourses and habituated 'systems of hearing' designed to undercut 'minority' voices?" (Sohan, 2009, p. 274). She finds that the dominant orientations to literacy don't permit her students to respond to codemeshed texts effectively. Such concerns are understandable. The dominant orientations to literacy are not friendly to translingual writing. We have to consider alternate orientations that present strategies of reading and writing that enable us to deal with textual hybridity.

In this chapter I argue that an understanding of writing as translingual requires a shift to a different orientation to literacy, that is, from autonomous to negotiated. Such an orientation treats the text as co-constructed in time and space—with parity for readers and writers in shaping the meaning and form—thus performed rather than preconstructed, making the material and multisensory dimensions of the text fully functional. It is such an orientation that I find NES and multilingual students adopting in my classes. Drawing from classroom ethnography, I demonstrate how the codemeshed texts of a multilingual student were negotiated for meaning. Going beyond the native/non-native and monolingual/multilingual speaker binaries, I also argue that both student groups already bring such an orientation to literacy from contact zones outside the classroom—from multilingual home environments and new social media, from precolonial community practices and postmodern digital communication.

Scholars in composition and related disciplines have hitherto conducted product-oriented analyses of codemeshed texts without exploring how they are negotiated for meaning. Codemeshing will be problematic in relation to traditional practices of reading and writing. To understand translingual literacy, we have to move from product-oriented analyses to process. We have to explore the processes of production, reception, and the negotiation of texts. We also have to move from writing being an independent activity to perceiving it as literacy or, in other words, a social activity that integrates reading, writing, and diverse semiotic resources. This is a missing dimension in the scholarship on codemeshed writing, which I address in this chapter in order to answer the questions of Bizzell, Sohan, and other concerned teachers.

Competing orientations to the text

The dominant orientation to literacy has been called different names by different scholars, that is: alphabetic literacy (Baca, 2009), autonomous literacy (Street, 1984), divided logos (Ratcliffe, 1999), essayistic literacy (Hesse, 1999), graphocentric literacy (Mignolo, 2000), ortho-graphy (Blommaert, 2008), rhetorical transparency (Stark, 2008), and scriptural practice (de Certeau, 1984). What they all have in common is not only a treatment of texts as featuring one symbol system (alphabets) and one modality (visual representation), but also a particular orientation to reading/writing activity. Dominant orientations to literacy are motivated by the following assumptions: the text should present self-evident meaning; meaning is a product waiting to be extricated from the text; the reader should remain detached from the text in order to employ objective interpretive approaches for accurate meanings; it is the writer's responsibility to encode meanings in such a way that the text can present its meanings with clarity and ease; if there is any activity in meaning-making, it follows the conduit model, whereby meaning filters from the writer's mind through the text to the reader's mind; and whatever time and space the text is located in and travels through, it has the power to convey the same meaning by transcending contexts.

I treat this orientation to the text (which I will call autonomous literacy hereafter, adopting Street's label) as *ideological,* as it is socially constructed, with implications for power relations. Michel de Certeau considers this model of literacy an "Occidental ambition" (de Certeau, 1984, p. 133). In fact, the orient's multimodal literacy practices were suppressed by European colonization activities, as reviewed in Chapter 3. Even in the West, autonomous literacy originated at a particular time. de Certeau locates its rise in the eighteenth century. He associates this literacy with the rise of empirical science, industrialization, and bureaucracy. Collectively, these movements display a trend toward a positivistic orientation to reality, transforming experiences into manageable and disciplined knowledge. Scriptural practice (de Certeau's preferred term, a metaphor evoking the efforts of clergy to control meaning in religious texts) was the instrument by which knowledge was made fit to be encoded, stored, managed, and imposed on others.

There have been more integrated understandings of discourse and textuality during other periods in the West. Krista Ratcliffe, in proposing a more integrated orientation to reading/writing and speaking/listening, traces how the separation took place in Western history. The legacy of the "divided logos ... the logos that speaks but does not listen" (Ratcliffe, 1999, p. 202) begins after the Greeks. Ratcliffe argues that *logos* actually assumes a more integrated notion of discourse, where speaking/listening (or more broadly, production/reception) processes were not separated. As an example, Ryan Stark demonstrates how pre-Enlightenment poetry and rhetoric demanded more participation from readers, before what he considers the "apotheosis of rhetorical transparency" (Stark, 2008, p. 271) in the writings of the Royal Scientific Society. Pre-Enlighenment authors adopted an enthymematic structure which demanded imaginative leaps of logic from readers for the co-construction of meaning.

The tendency of isolating the text and giving primacy to the writer's responsibility at the cost of the reader's agency has been exacerbated by disciplinary practices in various language-related fields. Structuralist linguistics separated grammar from context and performance in an effort to analyze and control meaning. It also gave primacy to orality and, thus, speaking at the cost of other skills. Mastering a language is still considered the ability to speak, in many models of language teaching pedagogy. Writing closely followed in importance as another productive skill that showed "the mastery over language and a means of authoritative expression" (Ratcliffe, 1999, p. 202). Following such trends, writing instruction has traditionally concerned itself with textual production, leaving reception (and hermeneutical processes in general) to literature, philosophy, and other fields (see Hesford, 2006). Rhetoric has similarly maintained this separation of skills. As Ratcliffe puts it: "Classical theories foreground the rhetor's speaking and writing as means of persuading audiences; these theories are only secondarily concerned with how audiences should listen. ... Classical and modern theories of rhetoric rarely delineate or question such production/reception differences" (Ratcliffe, 1999, p. 199). Such developments have left the text with an insufficient sense of negotiability, sociality, performativity, and space/time ecology. Worse still, suppressing readers' diverse "tactics" of co-constructing the text, the tradition of autonomous literacy has lent itself to the "strategies" of the dominant groups to control meaning (de Certeau, 1984).

The social and technological changes of late modernity compel us to relate to texts differently. Internet has introduced new forms of textuality and brought out our capacity to read and write differently. Nicotra (2009) uses multi-user tagging as an example to redefine writing as a deeply negotiated social activity, echoing the theorization of others on digital communication (see Johnson-Eilola, 2004; Wysocki, 2004). Such an orientation adds certain new dimensions to writing. Writing is not about one person producing a text that contains its meaning, but many people constructing spaces for the co-formation of text and, thereby, collaborative meaning-making. There is thus a keener appreciation of the materiality and spatiality of writing. Meaning doesn't reside solely in language but in all the resources of the text and context. There is also a strong sense of performativity, as the content is not given but co-constructed. Writing is not itself constitutive of meaning but provides the resources for the construction of meaning. More importantly, the status of readers and writers gets redefined, as everyone is both a reader and a writer, sharing mutual responsibility in the construction of meaning. Invention and creativity are not left to a single writer but decentered, as multiple readers and writers invent the text. Jodie Nicotra takes pain to explain that these features of writing are not unique to multi-user tagging. They are present in all forms of writing, perhaps hidden or suppressed by the dominant ideology of autonomous literacy. She therefore argues for "a new metaphor for writing that encapsulates how writing emerges spatially from dynamic, collective subjectivities in a network" (Nicotra, 2009, p. 259).

Though Nicotra presents the shift as being fundamentally from a time-bound to a spatial paradigm, we must note that the temporality of writing has traditionally been somewhat limited in literacy. Time, in the process tradition in composition has been addressed largely in relation to the cognitive activities of the author in the multiple iterations of a single textual product (see Flower, 1994, for example). Similarly, the reader response tradition in literature has limited temporality to similar processes in the interpretive iterations of the reader within the bounds of a single textual product (Tompkins, 1980). However, scholars in sociolinguistics are now theorizing the ways in which texts travel across time to different locations and take diverse forms and meanings in the context of globalization and transnational relations. The spatio-temporal circulation of texts shapes both their production and reception in complex ways. Cathy Kell (2010) is open to the possibility that a text which is treated as ungrammatical or incoherent in one context may gain significance and functionality when it travels to a different social and temporal domain. However, we have to be open to the possibility that texts that have meaning in one location and time may be silenced in another. Blommaert adopts the term "constrained mobility" to capture the difficulties of uptake in the translocal movement of the text (Blommaert, 2008, p. 194). Though the potential for silencing is there, we mustn't discount the agency of authors and the creativity of readers as they negotiate traveling texts for meaning (as demonstrated in my example below).

Also useful in Blommaert's project is the case that he makes for the aesthetic dimension of the text. A sensitivity to the materiality of the text should make us appreciate its aesthetics. Interpreting the mix of pictures and words, and the play with spacing and stylization of scripts, in the biographical/historical texts written by two locally literate Congolese authors, Blommaert interprets how their multisensory resources are important for the construction of meaning. Considering the reasons why writing lost its aesthetic and visual resources and got reduced to ideational content, he blames Enlightenment: "Language ideologies emphasising denotational functions rather than others merged with broader rationalist ideologies about the privilege of 'pure' knowledge in subjectivity" (Blommaert, 2008, p. 114). He goes on to protest against "the effect of a stratification of the means of visualization, in which *ortho-graphy* is ranked higher than all other forms of writing—in short, than *hetero-graphy*—and in which routinised practices of disqualification occur" (Blommaert, 2008, p. 117). He argues that in order to understand the rhetorics of translingual authors, we have to reclaim the lost materiality and multisensory dimensions of the text, together with its aesthetics.

Scholars of ethnic rhetorics are also rediscovering rhetorical traditions important for understanding negotiated literacy. Paradoxically, the contemporary digitization of the text and emergent textual modes have spurred a rediscovery and celebration of suppressed precolonial traditions. Mao makes an insightful distinction between the focus on the "what" in Western rhetoric and the "where" in Chinese. The distinction would suggest that Chinese interlocutors are not necessarily looking for a pre-constructed content in discourse, but are valuing the exprerience of co-constructing meaning. Others are theorizing the multilingual and multimodal literacy practices which enjoyed vibrancy in precolonial times and communities. As discussed in Chapter 3, the *manipravala* tradition of Tamils in South Asia (Pollock, 2006), *kene/dami* tradition of the Kashinawá in Brazil (de Souza, 2002), and the *tlaquilolitzli* in Mexico (Baca, 2009), suppressed during European colonization of these regions, involve the complex co-construction of meaning with a deeper appreciation of the text's materiality and spatiotemporal embeddedness, different from autonomous literacy.

In cultural studies also scholars are expanding their orientations to text. Pratt's (1991) injunction to explore the language and literacy encounters at the contact zone has generated an interest in understanding how these "literate arts" are rhetorically constructed and negotiated. While Pratt's model enables us to understand how language contact can engender new norms and literacies, it doesn't provide enough details about the production and reception strategies that facilitate the literate arts of the contact zone. Jacqueline Jones Royster (1996) addressed this concern when she called for a "code of cross-cultural conduct" to negotiate differences of race and gender. Her call has implications for understanding the ethics, linguistics, and rhetoric of negotiation in global contact zones. Krista Ratcliffe's theorization of rhetorical listening is an exemplary attempt to address Royster's call. Ratcliffe defines rhetorical listening as:

> a performance that occurs when listeners invoke both their capacity and their willingness (1) to promote an *understanding* of self and other that informs our culture's politics and ethics, (2) to proceed from within a *responsibility* logic, not from within a defensive guilt/blame one, (3) to locate identification in discursive spaces of both *commonalities* and *differences*, and (4) to accentuate commonalities and differences not only in *claims* but in *cultural logics* within which those claims function.
>
> *(Ratcliffe, 1999, p. 204; emphasis in original)*

The implications of rhetorical listening for translingual literacy are profound. It is not only readers' capacity for codemeshing and multilingualism that counts, but their willingness to engage with difference. We have to encourage them to move out of self-centeredness in assuming only their norms as relevant, and try to understand the diverse cultural values and logics that inform texts. They have to go beyond and behind the text to understand the cultural politics that dictate different forms of uptake. They should expect not only commonalties to aid in understanding a text, but also treat difference as productive and enabling. They shouldn't filter out the arguments and claims in essays but engage with the cultural contexts from which they emanate. To do all this, Ratcliffe asks that readers read "not for intent, but with intent" (Ratcliffe, 1999, p. 205). Similarly, she flips the activity and the word "understanding" to argue that one should "stand under" (Ratcliffe, 1999, p. 207) a text to let its difference flow over one's reading and interpretation.

There are connections between the emerging orientations to literacy reviewed above and the translingual practice I articulate in this book. However, there are also differences. The interpersonal and social dimensions are more pronounced in my translingual practices compared to certain orientations to the negotiated text. For example, de Certeau gives interpretation completely into the hands of the reader and ignores the writer: "He [reader] detaches them [texts] from their (lost or accessory) origin. He combines their fragments and creates something un-known in the space organized by their capacity for allowing an indefinite plurality of meanings" (de Certeau, 1984, p. 169). In such models, the birth of the reader requires the death of the author. This move reifies the reader/writer binary by shifting power from one party in the communication (writer) and giving it to another (reader). In translingual practice, there is mutual respect and engagement on all sides of the production/reception continuum. Though writers are mindful of interlocutors' agency and open to having them negotiate meaning differently, they still calibrate their utterances in particular ways to represent their ideas. They come with strong expectations about what they want to communicate, they care a lot about their objectives, and actively contribute to the negotiation. In this regard, we have to also distinguish certain post-structuralist orientations which subsume both readers and writers into texts and discourses (for a critical discussion, see Ratcliffe, 1999, pp. 199–205; Ashcroft, 2009, pp. 143–58). Some definitions of digital communication (as in Nicotra, 2009) court the danger of eliding agency from both readers and writers, as they focus on distributed intelligence and communication in the somewhat impersonal process of constructing a virtual text. While this shaping of the text by multiple parties and discourses resonates well with translingual practices, we must retain the agency of speakers/listeners and writers/readers in negotiated literacy.

An orientation consistent with translingual practice is that of the text as negotiated and co-constructed in time and space, with parity for readers and writers in shaping the meaning and form, thus performed rather than preconstructed, making the material and multisensory dimensions of the text fully functional. I call this *negotiated literacy*. This orientation may provide a better approach to the interpretation and appreciation of translingual writing. In this chapter, I show how the negotiation strategies I identified earlier—that is, envoicing, recontextualization, interactional, and entextualization—help unveil the practices that constitute negotiated literacy. Applying the findings from oral discourse in Chapter 5 to literacy might be considered overgeneralizing. We have to be mindful that literacy is a different modality of communication. The realization of the four negotiation strategies will be different.

Though some of the physical resources for meaning-making in the face-to-face encounter are absent in the more distant and detached literate negotiations, the physical body of the text and the record of serial drafts provide other resources of value. The materiality of the text provides clues for the interpretation of meaning (i.e., space, font type and size, visual resources, and pagination). Also the possibility of serial drafting and revision provide additional resources for entextualization of meaning, with authors trying out options and preparing readers for meanings through successive drafts.

The context

My textual analysis comes from a classroom ethnography of writing practices in a course on second language writing. The course was open to both graduate and advanced undergraduate students. I analyze the classroom negotiations around the texts of an undergraduate Saudi Arabian student Buthainah, whom we met in Chapter 1. I ask how this student's codemeshed writing was negotiated by her peers and instructor from linguistically heterogeneous backgrounds. I focus on both sides of the negotiation process: How is a codemeshed text interpreted by readers? And what does the writer do to facilitate effective reading? These questions allow me to analyze the processes of production, reception, and co-construction of translingual literacy. In adopting an emic perspective through the ethnography, I attempt to understand the strategies which students themselves employ to write and read such translingual texts.

I don't claim to have taught these negotiation strategies to my students in this class. All that I can claim is that I constructed a favorable pedagogical environment, a relatively safe site, to help students practice the strategies that they already bring with them. Rather than imposing my own literacy assumptions on students one-sidedly, I provided a context where I could negotiate with them the strategies they were familiar with. This doesn't mean that I didn't influence them in any way, but my teacherly intervention was also open to negotiation, as were the feedback and suggestions of their peers.

I adopted what I call a *dialogical pedagogy* (to be discussed more fully in Chapter 9) which develops learning through collaborative interactions between the instructor and the students. The readings and writings emerged out of dialog and dialectical interactions with one's peers and the instructor. Students posted at least six drafts of their literacy autobiography at various stages of development into their folder. The peers and the instructor were expected to read the drafts and post their feedback into the author's folder. The authors had an opportunity to respond to the feedback, reflect on their writing challenges, and pose further questions in their weekly journal entries as they revised the draft for another review. Though there were three textbooks on second language writing that were prescribed, learning from these textbooks was also collaborative, with classroom discussions and group activities complementing reflections, journaling, and writing on the Internet. At an early stage in the course, the students also read my literacy biography (Canagarajah, 2001) as an example for their writing. Though I did not codemesh extensively in that article, students had an opportunity to discuss the idea of codemeshing from one of my articles (Canagarajah, 2006a) which was introduced at a late stage to answer questions about alternate discourses in academic writing.

Could my pedagogy and my identity have influenced students into translingual practices? Pedagogical environments are not neutral. While teachers holding mono-lingualist assumptions may stifle students, dialogical pedagogies may facilitate alternate literacies. I saw to it that there was enough diversity in readings and activities for students to explore different textual strategies, despite my ethos. In this sense, there were varied affordances and resources in the classroom for students to adopt for their engagement and reflection. Though some of my own publications would have influenced students toward the translingual orientation, the texts by other scholars in the course adopted more conservative and normative positions. Furthermore, while there were affordances for translingual orientation, they were mediated by the dominant pedagogical discourses and institutional expectations regarding composition in an American public university. Students had to make their own decisions about how to write, negotiating the mix of affordances and constraints in the course. In retrospect, I find that my own feedback sometimes reflected the dominant discourses on writing. My negotiation of meaning with the writers educated me on translingual strategies and helped me arbitrate between the differences in orientation between NES and multilingual students.

The main requirement for the course was a serially drafted and peer-reviewed literacy autobiography. While the writing provided fascinating insights into the different orientations of multilingual authors, their negotiation with other students (half of whom were NES or Anglo-American) provided useful perspectives on the strategies of interaction surrounding the text. In addition to the serial drafts (identified as D1, D2, etc. below), the weekly journals students wrote (abbreviated as J), classroom activities (A), peer commentary (PC), and interviews (I) provided additional insights into their attitudes to writing. In addition to these forms of data, I adopted stimulated recall (SR) methods to ask students the reasons why they adopted certain strategies and choices in their writing. The method enabled me to understand their assumptions of textuality and communication without relying solely on my interpretation. In the case of Buthainah, I also had the possibility of conducting a member check (MC) procedure. I gave her an early version (EV) of my draft to get her response to my interpretation. All these forms of data enabled me to triangulate my findings.

I choose to focus on Buthainah because she displayed some of the most creative and controversial codemeshing in the class. In her literacy autobiography, she both discussed and enacted the translingual literacy she had developed in Arabic, English, and French. For performative reasons, she deployed codes from all three languages in her text. It was also a multimodal text. As she had a more expansive notion of literacy as multimodal, she included visual motifs, emoticons, and other symbols in her writing. The narrative of Buthainah was arranged in an episodic structure, through a series of developing situations in her literacy trajectory. The most striking feature is her use of Arabic verses to preface the themes of her sections. Buthainah interprets them unobtrusively a couple of paragraphs into the section. Thus she forces us to keep guessing the meaning, almost simulating the process by which translinguals negotiate meanings in contact situations. The translation also comes in different forms. While some are direct translations, in other cases she offers a paraphrase or an allusion. Through all these strategies, Buthainah is calling for a more than cerebral response to her narrative and text.

The highest manifestation of translanguaging in her essay occurs at a metaphorical and rhetorical level. The merging of the Arabic quotes with the struggles and achievements in English literacy raises some fascinating interpretive possibilities. It appears as if Arabic culture and literacy have motivated Buthainah to progress in English language and literacy. The Arabic verses are empowering sentiments that move her forward when she experiences discriminating labels and disempowering experiences in English education. At a broader level, this textual realization proves that the first (and other) languages students bring with them need not be a negative interference on their mastery of the English language and literacy. The resources in the translingual's repertoire can complement each other.

Textual negotiation strategies

Despite the atypical codes and rhetorical moves in Buthainah's essay, her peers and I were considerably successful in constructing meaning and appreciating her writing. What strategies helped us interpret her writing? And what strategies did Buthainah adopt to communicate her voice and rhetorical expectations through her choice of codes in her text? I proceed to show how the four strategies I introduced in Chapter 5 were realized in this negotiated literacy. The classroom ethnography enables me to see that the students adopted these strategies with considerable awareness and agency.

Recontextualization

Buthainah adopts recontextualization strategies to establish her voice, frame the text, and alter the footing to help readers negotiate her text effectively for meaning. In this particular literacy event, Buthainah has to deal with three specific forms of bias her readers will bring with them: 1. Autonomous literacy ideologies to interpret and assess her writing; 2. Native speaker norms to understand her English; and 3. Essentialized notions of culture toward her Arabic identity. Buthainah negotiates these biases to construct a different context for her writing. Though she accomplishes this recontextualization among her peers (the immediate audience) over multiple drafts, she has to take care to adopt other strategies within the body of the text for potential readers outside the class who don't have access to her drafts. We will start with the strategies adopted within the body of the final draft first, and consider the protracted strategies over multiple drafts in the section below on entextualization.

Consider her opening, quoted in Chapter 1. Buthainah starts the essay with an Arabic epigraph that also serves as the title for her essay. It is an Arabic proverb that is only translated in the second paragraph as "Who fears climbing the mountains—Lives forever between the holes." This is a bold opening that dramatically introduces the ethos of the text, and signals to readers that they have to adopt a different orientation to reading. The author is not going to provide all the meanings to them; readers have to work for them. In this sense, this text goes against the expectations of autonomous literacy. Buthainah was always conscious of demanding a different orientation to her writing. In a member check comment, she insisted that she "did not see my essay as a one-way informative essay. It is a negotiated essay" (MC). It didn't take much time for her peers to figure out that they had to read the draft differently if they were to decode the Arabic and other unique features of English. Tim, an Anglo-American student, observed:

> By not translating you are excluding a wider audience, your non-Arabic speaking audience from being able to engage fully with the text. Perhaps you are challenging them to bridge that gap as readers. That if they want to gain access to your writing (to a piece of you, perhaps?) they have to meet you halfway somehow.
>
> *(PC, 10/22)*

Meeting halfway is precisely what translinguals do in contact situations as they develop the "synergy" to construct a hybrid text between their different codes (Khubchandani, 1997, p. 94).

Secondly, the opening also suggests that it is not written with NES norms in mind. The Arabic and the deviations from SWE suggest that it is written according to translingual practices. Though Buthainah had ample opportunities in her drafts to correct some of the idiomatic and grammatical peculiarities (note "storms of thoughts stampede," "a few number of students," and "my literacy development shunt me") she declined. I will show later that she made a rhetorical justification to use them. More importantly, in her essay, her interviews with me, and in classroom conversations, she questioned NES norms:

> Although some people assume that "excellence" is associated with writing like a "native," I strongly disagree with such belief. Who is a native speaker anyway? And why should a second language English writer have to mimic "native" in order to be given the award of excellence.
>
> *(A, 09/10)*

Buthainah adopts other strategies in the body of the essay to reinforce her identity as a translingual and prepare the reader to negotiate her codemeshing. Starting from her thesis statement in the second paragraph, Buthainah represents herself as a "functional bilingual" (D6). She uses this term to contest the ESL and remedial writing courses into which she was placed after she migrated to the USA. She defines *functional bilinguals* as: "language users who may have [a] few problems with English, but were beyond the realm of ESL" (D6). Buthainah implies that she may not have the grammatical competence of the native speaker, but she has the communicative competence to function bilingually and achieve her interests in the repertoire of codes she brings with her. Also, though she may not have a formal mastery of the language for all purposes, she has the functional capacity to "perform" in the registers and contexts she chooses. Buthainah is not denying that there may be idiosyncrasies in her grammar or idiom. What she is claiming for herself is creative and critical communication in a rhetorically effective text. Her self-ascription should dissuade readers from adopting unfair criteria to judge her.

There is evidence that her North American peers did shift from their habitual NES points of view and adopted a translingual orientation to this text. For example, Mark, an Anglo-Canadian, said in his peer review: "Perhaps Buthainah is willing to help the reader but at some point somethings can only be known to those who are willing to learn and become Arabic English bilinguals" (PC, 10/28). Mark recognizes that Buthainah's grammatical peculiarities are creative influences of a translingual competence. Chrissie, an Anglo-American student, figured out that these peculiarities could be performative:

> As a student at an American University, she knows that following the "rules" of academic writing will get her far, but I think she does so with a sense of who she is. She obviously respects her L1 and explicitly shows us, the reader, through out the text with poems, and how expressions are beautiful in Arabic, but awkward in English (for example).
>
> *(PC, 10/28)*

These readers are prepared to negotiate the grammar for rhetorical and performative meaning rather than stop with an evaluation of its formal correctness.

As for the cultural stereotypes, Buthainah deals with them more directly in anticipation of her readers' responses. For example, referring to her trip to the USA for her education, she writes:

> When the paper works were complete, my family and I traveled from Saudi Arabia to United States by air plane [P.S. I wanted to travel on a camel, but they were all rented!].
>
> *(D6)*

I was struck by the post script. In my stimulated recall, I asked Buthainah, "This might be considered a digression by some readers. How would you respond to that criticism?" Buthainah replied:

> Yes, it could be to some readers. However, when someone writes about themselves, they have to consider the stereotypes and whats going on around them that may influence the comprehension or the interpretation of the text. I wrote that sentence because there are, still to this day, people who think that I, as a Saudi, ride camels to school. It is a joke that tries to remove that stereotype. In addition, a joke was needed here because I may have readers who hold negative associations toward my ethnicity. And I tried to elevate that tension that the reader may have, and hopefully, it will never occur.
>
> *(SR)[1]*

By bringing up the stereotype herself, Buthainah is compelling readers to face their biases. This way, she is also disarming readers of their prejudices and encouraging them to judge her more fairly. Such a strategy of self-deprecating humor has also been observed in LFE conversations. As mentioned earlier, Planken (2005) finds that speakers from Norway and Sweden joke about their own English accents and styles in order to make each party relaxed and free to negotiate their differences. There is evidence that her peers found Buthainah's move hilarious (Christie, Rita: PC, 10/26), perhaps in recognition of their cultural biases.

To adopt Ratcliffe's terms, these recontextualization strategies may be considered a form of "laying" (which Ratcliffe [1999] presents as distinct from "saying"). Buthainah is laying her identity and terms of engagement up front so that readers may negotiate the text with full awareness of its difference. Such strategies are also designed to realign relationships between interlocutors so that they are prepared to negotiate the text on equal terms, laying aside their status differences, biases, and inhibitions.

Interactional

Buthainah doesn't depend only on the reframing of the context to motivate her readers to negotiate the text. She adopts more direct strategies to invite, cajole, and even pressure the reader into negotiation. Though interlocutors from traditionally multilingual communities will be expected to negotiate the text actively, Buthainah cannot assume this in the case of NES who also read her text.

A striking feature in her writing is that Buthainah provides frequent parenthetical comments to the reader (some preceded by "Dear Reader" or "PS," as we saw in the preceding example). This strategy emerges as a way of inviting the reader to interact with her. When I commented in EV that her asides to the readers sounded awkward and came close to violating the formality of academic prose, Buthainah responded:

> I knew that I was taking a risk by addressing the reader. But, I wanted the reader to be included into my discussion. By addressing my readers, I am welcoming them to the discussion, which, in my perspective, [is] ongoing.
>
> *(MC)*

Buthainah intended the direct address to draw readers into a conversation. There was uptake. Fauzia mentioned in reference to one case of direct address: "I found myself laughing when I read this because you [are] talking to me directly. I wonder, however, are [you] keeping this as part of your style? I think you should, it really grabbed my attention" (PC, 10/22).

Through this strategy, Buthainah is not only inviting the reader to negotiate but signals that she is herself open to negotiating their difference. On another occasion, she mentioned that the parenthetical asides were a way of showing that she respected the readers' perspectives and valued their activity in interpreting the text. She explained:

> I really do respect the readers of my paper. And I know that there will be different interpretations of my text. However, acknowledging this fact and

informing the reader that I—as the author—know that they exist and that they are different thinkers and intellectuals than I am is a gesture of respect.

(SR)

Through this strategy she is acknowledging the otherness of her readers, and accepting them with all their peculiarities. Here again, there was uptake from the readers. Christie, an Anglo-American student, mentioned that this strategy "shows how much she values the readers opinion" (PC, 10/28). Such an impression would motivate readers to co-construct meanings with her. The strategy helps convey equal responsibility in negotiating the text.

Sometimes Buthainah tantalizingly held back or delayed important clues for interpreting non-English codes. In other cases, she offered only oblique cues for interpreting them. When I queried this strategy, Buthainah said: "I thought that if I kept it in Arabic, the reader would be eager to continue to reading to get to the meaning of this poem" (SR). It appears that she wanted to pressure the reader to keep reading and look for more clues for interpretation. This way, she encourages the reader to be more alert and proactive in creating meaning. She thus sustains the curiosity of readers and motivates them for more engaged reading. As Ratcliffe would argue, negotiated literacy involves reading "not for intent, but with intent" (Ratcliffe, 1999, p. 205). There is evidence that some readers were prepared to adopt this orientation in places where interpretive clues and translations were delayed. Mark said,

> To me, a non-Arabic speaker, this quote is a beautiful collection of alien writing, fascinating but incomprehensible. It is a statement to me that there is something Buthainah understands that I do not. It is a move that distances me from Buthainah but also leaves me intrigued and interest[ed] in reading more.
>
> *(PC, 10/28)*

The paradoxes are telling. For Mark, the alienation is beautiful, the incomprehensibility fascinating, and the intrigue interesting. In other words, the incomprehensibility and alienation pressure Mark to keep reading further.

A pointer to a more radical strategy was that Buthainah refused to translate a set of lines by an Arabic poet in one specific instance. For other Arabic verses, she had at least provided paraphrases or allusions elsewhere in her essay to help interpret their meaning. When I queried her on this enigmatic omission, Buthainah explained:

> Translating this poem would take so much of its value and providing a two sentence explanation will not do any justice for these few lines. The message of these lines is that ... [offers a paraphrase]. I feel that these few lines that I wrote above about this poem do not give it any justice. Leaving it stand alone is more powerful.
>
> *(SR)*

But this raises the question as to what Buthainah expected readers to do to interpret these lines and make the connection to her narrative.

Since writing is multimodal for Buthainah, an aesthetic appreciation of the lines is part of her expectation. Even if we cannot understand the meaning of Arabic, we can respond to the visual effect of the lines. For this, one has to do a holistic reading, and desist from extricating meanings from the lines. In such instances, Buthainah aestheticizes the written word and, thus, changes readers' orientation to words as rational communication. There is evidence of uptake from students. Eunja, a Korean student, mentioned in her peer review: "Written Arabic—How elegant language it is! (I'm not quite familiar with spoken one^^)" (PC, 10/22). Mark said: "I absolutely love the Arabic phrases in the text, please keep them, and I hope they're Arabic otherwise I feel kind of foolish" (PC, 10/22). Though both students don't understand the meaning of the lines, they are responding to their aesthetic effect.

Furthermore, the visual and aesthetic dimensions also convey the ethos of the text and the writer. There are many other features Buthainah used for this purpose, such as the motif she uses to divide her sections: ~ʘ~ʘ~ʘ~. Buthainah wrote a marginal note in my interpretation of this motif in EV: "It is a familiar shape that one may find in Islamic art. Since I am a Muslim, and Islam influenced me, it also influenced my literacy experience. Thus, using this particular motif was a hint to the reader to my heritage" (MC). Buthainah clearly wants to give some clues to her identity through such symbols, which includes the Arabic scripts.

Such multimodal resources, while communicating their own meaning, can also aid in the interpretation of the text. An understanding of her codemeshing requires going beyond the denotational meanings of words. Buthainah uses the ecological resources of the text to aid in intelligibility and interpretation. Scholars like Khubchandani (1997) have argued that translingual interactions are aided by gestures, tone, setting, objects, and interpersonal strategies for interpretive clues, and not words alone. I would like to focus first on what may be considered the *microecology* of the text (to borrow a phrase from Creese and Blackledge, 2010). There are other ecological resources beyond the text, and social negotiations that extend in time and space beyond the final draft, which will be discussed later. Buthainah deploys emoticons, provides visual cues, stylizes fonts, and represents auditory effects in her essay. Through all these strategies, Buthainah is calling for a more than cerebral response to her text. She justifies her choice of these non-linguistic symbols as follows:

> Symbols work as another way of expressing myself. I used Arabic, poems, French, and now symbols. Limiting myself to one language is – ironically – limiting. … But, experiencing more than one language, we are able to express ourselves in different ways or the best way. So, symbols serve as another "language" that words may not be the best tool to express.
>
> *(SR)*

As I will argue below, the semiotic resources from the microecology of the text also help to build alignment that translinguals depend on to co-construct meaning.

As we discussed earlier, translinguals orientate to communication in more than rational terms. Buthainah gives ample examples of such a predisposition in her literacy narrative as she explains how she was socialized into a multisensory orientation to language and texts from a young age. References like this would indicate to the reader that language and texts mean more than denotational meaning for Buthainah. There is evidence that at least some students opened themselves to a multisensory reading of her essay. Chang noted: "When I was reading your autobiography, it felt like you were talking directly to me in person. Things like 'Dear reader,' emoticons, textual facial expressions (I don't remember the terms), 'thank god,' italics that emphasize your tones ... all make your story flow vividly into my ears. Well ... maybe more like I was talking to you on MSN since it's all text" (PC, 10/22). The analogy to the Internet chat forum is interesting. It suggests that some students are drawing their classroom negotiation strategies from their socialization in digital media sites.

To return to the case of the untranslated Arabic, while these multimodal resources will help readers guess the meaning of codemeshed items in context, Buthainah also expects readers to adopt the well-known translingual strategy of the "let-it-pass" principle. Some students did adopt this strategy. Asked how she dealt with the untranslated Arabic, Rita said that she "decided not to worry about what I couldn't understand" (I, 05/09). She later elaborated that she looked for other clues for interpretation and meaning negotiation both within and outside the text (such as conversations with the author and her peers in the classroom). What this strategy does is to also convey to readers that meaning is not a product one can fully control or possess. Ratcliffe discusses how the orientation to interpretation based on "mastery" of meaning has created certain unhealthy orientations. It has stifled the art of nego-tiated meaning construction. The "let-it-pass" principle reinforces the notion that interpretation is collaborative and protracted. It instills values like solidarity, patience, humility, and tolerance among interlocutors—values that scholars have pointed out as essential for the success of lingua franca communication.

There are also some performative motivations behind Buthainah's strategy of forcing the readers to work for meaning and interpretation. In further explaining her reasons for not translating the Arabic, Buthainah said her intention was "giving a sample or a taste of the experience that language learners go through to those who never experienced it, which may help them understand these stories and experiences better" (MC). She wanted reluctant readers, especially NES, to go through the experience of being disadvantaged by an alien code, humbled into learning it, and encouraged to negotiate for meaning. Through this process, she also forces NES to adopt the strategies translinguals use in contact situations. This would involve a reversal of power. Readers who expect authors to make meanings clear to them will find that it is their responsibility to create meaning. NES will find themselves in the position of constructing meaning with multilingual writers on an equal footing, without the condescending view that it is the multilinguals who are deficient in language skills. There is evidence that Buthainah succeeded in her performative objectives. Recall Mark's observation that "somethings can only be known to those who are willing to learn and become Arabic English bilinguals" (PC, 10/28). Through this strategy, Buthainah hopes to make readers change their footing and frame, and collaborate in constructing meaning. As Ratcliffe suggests, negotiated literacy involves self-criticism and reflexivity (Ratcliffe, 1999, p. 204). Readers should engage with their biases and assumptions as they encounter the writer's otherness.

In deploying all these strategies, Buthainah adopts an enthymematic orientation to writing. She expects the reader to fill in the gaps to make meaning rather than expecting all the connections to be made self-evident (if this is at all possible in writing). The reader is compelled to make some leaps of logic and imagination to construct meaning. Buthainah uses this strategy consciously. When I mentioned in EV her frequent asides, "They don't display the careful and economical expression of thought valued in academic literacy," Buthainah explained: "Actually, they are supposed to … trigger the reader to look at the other side of the statement" (MC). In other words, Buthainah doesn't expect readers to remain satisfied with the literal meaning, but to infer its implications. In a similar way, in cases where literal understanding is not possible, Buthainah expects readers to fill the gaps through strategies such as the "let-it-pass" principle, aesthetic and multimodal reading, and strategic alignment. Buthainah thus composes a *writerly* as opposed to a *readerly* text (in Barthes's 1974 terms), that is, an essay that *requires* (not just expects or invites) readers to invent meaning imaginatively and actively.

To construct meaning across such differences and seeming gaps in communication, one has to strive for alignment. It is clear that Buthainah was being mindful of offering enough affordances for this purpose. Providing another reason for not translating Arabic, she explained:

> If I translated everything, then the readers would simply go through it. But, if I did not translate it or provide an immediate translation, then, I am encouraging the reader to question the relationship between the poem and the stories being told and promote critical thinking.
>
> *(MC)*

Though Buthainah refers to affordances within the text here, I will show later that she is prepared to move outside the text and help interlocutors look for social and contextual alignment as well.

We can now return to the untranslated Arabic epigraph to consider how the alignments in the context helped us reconstruct the meaning. The passage in question is the following:

~◈~◈~◈~

بقدر الكد تُكْتَسَبُ المعالي   ومَنْ طلب العلا سهر اللّيالي

يروم العز كيف ينام ليلاً   يغوص البحر من طلب اللآلي

ومن رام العلا من غيركد   أضاع العمر في طلب المحال

الإمام الشافعي رحمه الله

When I was in fourth grade, I became sincerely interested in enrolling in the Communication Club (CC). Students in the club have the opportunity to give a speech in front of all of the attendees at the school. The advisor for the club, however, restricted those who may enter that club by requiring the interested candidates to submit an essay about nutrition. Since my desires to be a member of that club were high, I did not mind writing the essay and submitting it for an evaluation. I understood that whatever knowledge I will gain by being a member of CC would be helpful. That writing competition was my first of many that ended with success, ma sha Allah. Later in the week, the advisor informed me of my acceptance. Upon hearing my acceptance, I was thrilled to be a part of the Communication Club. [P.S. Later that year, I found that CC lacked the factors of entertainment and coolness.]. ...

(D6)

The six lines in Arabic, arranged symmetrically and ending with what appears to be the name of the writer at the bottom, appears to be poetry. It is followed by a narrative about Buthainah's attempts to gain entry into a coveted Communication Club in her school. It is clear from her section divider that this is a new and separate vignette. The Arabic lines therefore refer to what follows rather than what precedes it. We have to infer the meaning from the narrative that follows in English. Putting these clues together, we can intuit the following: these lines refer to achieving success by struggling against all odds; they motivate hard work; Buthainah finds inspiration for her English language and literacy acquisition through Arabic culture and values. Such an interpretation is confirmed later by Buthainah's comments in the member check procedure: "The message of these lines is that who desires the best, need to work for it. He/she needs to stay up late working for it just like how divers have to search for the natural pearls. And those who try to get to the top and not work for it, they will waste their life getting nothing" (MC). Though we have been considerably successful in deciphering the meaning of the lines, it is also clear that the metaphor of pearl divers eluded us. We had to await further interactions with Buthainah and other strategies to unpack the meaning of this metaphor.

It became evident that Buthainah treated interpretive interactions as taking place outside the text as well. Buthainah assumes that her explanations and interactions in classrooms, interviews, and the peer critique are part of the negotiation of meaning. The text is part of broader social action. For example, Buthainah accommodated face-to-face interactions as part of textual meaning-making. Her peers too began to count on such negotiations for meaning. After raising some questions about the verse, Tim wrote, "I think discussing this with you and hearing your thoughts would be more helpful. Hopefully we can do this on Wednesday" (PC, 10/27). He was counting on a face-to-face conversation to unpack the meaning of the Arabic verses during class. Rita also said, "I trusted my classmates to explain what was important" (I, 05/09) when I asked how she dealt with the untranslated Arabic. In her case, Rita is counting on others in the class too to help her. For her, meaning-making is collaborative. Though Buthainah was prepared to engage in these conversations, and answered many such queries in the electronic forum and in the classroom, she refused to translate her Arabic verses on the text (as proven by their presence in the final draft). It appears that Buthainah was satisfied with these social interactions for unpacking the meaning of these verses. Such examples suggest that literacy for Buthainah is part of social practice. The negotiation of written meaning occurs on an expanded communicative context, one that includes conversations. It became evident that such interactions helped some students understand the meaning of the metaphor "pearl divers" in the text in question.

There is also a strong temporal dimension to the meaning constructed through these negotiations. As Ratcliffe points out, negotiated literacy doesn't assure correct meanings, but encourages the practice of interpretation as "ongoing" (Ratcliffe, 1999, p. 207). As we saw in relation to translingual communication, the synchronized trajectory of negotiation and collaboration is important for the meaning constructed. The reader's erroneous attempts at meaning-making are factored into this interpretive process. There is a performative dimension, as readers are taken through the hermeneutic cycle, through inferences, revisions, and reconstructions. As readers engage with Buthainah's text at different times, and perhaps serially, they will come to different understandings of her essay. Christie changed her opinion dramatically on the place of Arabic quotations in Buthainah's drafts. She mentioned in her peer review: "Although, last week I wrote that she explain her Arabic poems, I now feel that they are a key part to her narrative. She is indirectly showing us, the reader, who she is through these poems ... Perhaps it is up to us to figure out the significance of these words?" (PC, 10/27). She had earlier advised Buthainah that "transcribing the poems would be beneficial to your paper – it would give us a sense of how important these poems are to you as not only a learner but as a writer as well" (PC, 10/22). After repeated readings, and a revised understanding of Buthainah's strategy, Christie develops a richer interpretation of the narrative. She gains new insights into Buthainah's ethos, merges the author's identity with her literacy trajectory, and factors in the feelings associated with reversing the reader/writer roles and power relationships. From this perspective, meaning is progressive and temporal in Buthainah's essay. More important than capturing a paraphrasable content is the route readers/writers take in negotiating meaning. For translingual literacy, it is not the *what* but the *where* that counts; or, rather, the where makes up the what.

Envoicing

Buthainah's reliance on alignment for intelligibility makes her daring and creative in her grammatical choices. As she assumes that the reader would negotiate for meaning, Buthainah engages the reader more boldly. In adopting this orientation to language, it is also clear that she is moving away from NES norms. She is appropriating English according to her values and interests and seeking new indexicalities for these language resources. Similarly, she meshes resources from other languages and other semiotic media, as we saw earlier, for her voice. In doing all this, she assumes that readers will adopt a translingual orientation to interpret her semiotic resources according to her altered frame and footing.

For example, when she overused the word *adore*, I asked if she considered the possibility that NES will find this a cliché. She replied:

> I would respond by saying that I have a different insight into this word [than] a monolingual native speaker of English because I am a multilingual. What the word "adore" evolved to be is different from what it is to the native speaker. In addition, the context in which it is used may characterize the word as a cliché—but, in this context, I do not see it. Also, I honestly do not like to see the native speakers as the other. It feels odd to consider them that way in the question of "how THEY think." … it is very clear that I am "different" from the native speaker.
> *(SR; emphasis in original)*

I am assuming that "evolved to be" refers to the meanings *adore* acquired through reader negotiation. And "in this context" probably points to the translingual (not NES) norms in operation. Buthainah indirectly criticizes my bias toward NES norms in the way I frame my question. From her perspective, the status of a word as a cliché depends on the interlocutors concerned. *Adore* might be a cliché for native speakers, based on their history and contexts of usage, but the word may not have the same connotations for translinguals who renegotiate meanings. It appears that Buthainah is claiming a new indexicality for this word.

There is a similar reorientation required for idiomatic uses. I had raised a question about the possibility of non-idiomacy in the opening of her essay where she uses the phrases: "storms of thoughts stampede," and "my literacy development shunt me." Buthainah replied: "Actually, I am surprised to hear that because … it provides the readers of a visual for what I felt at that time. I do not see why only bulls stampede—this verb can be used figuratively as well. I do not think that this is an issue of native speakers of English, I think that it is a stylistic choice" (SR). Again, when I referred to these phrases as "peculiar" in EV, she responded: "Honestly, I do not see how they are peculiar. I find them creative" (MC). It is clear that Buthainah is experimenting with new uses for these phrases, enabled by her sense of ownership of the language. The uptake has varied. While some (including NES) have gone further than me in appreciating the creative imagination behind these lines, a few have remained unconvinced—a matter to which I return below.

It is Buthainah's translingual orientation that also gives her confidence in her spelling and grammatical usage. In the opening quoted in Chapter 1, some will identify expressions like "a few number of students," "an illustration … shunt me," and the missing question mark in "which experience should I value," as ungrammatical. Readers would have identified other such deviations from NES and SWE norms in other excerpts. It is possible to imagine that Buthainah would argue that the translingual orientation would help readers to negotiate her choices effectively to achieve intelligibility. Moreover, as scholars like Ashcroft suggest, such uses can also be *metonymic* (Ashcroft, 2009, pp. 125–82). They are there to symbolize or represent the difference of translingual writers and their voice. In this sense, grammar is a strategy to perform certain rhetorical functions.

My interview confirmed that Buthainah treated grammar as rhetoric. Asked about possible errors, Buthainah redirected my attention to the interactional goals of her writing. Regarding one case, she said: "I was so engaged in developing the content that I did not notice it" (SR). A focus on grammar as form would have limited Buthainah's writing. She would have focused on possible errors (from an NES perspective) and not allowed herself to freely draw from diverse grammars and meshed them to achieve her rhetorical goals. For example, significant choices in Buthainah's codemeshing are motivated by her desire for identity. This attitude also provides her a strong investment in writing. She focuses not on correctness, but voice. Reviewing what she had learnt in the course, she explained in an interview:

> I learned about the diversity of writing for one genre. All of my classmates and I were required to write about our lives, the way each person recalled these memories portrays not only the diversity of ethnicities, but the diversity of writing, Priority for voice and identity rather than encoding of meaning.
>
> *(I, 12/09)*

Buthainah makes a distinction between the constitutive and performative sides of writing, giving more importance to the latter. When I observed that her few French mixings didn't add much to the meaning of the essay, she responded:

> The reason I used "moi" is because it was part of my literacy history. I took three courses of French, and it seemed silly to ignore one part of my literacy development, and accept some. It seems hypocritical in a way. If, as you said, some readers would say that "don't serve any significant rhetorical functions in the essay" (unlike the Arabic quotations) I would say that the French langauge served a role in my literacey development. It may not be and will not be as influential as the Arabic language, but its there.
>
> *(SR)*

It emerged that the choice was based on concerns of identity representation and the ethos of the text, and not on meaning alone. The words also represent her translingual literacy background. Therefore, the words are important for what they *do*, more than what they *say*.

There is evidence that her peers negotiated her unconventional language choices fairly well. In fact, no one complained about her English. They always made sense of Buthainah's arguments and discussion, and never raised issues about her grammatical or spelling usage. Though some students asked for a translation for the Arabic, they never asked her to "translate" her English. Chang observed about her early draft: "She realized the power of a new language when she was young and her way of dealing with it was study hard to have a share of it … Therefore, she had the motivation to learn any new word she came into, to grasp this knowledge of language and to use it independently as her own voice. Besides, she also knew that her messages conveyed through language are still open for the audience's various interpretations"

(PC, 10/28). It is clear that Chang appreciates Buthainah's ownership of the English language. He is also open to co-constructing meaning in context, understanding that "various interpretations" are acceptable. It is possibly Buthainah's recontextualization cues that enable Chang to respond favorably to these rhetorical effects and expectations.

Many students also appreciated the performative intentions and effects behind her language choices. Fauzia notes:

> She feels that language is the best tool/approach to use when in need. I feel that she is assertive in that she had the experience of not understanding a language. Thus, in her AB [i.e., autobiography] she turns the table on the readers – having Arabic text that the majority will not understand. She seek to be on top of everything and having a power. In this case, her power tool is language, especially Arabic. Even though, she loves presenting her power tools, Arabic, she is, at the same time, talk about how she likes learning new languages.
>
> *(PC, 10/28)*

Thus Fauzia realizes that the Arabic expressions and enforced difficulty are to make readers (especially NES) understand the importance of negotiation and reversal of power relationships.

Buthainah's orientation to language and text confirms the strategies translinguals adopt in contact situations. By focusing on the activity at hand, translinguals make grammar subservient to the objectives of communication. Rather than letting grammar control communication, they focus on the pragmatic strategies that will enable them to reshape form, making even "deviations as the norm" (Khubchandani, 1997, p. 94). Thus, translinguals are more open to the possibility of emergent grammar (Hopper, 1987), letting new norms emerge from the negotiation process and objectives of the interaction. Furthermore, the importance of form in intelligibility is reduced as communication is multimodal. Translinguals use ecological resources as cues for interpretation and communication. More importantly, since meaning is co-constructed, form doesn't hold unqualified power in translingual communication. Grammar is incidental to meaning-making. It is an affordance for performing social and rhetorical acts, and doesn't become an end in itself.

It is clear that Buthainah claims ownership over English, appropriates English for her purposes, and uses it with a critical and creative orientation. Her usage is informed by the relativity of language norms in contact situations. Since Buthainah expects situated negotiation, I haven't flagged what might appear as grammatical, spelling, and idiomatic deviations in Buthainah's essay when I quoted them. I generally understood what Buthainah was communicating in her drafts even when her choices appeared idiosyncratic. In other cases, I exercised my "capacity and willingness" (Ratcliffe, 1999, p. 204) to negotiate meanings with her. It is only when one chooses to be prescriptive and refuses to negotiate with the writer and the text that language choices become a problem or fail to make sense. However, achieving new indexicalities is not easy. It is a two-way process and requires sedimentation of codes through repeated use.

Buthainah is not always successful in gaining uptake. We will discuss what Buthainah can do better later.

Entextualization

As mentioned earlier, such interpretive negotiations occur not only around and after the final product, but through the entire composing process. Buthainah uses the serial drafts to shape the interpretation in significant ways. We will consider in this section how Buthainah uses the temporal composing process of entextualization to prepare readers for effective negotiation and gain uptake. For example, Buthainah often directly queries her peers to understand their comfort level with codemeshed writing. She also uses these queries to calibrate her own meshing of codes to suit her audience. At the end of her third draft, for instance, she adds a note to her peer reviewers: "p.s. ... Should I translate the poems?" (D3). Though all students posted their drafts for peer review, Buthainah was the only student to go the additional distance of querying her peers on her choices. On another occasion, she writes in her journal:

> Alright, I submitted my first draft and I have a loooot of questions. ... Should I talk about my English literacy only? Or should I talk about my English, Arabic, and French literacy?!? Should I address my readers? Or should I ignore the fact that this is a personal essay?
>
> *(J, 09/15)*

Students who read the journal entry did offer their opinions. Receiving conflicting responses from her peers (i.e., some asked her to translate the poems, and others not to), she used her own discretion in the end.

Though Buthainah boldly refused or delayed translation, demanding more from her readers in many cases, in others she increased the range of codes included in her successive drafts as the capacity of the audience progressively increased. In the first draft, for example, Buthainah doesn't codemesh at all. Her essay is a straightforward narrative in English. The only indication of codemeshing are two smiley faces. It is in the second draft that we see the first signs of linguistic experimentation. She begins her essay thus:

> "Oh God! Give me more knowledge" – My education dictum through the years is a verse in the Quran stating: "وَقُل رَّبِّ زِدْنِي عِلْمًا"
>
> *(D2)*

Note that she begins with the English translation first and gives the Arabic original next. In her later drafts, not only will she begin with the Arabic quotation, she will also delay the translation. Yet, some cases of codemeshing are deployed only gradually. Even in her fourth draft, she writes "Thank Allah" and not *"ma sha allah."* Such careful meshing shows that Buthainah is sensitive to the capabilities of the audience in negotiating her text. She gradually builds the capacity of the audience to interpret her codes by progressively assessing the uptake of the readers. The text takes its shape temporally in relation to the responses and co-construction of the readers. The evolution of her text also shows that she is mindful of power differences in the contact zone. She recognizes that NES norms and autonomous literacy are the dominant conventions in this context, and inserts her difference gradually. Also, true to the translingual practice of mutual accommodations in communication, Buthainah is prepared to codemesh responsively. In all this, her extextualization strategies show careful thinking about the nature and extent of deviation from SWE.

The challenge for Buthainah is to assert her own voice and rhetorical designs even as she leaves the text open to the reader's agency. For this reason, Buthainah introduces her codes in less explicit and oblique ways in many places. For example, her opening in D4 is as follows:

وَمَنْ يَتَهَيَّبْ صُعُودَ الْجِبَالِ ~~~ يَعِشْ أَبَدَ الدَّهْرِ بَيْنَ الْحُفَر

Who fears climbing the mountains ~~~ Lives forever between the holes

However, in the final draft, she introduces the English translation in a more oblique way in the second paragraph: "My parent's face discolored and the sense of disapproval appeared in their tone of speech. To encourage me, they recited a poetic line that I did not comprehend as a child but live by it as an adult. They said 'Who fears climbing the mountains ~~~ Lives forever between the holes.'" The reader has to align the self-standing Arabic epigraph with the parents' aphorism two paragraphs later to figure out the connection in the context of the narrative. Thus she provides space for—and anticipates—the interpretive work of the reader.

Consider the design behind another reference that becomes more oblique in later drafts. The reference to the travel by camel appears as follows in D4: "When the paper works was complete, my family and I traveled from Saudi Arabia to United States by air plane—not by the stereotypical Arabian camel [I wanted to travel on a camel, but they were all rented]." In D6 the phrase "not by the stereotypical Arabian camel" is removed. With this omission, the parenthetical statement now appears as a more enigmatic or tongue-in-cheek comment, as the author's position is left unclear. Some readers may initially read the lines literally (assuming that traveling by camel is Buthainah's preference) and fall victim to their cultural stereotypes, realizing only later that the author wanted to expose their own biases. We can see in such examples that Buthainah's strategy goes counter to the objective of revisions in the autonomous literacy tradition. In that kind of literacy, revisions are supposed to make the meaning more explicit and transparent. Buthainah's progressive indirection and obliqueness is to serve her performative objectives and give allowance to readers' interpretive work. Similar to the pre-essayistic tradition before the Enlightenment, she gives readers "room to roam" (Stark, 2008, p. 269) and resources for alignment. In constructing such a writerly text, however, Buthainah is also taking more risks, moving away from an effort to control meaning.

Buthainah also allows herself to be shaped by the readers' responses. She finds certain interpretations useful and builds them into her essay. For example, it is remarkable how she adopts peer suggestions to reformulate her thesis. Many students had been left with the question of how her trajectory of literacy shaped her present educational status. Buthainah had ended her narration with high school. Therefore, Chrissie suggested: "I think talking about college years would be good. YOU ARE AN ENGLISH MAJOR. … I wonder if you have anything to say about that. … you know how you were schooled or molded into writing a specific way" (PC, 10/22). Rita similarly asked: "I'd be interested in hearing a bit more about your transition from 'ESL student' to 'English major.' Was that something that you knew you wanted to do for a long time? How did you decide that that was the major you would pursue? How do you relate to ESL learners now as a result of that transition?" (PC, 10/22). Buthainah weaves this component into her trajectory to enhance her theme of oppositional learning. This is how she begins the final paragraph of her final draft: "Many—including my ESL teacher—did not expect me to major in English Literature. … Nearly all of the Saudi students at the university are majoring in degrees related to engineering, business, science, and, sometimes, education. … Thus, I challenged people's beliefs with my parents' support and majored in English Literature at Penn State University the following year" (D6). She develops the point in her concluding lines to provide a powerful culmination for her theme of empowerment through literacy: "Since I strongly believe that knowledge is the key to freedom from ignorance, I wanted to expand beyond my English department. In addition, I wanted to help those who may undergo the same *ESL journey* that I experienced especially those who are considered functional bilinguals, and the only way to do so was to be part of that group once again and join that field" (D6). Though she accommodates the views of readers into her draft, she does it in her own terms and in line with her resistant perspectives and critical objectives.

Buthainah thus adopts a dynamic entextualization approach of: (1) accommodating feedback; (2) being sensitive to readers' capacities; (3) challenging them to step out of their comfort zones; and (4) reconfiguring the text according to these factors. There is evidence that Buthainah is aware of the value of such a negotiated composing process. In a course-end interview on the collaborative, process-oriented writing, she stated: "Yes, it was helpful because I was debating on whether I should include Arabian poems or not. And if so, shall I translate them? I got many responses, and settled with keeping the poems un-translated" (I, 12/07). Though Buthainah finally makes her own choices about how to shape the final product, the interaction with her readers helps her to make her decisions wisely and confidently. The entextualization process helps her to calculate the responses and counter-strategies of her readers.

Translingual literacy succeeds because words and texts are made open for co-constructed meanings in the broadest social, temporal, and spatial contexts. Readers and writers are open to new indexicalities from the diverse semiotic resources meshed in the text. I must emphasize that this mode of negotiated literacy is dialogical. While Buthainah pressures her peers and instructor to read in specific ways in certain instances, in others she draws back to modify her uses in response to their feedback. Her voice is a negotiated outcome.

Conclusion

The negotiated literacy articulated above casts a different light on the problems posed by instructors in the beginning of this chapter. Would codemeshing affect intelligibility? What do we do when the codes meshed by a writer are unknown to readers? Would the deviation from universally accepted norms and forms harm textual coherence? These are "problems" only when one refuses to negotiate with writers and writing. For those who actively engage with writers to negotiate meaning, collaborating in the construction of the text, form and content are what they mutually make of them in their situated contexts of communication. Without adopting a negotiated literacy, we won't be able to interpret meanings appropriately in a codemeshed text, or appreciate its rhetoric, logic, or grammar. Meaning doesn't reside inside the text or in the language. And it is not the responsibility of the author to give meanings on a platter. Defining communicative success as collaboratively achieved, both interlocutors should be responsible for negotiating effectively. Furthermore, the socially embedded and ecologically situated nature of the text opens it up for influences from outside. Meanings are generated by the interplay of people, objects, spatiotemporal contexts, and textual ecology.

All this doesn't mean that there will always be agreement on the meanings and significance of a text. Though I show that there is strong uptake of Buthainah's strategies in my discussion above, it shouldn't be taken to mean that everyone understands and appreciates her text the same way. As Ratcliffe explains, what negotiated literacy guarantees is not mastery or uniformity of meaning but a *willingness* to engage with each other in meaning-making practices relentlessly (Ratcliffe, 1999, p. 204). She further says: "Although rhetorical listening does not guarantee that everyone will concur about definitions, intersections, and applications of the political and the ethical, it does guarantee that such considerations will be at the forefront of meaning-making. This is an ongoing process" (Ratcliffe, 1999, p. 207). From this perspective, authors and readers are not anxious about making the same meaning all the time and in all contexts. Most students appreciated that the meaning of the essay was different to different readers, and they were comfortable with the plurality of meanings. In this sense, they came to share the view of translingual communication as situational and open to intersubjective construction. In fact, as Buthainah assumes that negotiation is "ongoing" (as she once says, echoing Ratcliffe's words), she is relaxed about her choices. Similarly, many students who are critical of Buthainah's writing at certain points change their opinion later (as we saw in the case of Christie), as they gain more background knowledge, understand Buthainah's expectations, and are willing to exercise their capacity. In other words, it is not uniformity of meaning but the capacity and willingness to keep negotiating for meanings that interlocutors strive for in negotiated literacy. However, we must note that uptake is not always guaranteed. The questions which the students and I ask in the feedback show our confusion and skepticism at times. We are not always convinced that her French meshes or that her new idioms are rhetorically successful. I will show in Chapter 9 that Buthainah herself confessed that not all her choices were intentional or consistent. At times Buthainah is too agentive, and fails to offer enough cues for alignment and re-indexicalization. Buthainah is by no means perfect. She can develop her proficiency further.

We must also note that negotiated literacy involves redefining constructs such as coherence, error, and rhetorical effectiveness. For example, when we realize that literacy is performative, we have to ask if we should judge the text based on how it is constructed or what it does. Though we may fault the writing on mechanical or grammatical grounds, it could be highly effective in the social and rhetorical functions it accomplishes. In fact, the seeming textual or grammatical deviations may precisely be the reasons for its rhetorical effectiveness. For example, the idiomatic differences, grammatical deviations, and spelling idiosyncrasies are important for the social functions intended by Buthainah. They are important for her voice. They are the means for reversing the power relationships with NES and changing their footing. From this perspective, the deviations are performative, and important for the text's rhetorical effectiveness. Furthermore, other controversial moves such as the direct address to the reader and seeming digressions (i.e., the reference to traveling by camel) can also have performative reasons. They initiate enthymematic responses. Such effects thus provide a coherence to the text that a mere consideration to form would miss.

One of the performative effects achieved by Buthainah's strategies is to make us self-critical and examine our own rhetorical biases and language ideologies. As Ratcliffe points out, "For when listening within an undivided logos, we do not read simply for what we can agree with or challenge, as is the habit of academic reading (in its multiple guises). Instead, we choose to listen also for the exiled excess and contemplate its relation to our culture and our selves" (Ratcliffe, 1999, p. 203). At the very least, Buthainah's writing compels us to ask the following questions: From whose perspective is something ungrammatical? What if the norms of use by NES are irrelevant in certain multilingual interactions? Shouldn't we treat some of the new meanings which translinguals construct as creativity rather than error? At what point do we decide that the language stops changing and that we should hold atypical uses as errors? Who has the right to change language—and whose usage should be prohibited from language change? Why do we treat language as a shibboleth rather than an affordance for meaning-making?

In all this, we find that we need a new literacy for understanding translingual writing. My articulation of the practices of negotiated literacy answers the questions of teachers quoted in the beginning. If we adopt an orientation of negotiated literacy, codemeshing won't seem difficult to interpret. In contexts where shared norms are difficult to expect, whether in speaking or writing in the global contact zones, translingual practice invokes a different orientation to text construction and interpretation. We also find that both NES and multilingual students already bring such strategies of negotiation to the classroom. They have been socialized into such literacies from contact zones outside the classroom. Teachers can design pedagogical environments that tap into these intuitive strategies as they learn from them and also help students develop them further through practice.

8

RECONFIGURING TRANSLOCAL SPACES

We have analyzed translingual practices in the largely micro-level contexts of conversations, literacies, and classrooms in the previous chapters. Though there is value in analyzing power negotiations ground-up from these interactions, it is unwise to ignore the macro-level contexts of communication. In this chapter, we expand our orientation to the geopolitical contexts of texts and talk. Translinguals often adopt strategies to reconfigure contexts to suit the negotiation of codes. We will consider how power, identities, and language ideologies are negotiated in translocal spaces, and the implications that they have for the ways in which English is taken up, given value, and gains indexicality.

The notion of context is limiting in current approaches to global Englishes. As scholars consider English in relation to the communities it travels to, they tend to look at context as bounded, static, and centered. For example, each English variety is given a corresponding national or community locus to house that variety. Even lingua franca English is given a community, albeit a multicultural "imagined community" (as in the ELF models we discussed in Chapter 4). Other models, such as WE, provide English varieties with a static and bounded geographical context as, for example, nation-states. There are many limitations with such orientation to the context of English. It assumes a homogeneity and sharedness which are not always available when English is mobile. Furthermore, contexts are overlapping, porous, and even conflictual. Rather than governing language, they are reconstructed by language. We need a more complex and dynamic orientation to context in order to understand the spatiotemporal mobility of English. English flows across layered and changing contexts, traversing competing norms and values, to take on new grammars and meanings.

Most analyses of global Englishes also filter out the spatiotemporal migrations of the language by focusing on the traces left in the language system. Their focus is on the diversification of the system of English in different spatiotemporal locations.

Therefore, they analyze varieties such as Sri Lankan, Nigerian, or ELF varieties as the outcome of such migratory processes. However, the language system is not always rich enough to capture or explain the processes involved in the spatiotemporal migrations of a language. The varieties constructed by dominant schools are heavily sedimented and mask the processes underlying their formation. We are left with static systems of English that miss much of the complex information on the dynamics of mobility. The bounded notions of context have thus had a conservative influence on global English models, positing limited diversity for English varieties.

In order to understand how English gains new meaning and patterns in mobility, we have to unmoor its resources from the strictures of geographical context and community. We have to follow their trajectory to understand the way in which they engage with spatiotemporal contexts. We have to ask how these resources gain uptake and indexicality as they travel to new contexts. The question is complicated because language is not completely a case of free-floating signifiers. Language resources do come with histories and values belonging to the places they inhabit. Similarly, contexts are not neutral; they are power-ridden. It is important to ask how those who take their language resources to a new context, and those who inhabit that context, negotiate the meaning and value of these resources. I would like to insert the notion of mobility into contexts and codes to consider the implication for translingual practice.

I consider these questions in respect to skilled migration in this chapter. As migrants move from their lands to others places looking for education and employment, they are also taking their Englishes with them. How do the English resources that they bring with them fare in the new contexts? What happens in these contact zones? I first review the influential model Blommaert (2008, 2010) has provided to study traveling codes in geopolitical contexts. While sharing the theoretical assumptions motivating translingual practices in this book, Blommaert's model features slight differences that have implications on how I view contact zones and human agency.

The uses of scales

We face many questions as we unpack the different layers of context. Context is a relational construct, that is: is a particular context home or alien? Contexts are overlapping, that is: is a particular context local or global, when we know that the global interpenetrates the local? Context is dynamic, that is: how do space, time, and social structure interact in reshaping context? Context is mediated, that is: how do nation, profession, class, religion and other domains constitute a particular context?

Blommaert introduces the metaphor of *scales* to usefully unpack the many layers of context. It is a valuable borrowing from fields like geography (Uitermark, 2002) and political economy (Wallerstein, 2001) for the purposes of sociolinguistics. Blommaert interprets and applies scales in a particular way to aid language mobility. He states that "scales offer us a vertical image of space, of *space as stratified* and therefore power-invested; but they also suggest deep connections between spatial and temporal features" (Blommaert, 2010, p. 34). In this manner, scales are relational constructs that allow us to see contexts from different perspectives and relationships. Dimensions of space, time, and society are not kept apart. Space and time shape each other in radical ways as the macro gets instantiated in micro-level relationships. The scalar metaphor thus cuts across spatiotemporal dimensions and accommodates them into combined units for analysis. We have to also remember that contexts should not be treated as static. Interactants construct the context that is operative in their talk by invoking different scales of time, space, and social life. Scales allow us to address how interlocutors invoke scales of different levels, orders, and dimensions to shape their interactions—as we saw in the way they strategically frame their texts and talk for different footing in the previous chapters. In this sense, scales offer a richer orientation to context. The approach also allows us to identify for analytical purposes the ways in which scales of different hierarchies subtly come together in "layered simultaneity"—as in the case of lamination discussed earlier.

Furthermore, the scalar metaphor reminds us that mobility is not across neutral social and geographical spaces. These spaces assign values and statuses to the codes that people take with them. In other words, scales explain how difference is turned into inequality. Such an orientation allows us to address the challenges in communication, integration, and success for migrants in diverse environments. Migrants may experience a lack of access to the codes enjoying power in certain spaces, and a lack of uptake for the codes they bring into new spaces. As Blommaert puts it, "People do not just move across space … they move across different orders of indexicality" (Blommaert, 2010, p. 41). The scalar metaphor helps explain how the different indexical orders correspond to different scale levels of interaction involved in migratory contact between people. Thus the metaphor helps us address power relations when language resources are negotiated in shifting contexts.

What is unique in Blommaert's application is his emphasis on scales as vertical and hierarchical, as evident in his statements above. In some ways, this orientation reflects the origins of this metaphor in the neo-Marxist tradition of the social sciences. However, Blommaert provides additional reasons for this heavy emphasis on power and inequality:

> Different scales organize different patterns of normativity, of what counts as language. This may quickly be turned into an image of chaos and fragmentation (and quite a lot of post-modernist literature would make this interpretation), but … such interpretations are not helpful. The processes we see are not chaotic but ordered, although they are of considerable complexity.
>
> *(Blommaert, 2010, p. 37)*

It appears that Blommert would like to resist what he considers to be a postmodern interpretation of language and context, presumably informed by notions of hybridity or fluidity. He perceives such lines of interpretation as leading to the chaos and fragmentation of indexical orders. Therefore, he defines social and geopolitical spaces as clearly stratified. Blommaert's emphasis is useful in a context where postmodern theorists treat languages and identities as relative and free-floating. Blommaert is right in seeking a keener sensitivity to issues of power and social stratification when we consider the way mobile resources gain uptake in different contexts. However, his application of scales appears somewhat static and rigid for my purposes. The possibilities for power to be negotiated by diverse agents and agencies in mobility appear limited. Also, there are few qualifications on the scope and reach of power across diverse social spaces. In other words, Blommaert's notion of scales doesn't leave room for agency and maneuver. The possibility that language norms may be renegotiated, or that spaces can be reconstructed by people in communicative situations, needs more appreciation.

Blommaert does accommodate the possibility of different orders of hierarchy in different domains. In fact, within the same space there could be different language norms in operation. Blommaert adopts the term *polycentricity* for this phenomenon. However, these polycentric norms are not allowed to overlap or to lead to tension. Language norms are stratified according to different contexts and functions:

> We thus see various orders of indexicality operating in the same polycentric environment, often without manifest overlap or confusion but "niched" and confined to particular sets of communicative tasks.
>
> *(Blommaert, 2010, p. 61)*

The acknowledgement of language norms as polycentric, therefore, doesn't lead to power being contested. Norms and statuses differ according to particular communicative tasks or genres, leaving the broader social hierarchy clearly stratified.

As a result, scales are predefined and do not provide scope for revaluation. Blommaert defines scales according to space and time in the following way:

	Lower scale	Higher scale
Time	momentary	timeless
Space	local, situated	translocal, widespread

(Blommaert, 2010, p. 34)

Among the values which Blommaert uses to characterize scale levels, lower scale is associated with "diversity, variation" and higher scale with "uniformity, homogeneity" (Blommaert, 2010, p. 35). That is, since scales are hierarchically stratified, there is a restricted set of universally accepted norms at the higher scale level.

According to this stratification of scales, language statuses are predefined according to the socio-economic status of the communities. For Blommaert, prestige languages of the West (i.e., English) are of a higher scale, while the languages of underdeveloped communities (i.e., Swahili) are of lower scale. Similarly, elite varieties of a language (i.e., native speaker varieties of English) are of a higher scale, and non-native varieties (i.e., Chinese or Nigerian English) are of a lower scale. Therefore, "prestige varieties of language" are treated as "high-mobility resources" (Blommaert, 2010, p. 12). Such varieties "allow mobility across situations and scale-levels" (Blommaert, 2010, p. 12). These definitions set clear standards for the types of language or language varieties that are preferable for success in mobility. Elite European languages are the portable resources in migration for multilinguals from Asia, Africa, and South America. Their local languages do not travel well.

In the context of this clear social and linguistic stratification, migrants find their roles and statuses predetermined. Blommaert states: "Mobility, sociolinguistically speaking, is therefore a trajectory through different stratified, controlled and monitored spaces in which language 'gives you away'. Big and small differences in language use locate the speaker in particular indexical and ascriptive categories (related to identity and role)" (Blommaert, 2010, p. 6). In other words, migrants enjoy few possibilities for renegotiating their statuses or gaining a different valuation of the language competencies that they bring with them. Those who speak languages of lower scale levels find their statuses and roles already determined by the social context. From this perspective, migrants don't enjoy agency in relation to existing language norms and indexical orders.

While those who speak less prestigious languages enjoy limited mobility, those who speak the more prestigious languages can "jump scales" (Blommaert, 2010, p. 36). That is, the latter can make their norms and values applicable at different scales levels. As Blommaert explains, "some groups can jump scales while others cannot, and 'outscaling' is a frequent power tactic: lifting a particular issue to a scale-level which is inaccessible to the other" (Blommaert, 2010, p. 36). From this perspective, the powerful enjoy more resources for renegotiating scale levels, unlike the powerless who are stuck to the statuses and roles assigned to them.

It is not that the powerless don't have any space for renegotiation. The type of negotiability available for the powerless is limited in significance. Though they have agency to move across scales or index different scales in their communication, they don't have the possibility of changing the orders of indexicality or the hierarchy of scales. For example, Dong and Blommaert (2009) perform a fascinating analysis of a Chinese vendor to show how he switches codes and invokes different scales to establish his identity and footing differently with Dong in his conversation. The vendor, however, moves across scales and language norms that are already available, rather than renegotiating their values and statuses for new identities or complicating the orders of indexicality.

Furthermore, Blommaert's model is based on the assumption that the powerless have to switch to the changing scales, but the powerful (i.e., dominant institutions, "owners" of a language, or the traditional inhabitants of a social space) do not have to reciprocate. It seems that the powerful expect migrants to adjust to their norms, and not vice versa. This is a one-sided negotiation or, rather, accommodation. Is it possible that people have to increasingly co-construct norms and values in the many global spaces today because of the more cosmopolitan values and a more complex articulation of power? Could the negotiation of power be two-way?

Despite its value in addressing language contact and mobility, and adopting a much needed spatiotemporal focus which is lacking in other models of globalizing English, Blommaert's scalar metaphor suffers from some limitations:

a. This metaphor is too normative. The norms at different scale levels are not open for renegotiation, resistance, and reconstruction. However, norms are not always

clear-cut in social life. Negotiability is relevant in situations where there are conflicting norms. Different parties and dynamics in an interaction may throw norms
up for grabs. Norms are often brought into being through situational negotiation.
Such an orientation doesn't have to give in to postmodern fragmentation and
chaos, but has to accommodate a more dynamic view of norms.

b. The metaphor is too impersonal. People move across predefined scales and spaces.
The hierarchically ordered spaces determine their mobility and status. The metaphor
thus shows insufficient sensitivity to the ways people negotiate spaces, bring them
into being, or modify them in their favor. Rather than scales shaping people, we
have to consider how people invoke scales for their communicative and social
objectives.

Scholars in geography and political science from whom sociolinguists adopt this
metaphor use scales in more complex ways. For example, Uitermark reminds us:
"One scale should not be privileged over others as the starting-point for analysis and
[...] scale should be considered as a process rather than an ontological entity or a
pre-given outcome of social processes" (Uitermark, 2002, p. 751). From this
perspective, we should treat scales not as predetermined but as being open to negotiation. Scales are relative to the different issues and participants under consideration.
Their values and statuses change in relation to the issues being analyzed. This is
exactly the value of adopting scales. We are able to perceive contexts and norms in
relation to changing spatiotemporal realities. Uitermark's position echoes what others
like Swyngedouw have argued:

> [S]patial scale is what needs to be understood as something that is produced: a
> process that is always deeply heterogeneous, conflictual and contested. Scale
> becomes the arena and the moment, both discursively and materially, where
> sociospatial power relations are contested and compromises are negotiated and
> regulated. Scale, therefore, is both the result and the outcome of social struggle
> for power and control.
>
> *(Swyngedouw, 1997, p. 140)*

From this point of view, we should also be open to codes reconstructing scales. In
other words, scales don't determine indexicality in a one-sided way. Codes can be
used strategically to index new values. Social scientists also suggest that we should
consider activities of re-scaling, such as the redefinition of the translocal space to
accommodate new orders of indexicality, as having implications for changing the
attitudes and perspectives of participants. Uitermark argues that beyond considering
the implications for power differences, we should also be sensitive to "the effects
processes of re-scaling can have on institutionalized behaviour—the way actors talk to
each other, what options are considered viable, how people interpret particular
events, and so on" (Uitermark, 2002, p. 748). While these social scientists illustrate
how people change their behavior in relation to macro-level and top-down institutional
changes that alter the scales of reference and result in behavior changes, I would like

to explore how such rescaling can occur bottom-up in the renegotiation of codes. In this sense, the re-scaling that my subjects are participating in and their creative ways of redefining norms can have implications for attitudinal and institutional changes in dominant communities. Though employment and educational policies currently treat privileged native varieties of English as the norm for translocal spaces, we have to be open to the possibility of policy changes in the context of ongoing rescaling in everyday talk and texts in globalization and migration.

An alternative spatiotemporal orientation

As I will proceed to show from my research with skilled migrants in traditionally English-dominant communities, their orientation to translocal spaces is very different from what emerges in Blommaert's model. The experiences and views of my subjects point to ways of developing a more complex orientation to traveling codes and social spaces in the global contact zones.

Background

The data in this chapter comes from African migrants who have settled in English-dominant countries—UK, USA, Australia, and South Africa—for professional training and work. The focus of the inquiry was how language skills facilitate success for skilled migrants in their professions in host communities. The study has implications for the communicative competences and resources skilled migrants require in order to engage productively in professional and development endeavors in the context of globalization. This question is important for several reasons. Though proficiency in the medium of communication in the host community is assumed to be an asset according to human-capital perspectives, language hasn't received in-depth exploration in studies on skilled migration. The few studies we have show that there is a correlation between expertise in the dominant language and levels of success as measured by the income of migrants in the land of settlement (Adsera and Pytlikova, 2010; Bleakley and Chin, 2004; Chiswick and Miller, 1995, 2002, 2007; Dustmann, 1994; Dustmann and van Soest, 2002; Dustmann and Fabbri, 2003; Kossoudji, 1988). Such studies also show that those migrants whose native languages show the greatest distance from the languages in the host community are least successful in professional adjustment and success (see especially Adsera and Pytlikova, 2010). Needless to say, English and the elite varieties of that language are the assumed linguistic capital in such studies, given the global status of English in higher education, development, and professional communication. Research based on these orientations contributes to the popular discourses of "Global English" and leads to its frenzied acquisition in many countries, as governments prepare their citizens for higher education and professional advancement and, thus, migration and remittances as the path to development. However, these studies are not sensitive to the fact that English constitutes many varieties and norms, some well sedimented in post-colonial communities. Also, since these studies are correlationist and demographic, they don't explore the language attitudes and negotiation strategies of migrants. As a qualitative study aimed at tapping into the narratives of migrants, my project elicited the views and experiences of the migrants from an insider perspective.

The study involved a total of 65 participants from Sub-Saharan Africa.[1] The objective was to obtain in-depth narratives and opinions on the ways skilled migrants negotiate language differences in inter-community relations. The data-gathering method involved face-to-face, telephone, and email interviews. I focus in this chapter on a specific question related to the negotiation of orders of indexicality and scale levels. The statements and narratives below were provided in relation to the following question: "Do you experience any tensions between the variety of English you speak and the other varieties spoken in the host community? How do you handle these differences? Would you say that these have any implications for your work and social life?" In asking this question (and using the loaded term "tensions") I assumed that there would be inequalities, discrimination, and unintelligibility experienced by the informants as they confronted the orders of indexicality in the West. This expectation was in turn based on the assumption that the informants would mostly retain their home/community English varieties in their interactions as they are adult migrants. I hoped that the question would elicit the ways migrants negotiate these tensions.

In retrospect, it appears that my questions share Blommaert's perspectives on language contact. The wording of the question implies the following assumptions (to translate them according to Blommaert's model): The types of English the informants speak (i.e., local varieties of educated English, creoles, lingua franca Englishes, and hybrid forms) will be treated as out of place in the translocal spaces of communication in professional and social contexts in the West. These migrants' codes will be treated as belonging to the local scale level of their home countries. They will be deemed less portable resources. The high prestige resources are British, Australian, or American educated varieties of English, spoken by NES in the host countries. These are the "widespread" and "timeless" language norms, enjoying universal acceptance, suitable for the translocal scale. The migrants' own Englishes will be treated as "situated" and "transient," as these are contact varieties whose norms are fluid and unstable. The informants will have to adjust to the indexical order of the translocal scale, moving away from the norms of their national and home community scales in order to be intelligible or successful.

Translocal space redefined

Contrary to my expectations, almost all the informants took issue with the word "tension" in the interview question. Though some acknowledged that their inter-locutors had difficulties with their accent or made it appear so, they themselves were proud that they could negotiate the changing norms effectively for intelligibility and professional success. No one expressed a desire to shift to the high prestige or native varieties which were normative in the host communities. It became clear that the informants were interpreting the translocal space, orders of indexicality, and scale levels differently.

To begin with, the informants treated the translocal scale as characterized by diversity and plurality, and not by homogeneity and uniformity as Blommaert defines them. Rejecting my assumption of "tension," the following two informants clarified the nature of the contact as follows:

1. TN (Zimbabwe, male, health care worker in Sheffield)[2]: Not that I have noticed. I think there is an acceptance that people speak English differently with different accents. It could be that there are different dialects of English in communities and this is coming to be accepted.
2. Gabra (Ethiopia, male, dental school administrator in Seattle): It was a cultural shock to come here and see the different English spoken by different people. And the beauty of America is the difference. There's lots of cultures, so it's awesome that you're not saying, "Oh, my way is right or his way or her way is right," you know. Everyone is right as long as you communicate in English and the message gets across.

Both informants see the translocal space as open to diverse varieties of English. They bring with them a language ideology of tolerance toward diversity and the acceptance of differences. It is significant that they characterize this space so in different geographical places, that is, the UK and the USA. Though Blommaert acknowledges the multilingualism of translocal spaces, he still treats the norms as defined by elite NES. However, my subjects describe the presence of diverse norms, or at least their desire to construct new norms, in these spaces. They see an accommodation of the different Englishes people bring with them. The translocal space thus features plural norms. Interestingly, both informants don't express the need to shift to the elite varieties of UK or US English. Gabra emphasizes intelligibility and communicability despite or through the dialect differences. This is the strategy he adopts toward communication (i.e., "Everyone is right as long as you communicate in English and the message gets across"). Rather than shifting to one norm, and focusing on correctness of form, migrants hold on to their own language norms and focus more on intelligibility. We will see from examples below that the informants adopt a range of interactional strategies to get their messages across, while retaining their distinctive varieties of English. What emerges from the view of these subjects is that the translocal space is defined as polycentric, that is, multiple language norms can co-exist without affecting intelligibility and communication.

The informants particularly note that rather than everyone adopting one (presumably high scale) norm, they accommodate to their interlocutors' codes while retaining their own. In this sense, they see communication as a two-way process of mutual negotiation of language differences, rather than a shift to one norm of indexicality:

3. GHM (Uganda, female, school administrator in Bristol): I don't feel any tension about my ability to communicate in English and I think that it is sloppy when people say that they do not understand a person due to accent etcetera, as I speak

a little of many different languages and try my best to communicate with everybody and expect all to do likewise.

4. MA (Nigeria, male, university administrator at Penn State): Probably by paying more attention, just like they have to pay more attention to me as well, it is a two-way street, because of my the combination of Nigerian and British accent and all sorts of things. People had to listen to me more closely to understand what I said OK? With the same token, I had to listen more carefully to them in order to understand them, [...] It was both ways, so I will, just by paying more attention.

It is clear from GHM that insisting on one's own norm and complaining about other people's accents is criticized in these spaces. There is a strong ideological preference expressed by many others in these interviews that asking for repetition or signaling a lack of uptake is undesirable. Interlocutors are expected to collaborate and, presumably, adopt the "let-it-pass" principle to accommodate non-intelligibility. People also expect their interlocutors to accommodate the norms of others by taking extra effort, such as MA's strategy of "paying more attention." This might be considered an interactional strategy. We will see below that the informants expect NES to also adopt the "two-way street" orientation and not insist on their own norms. That is another communicative preference (or ideology) they bring with them. It is also interesting that both informants are comfortable describing their competence as one of "fragmented multilingualism" (Blommaert, 2010, p. 9) or translingual practice (to use a less pejorative term). GHM speaks "a little of many different languages" and MA adopts a "combination" of accents. This too is part of the pluricentricity in translocal spaces. Rather than valuing competence in whole languages, the informants focus on bits and pieces of language as portable resources for success in translocal spaces of super-diversity.

The skill that is most valued in these spaces is the ability to shuttle across norms. The informants accommodate the different norms of English that people bring from different places to the translocal space. In the following excerpt, a Tanzanian professor recounts how she accommodates the varieties her students bring with them to the American classroom:

5. ML (Tanzania, female, professor of labor studies at Penn State): Well, I do feel because we all have some sort of accents, and so I could if I want, I can play with it if I want to. I do do that sometimes. I can if I talk with African Americans, I can talk with them with really about (xxx). If I talk with other people non-Americans, then I can't do that. With Nigerians speak pidgin. And so more or less, if I talk with Indians, I do I will try to so that, I'm with the part of that culture. ... So how do I do it? I'm versatile. I just go with the flow, or I look at the makeup of my class sometimes and I do. They like it sometimes when I talk like them. Anyway, we cruise [...]

What ML values as portable resources are her repertoire of accents, not a proficiency in an elite variety of English. This helps in "crossing" to bond with diverse student groups. It is clear from what ML says that she accommodates to the varieties her interlocutors bring with them. She doesn't hold on to her norms rigidly. She moves closer to the norms of her interlocutors, with some changes in her own accent. These are her interaction strategies for achieving intelligibility. If such accommodation happens in both directions, it is possible that the parties will come out of their own varieties and co-construct new intersubjective norms for these translocal encounters. These norms will depart from the privileged varieties of NES and approximate translingual practice as I have defined it in this book. In this sense, the indexicality of the codes and accents people bring to translocal spaces is co-constructed according to the communicative situation.

Such processes of co-constructing indexicalities are important because the translocal space is not limited to a specific geographical domain (or *place*, hereafter, to distinguish it from *space*, which I define as social and co-constructed). My informants consider their profession as involving mobility across different places with diverse local norms of English. Their work would take them to different native-English speaking communities (such as the UK for my subject below, who is now located in the USA) and post-colonial communities (such as India). In such cases, holding on to US norms (or any uniform norm, however elite it might be) is not necessarily an asset for communication. Informant MA, in rejecting the notion that language difference causes tensions, mentions how he has transcended the norms of places by developing the ability to negotiate diverse varieties of English:

6. MA: (Nigeria, male, university administrator at Penn State): In my current [position], it doesn't. Like I said before, that will disappear with time. In other words, it used to be a barrier, it's no longer a barrier because naturally, right now, I can cope with any varieties of English. Because I deal with people who speak different accents, because I travel all over the world, and when in India, for example, then I'm in China, when I'm in Britain. And so now my ear is tuned towards different accents, or what they call accent.

MA is articulating his receptive competence here, unlike ML who was describing her productive competence earlier in #5. MA is not saying that he can speak the locally dominant variety of English. He can achieve intelligibility with them. In this conversational strategy, while both speakers may retain their varieties, they have the capacity to understand the other person's variety. Openness to others is the disposition he brings to such contact zone encounters.

It is clear that the translocal space is being defined differently by my informants. This space is transnational, supralocal, and cosmopolitan. The language norms in this scale level are polyaccented, multilingual, and plural. This scale level accommodates diverse local norms. It is in this sense that it is *trans*local, that is, it goes beyond local norms and indexical orders, and accommodates the norms of diverse localities. My informants deviate from Blommaert's orientation in that it is the native-speaker privileged varieties that are the norms for this scale level of communication. Privileged varieties of British English in the UK and American English in the USA belong to the national scale level. They belong to the *place*. My informants don't treat it as the norm for the *space* of transnational contact. Though NES, like everyone else, have a right to their own variety in local contexts and should retain it for their voice like others, in translocal spaces they are expected to negotiate the norms others bring with them (even if they might be non-native). In these spaces, privileged native varieties are treated as belonging to a lower scale. They are disparaged. They index parochial values and self-centeredness, as it becomes evident from the statement below:

7. OI (Sierra Leone, female, professor of English at Penn State): One thing I have realized personally for a while is that I always loved, may be because I grew up in a multilingual society where you always knew there other languages all around you, and so you had to way of opening up of other things. I have a feeling that we it is easier for us to translate and become something else and understand. But Americans tend to be so unique, language, so just like one language and sound one way. ... But I don't know but I feel like the Americans if you don't say exactly the way they say they can't hear. So it forces you to actually sound like them you know.

The insistence on American English means to OI a preference for uniformity and one-sided imposition. It is clear that OI considers her own ability to shuttle across scales and norms as a proficiency that is superior to that of her American interlocutors. There is thus the possibility for traditional norms to lose their high status in these translocal scales of communication. What is more important is the higher scale of accommodating language differences that OI represents, compared to the lower scale of insisting on one's own local norms by her interlocutors. Though she accommodates to the order of indexicality dominant in the US context, it is clear that she is critical of its imposition and desires a two-way negotiation.

It is not NES alone who impose monolingual ideologies; migrants too can sometimes impose their local norms on others in these translocal spaces. They can adopt this strategy as an exercise of power and a claim of status difference. We must note therefore that the polycentricity of the translocal space is not given, it is achieved. It has to be negotiated between the interlocutors. TW acknowledges how some may impose their norms on others as a deliberate exercise of power:

8. TW (Zimbabwe, male, juvenile prison officer in Sheffield): I think that people who get cross against each other in this country are fools because who doesn't know that English isn't our first language? It is people who are trying to be smart for nothing who may say "Excuse, what did you say?" Most people listen intently when they are speaking to each other because they know that this is not our country and we are bound to make mistakes in the way we say some words.

It is clear that a majority of the migrants (i.e., evident from "most people") adopt a different footing to their communication. They relate to each other with their shared non-nativeness. Once again, those who insist on uniform norms are disparaged. Their insistence on their own variety indexes ethnocentricism and "trying to be smart." It appears that the interlocutors in both 7 and 8 (NES in the former and migrants in the latter) attempt to jump scales. They are trying to impose their own norms on others. However, this attempt is contested by the informants. They interpret the imposed norms as local and parochial, and not belonging to the higher translocal scale. The interlocutor's exercise of power is resisted. In this manner, the footing and framing of the talk is expected to be always negotiated. Listening intently is an interactional strategy migrants seem to use to achieve intelligibility after the footing is re-established to accommodate their mutual differences.

What gives confidence to migrants to treat the translocal space as polycentric—that is, accommodating diverse local and national norms—is their different language ideology relating to these spaces and scales. I found that my informants adopted strong opinions against asking for repetitions in this space. Interlocutors are expected to take difference as the norm and negotiate it, rather than flag the difference by asking for repetitions. It is clear from 8 above that asking for repetition is taken as "trying to be smart." This interpretation is affirmed by TR below:

9. TR (Zimbabwe, male, accountant in Sheffield): If someone asks me to repeat myself, I feel offended and slighted; it's as if someone is questioning my command of the language. I think the others feel the same way when I ask them to repeat themselves as well. It is a difficult situation to be in but once you have spent a few days with someone, you get used to the way they speak and get on with it. What I don't like is colleagues that I have worked with for years asking me to constantly repeat myself, I find this to be annoying and frustrating as I always think that they should understand the way I speak as I have been with them for a while. It makes me think that they are reminding me that I am a foreigner and I don't talk like them.

Those who ask for repetitions are trying to frame the talk according to their own norms and demand a footing favorable to them. This insistence is an attempt to index the other's talk as alien ("reminding me that I am a foreigner"). TR is happy that he doesn't ask for repetitions in his conversation with speakers with different accents. He is proud of his ability to achieve intelligibility. He considers the need to ask for repetition or clarification a strategy to exercise power. Paradoxically this act indexes a linguistic deficiency and poor disposition. To ask for repetition is rude and exposes one's weak negotiation skills. The language ideology my subjects bring is for talk to be supportive and collaborative in translocal spaces. TR expects his colleagues to understand him.

It is also clear from TR that NES sometimes insist on their right to impose their local norms and make him feel as if he doesn't belong to this place. These examples suggest that the translocal space is not a neutral or democratic site. There are always power differences being negotiated. The framing and footing of the interaction has to be always recontextualized. Migrants may sometimes be deferential to the norms of the NES of the specific place. They acknowledge the code as inheriting certain values and norms. In this sense, we can consider the translocal space as representing power as defined in two different time scales. The colonial notion of power is based on the superiority of native speaker norms both in national and transnational contexts. However, that belongs to an earlier time scale. The migrants contest that indexical order with a post-colonial time scale. In this scale, especially in translocal spaces, people negotiate plural norms.

Translocal space mediated

Just as the translocal space is mediated by different time scales (which are always contested), there are also different social and institutional scales that mediate this space. These considerations suggest that we shouldn't think of translocal spaces as coming with uniform norms. To think of these spaces as homogeneous with clearly ordered norms is problematic for several reasons. Even in the UK or the USA, *places* where NES have a clear right for their own norms, there are *spaces* occupied by migrants alone. In these spaces, there are other orders of indexicality in operation. In this sense, a (geographical) place with its own historic norms can still accommodate social spaces where migrants can establish alternate language norms. Thus, native varieties may enjoy elite status in the place (i.e., local scale), but polycentric translingual norms may define the social space (translocal scale). The higher scale becomes a paradoxical space where the norms of diverse local places are accommodated, but subjects are able to transcend their local norms by shuttling between varieties and co-constructing more egalitarian norms and practices for communication.

Consider the perspective of a Zimbabwean nurse in Sheffield. Asked whether she faced any language tensions, she said:

10. SN (Zimbabwe, female, nurse in Sheffield): No. I have friends from the Philippines and although they have their own accent, this doesn't cause any tension at all. We understand that we are different. We know that we met because we are looking for money, you know. There is no point in hating each other when we are after the same thing.

It is clear that in these spaces, made up of migrants, there is a different order of indexicality. The shared multilingual norms of the migrants index solidarity and acceptance. The use of their respective norms displays acceptance of their own varieties of English. There is an acceptance that their accents are different from the dominant ones. Therefore multilingual migrants maintain their own norms, which deviate from elite varieties, for communicating with each other. Note also that there are different orders of indexicality laminated in the same space. While the local native speaker norms are present, the migrants impose on it their own multilingual norms. They have to signal to each other which norms apply through recontextualization strategies. However, some like the interlocutors in 8, may insist on the place/local norms.

There are other contexts where both NES and multilinguals may jointly co-construct new norms that deviate from the norms of the place. What happens in spaces where

NES are a minority in their own place? What happens in communicative contexts where they join multilinguals? Would they insist on their own varieties or accommodate multilingual and lingua franca norms? As they work with other multilinguals, NES may develop new speech repertoires and norms out of their joint practices. Consider the experience of a Zimbabwean teacher in Sheffield:

11. NN (Zimbabwe, male, teacher in Sheffield): I live at a school so I have got very strong bonds with other teachers. Our college is outside town and there are houses there for teachers who want to live there. I think as a community, we are very united, maybe it's because we are isolated from the other communities and we just have to get along well. It could also be because the majority if not all of us who live here are foreigners, the other guys are from South Africa, India and Trinidad, so it is easy for us to get together really. We speak different English, we speak it differently but we understand each other. We don't need an interpreter which is good and over the years we have grown to understand each other clearly than maybe was the case at first. ... I haven't come across what I can say is tension between us or indeed with Britons. I can understand them perfectly and my students can understand me.

It is clear that NN includes NES also into this translocal community. Even the "Britons" here can work with the language norms brought by the migrants to their school. They seem to successfully negotiate the language differences, just as multilinguals do. They have been able to transition from the national or local community scale to translocal scale in their interactions in what appears to be a multicultural campus in the British school. How did NES manage to recontextualize to the more diverse translingual norms? It could be because the migrants are the majority in this location, as NN mentions. That this community is relatively isolated ("outside town") may have also helped both the migrants and Britons to move to a new framing and footing for their interaction.

There are other situations where a mainstream space of work (with its own language norms) features multilinguals interacting with each other. What happens if the boss in one's workplace in a mainstream institution is another migrant like oneself? What scale level is in operation in this context? The place would dictate a local scale of native speaker norms; the institutional scale may also come with an indexical order privileging educated varieties of English. However, the interlocutors are both migrants who frame their talk according to lingua franca norms and adopt a different footing. In this case also the lamination of diverse indexical orders can be suitably negotiated to invoke norms advantageous to the migrants. Consider the experience of Borundi (from Burundi, a male, social worker in Bradford) who said that his supervisor was from Ghana and, therefore, they negotiated their local Englishes in the workplace. In this regard, the translocal space is what participants make of their interactions. The physical and institutional contexts of the place don't fully determine the language norms and interactional order of migrants.

Even in institutional contexts where there are interactions between NES and multilinguals, there are competing and overlapping scales that can mediate the orders of indexicality, calling for negotiation strategies for recontextualization. The following is the experience of a physician from Zimbabwe with his NES clients. Since he has institutional authority, he feels he has the upper hand. Besides, he feels that what matters in such contexts is one's professional expertise regardless of the language norm:

12. ET (Zimbabwe, male, doctor in Sheffield): I think because it is such a professional job, people are prepared to overlook the language issue. They would rather have an excellent physician who speaks little English than see him go to another country e.g. the USA. Besides, I think the patients wouldn't mind whether the physician who treated them, saved their life was speaking broken English or fluent English as long as they are good at what they do, that is all that matters. I think medicine and other technically demanding fields don't really need someone to be fluent in English, as long as they can make a diagnosis that is all that matters. It's more like football, Ronaldo didn't speak a word of English, neither does Messi, but they are technically very good at it. Most teams now are composed of footballers from different countries who all speak different languages but they still deliver. That is what medicine is like.

ET implies that the footing of the talk is shaped by the expertise of the professional. The status of the language variety or indexical order has to be considered in relation to the role it plays in the domain concerned. ET holds that the ability of someone to perform well professionally (as a form of practice) has implications for the acceptability and estimation of his/her language. The migrant professional may have greater chances of gaining uptake for the framing and footing of the talk in terms of translingual norms as the encounter takes place in his professional office. The awareness of this alternate order of indexicality and scale level (institutional) gives confidence to this subject and to other migrant professionals that they can negotiate the indexical order in their favor. Of course, if ET meets the client out in the street, the local place scale will have more claim, and he may have to negotiate language norms in the interlocutor's terms.

The next informant, TW, also feels that his institutional status provides him with the power to use his own variety of English confidently. As he works in a juvenile prison, he is dealing with inmates who are dependent on him. He has authority over them. Also the communicative functions he performs don't require complex or "advanced" uses of English. It appears that the interlocutors are from a lower social class. In addition to the institutional scale, then, there is also a social scale of class differences that mediates this translocal interaction. All these factors mediate the way his language resources are treated in this domain of activity. The laminated frames for the talk here with different orders of indexicality (between local educated varieties, class-based dialects of the NES, and indigenized English of the migrant) can be negotiated to the advantage of the migrant:

13. TW (Zimbabwe, male, juvenile prison officer in Sheffield): I cannot describe myself as proficient in English, I speak broken English but I get by, the young people

understand me and the managers understand me. Maybe because I work in a juvenile prison helps, you don't really have to talk to the inmates in a manner that elicits a prolonged conversation, it is just to give out instructions and there are specialists who do the other stuff with them. My job is to lock them in and check on them periodically so that they don't commit suicide. I am not there to do anything else, psychologists and teachers do that. There are all these other professionals who work with them, I am just there to ensure compliance and their health and safety, everything else is for others. That way, I don't really need fluent English, they can understand when I say move, then they move, or when I say visiting time is over, I use gestures which they can see as they have eyes. They understand that language better anyway and some of the inmates although they are white they can't really speak real English, they speak street English. So they can't say anything to me about my English because it would be a question of the kettle calling the pot black.

It is a fair question whether the street speech of the NES inmates or the Zimbabwean English of the migrant is of higher status in this context. There are uneven scales here. Even if we cannot decide if one type of English is superior to the other, the more important point is that the meditating factors (i.e., social class difference, institutional role differences, and national identities) lay the conditions for a dynamic negotiation of conversational norms. The fact that other scales are available helps TW to frame the talk differently with a different footing.

It is important to note from this example that a place may have many different varieties, and not all of them are prestigious. Therefore, even among native speaker varieties, there are differences in status. What TW characterizes as "street speech" in 13 is not necessarily of a higher status than the educated varieties of (non-native) English spoken by many migrants. The order of indexicality is not straightforward. The polycentric nature of norms and variability of scales becomes evident when NES use colloquial forms and migrants use educated speech. Typically, skilled migrants have been schooled in the latter and find it difficult to acquire local varieties of informal speech. However, the question remains: Which variety has prestige? Widely intelligible formal varieties or locally restricted slang? This is the dilemma Amare faces and perhaps uses to her advantage:

14. Amare [Ethiopia, female, nurse in Seattle]: Well, you know, especially when I was first here, it was frustrating because, I remember the first job I had. Um, the company supervisor was telling me he couldn't understand me. And I was saying, "He is speaking broken English, but I am trying to speak very current and grammatically correct. What is the problem?"

The different scales available help her to argue favorably for the acceptance of her variety of English. She attempts to frame her talk according to a different scale of indexicality, that is, one that has to do with education. The NES, in this case, uses a less educated variety.

We must add to these mediating factors the fact that there are diverse native speaker varieties, such as UK, USA, Canadian, or New Zealand English, which further complicate the orders of indexicality in translocal spaces. Migrants from post-colonial communities, where British norms were imposed earlier, may invoke that variety to contest the imposition of US English norms in US contexts:

15. Amare [Ethiopia, female, nurse in Seattle]: You know, I don't have a problem with a British person because we were raised in their accent and their teacher. So whenever they speak, they speak grammatically correct and things like that. So we don't have problems with British most of the time. Because when I am back home, I always listen to BBC programs, so that also helps me a lot.

It is interesting that Amare considers British English as "grammatically correct" and therefore more elite or preferable. I found many other informants holding up a particular NES variety as more prestigious and therefore more suitable, treating the locally dominant variety as lacking in prestige. In this sense, different national scale levels can be invoked in the translocal space to negotiate language norms and indexical orders. This can be treated as a recontextualization strategy to pluralize the norms and frame the talk and footing to one that favors renegotiation. It is also a tactic of resistance, using one elite norm to contest another.

What we find from these examples of mediating scale levels is that the indexical order of the transnational space is not predetermined. It has to be negotiated. Since there are power differences between speakers and between the different scales invoked by different parties in translocal spaces, the framing and footing of the conversation have to be renegotiated. While the powerful may attempt to jump scales, imposing their norms on others, the powerless may contest this attempt with their own negotiation strategies. The migrants attempt to define translocal spaces in more egalitarian terms where plural norms can be negotiated equally. The examples above show how migrants may jump scales themselves by invoking other scale levels, contrary to Blommaert's position that only the powerful can jump scales. In using their class/ education status over NES, migrants may employ a social scale to their advantage over place/national scale (as in 13 and 14). In using their professional authority over their clients, they may use the institutional scale over the place/national scale (as in 12). In using colonial British norms against US English, they may use the time scale against place/national scale (as in 15). In all these ways, they display their agency to redefine the translocal space to their advantage. The laminated nature of these scales provides them with ways of reframing the talk and negotiating the footing to make spaces for the Englishes they bring with them.

Achieving intelligibility in polycentricity

If migrants negotiate scales strategically, it is not to impose their own place norms on others. The goal is to create a more egalitarian space where they can all mutually negotiate their norms for intelligibility and communication. As we saw before, each person can retain his or her norm as they work with the interlocutor to achieve their communicative objectives. It may be asked how one can communicate when there are few or no shared norms for this communication. My informants recounted many communicative strategies which they employ to negotiate their norm differences and achieve intelligibility. In other words, they don't depend on codes alone but on negotiation practices. Their narratives provide glimpses into their strategies. We have already seen the many recontextualization and interactional strategies that they suggest in their interviews. MA (4) uses strategies such as paying more attention, listening more attentively (confirmed by TW also in 8), and treating conversation as a "two-way street." In 6, MA talks about using adaptive strategies to get used to diverse accents. TW (13) taps into the multimodality of language and uses gestures to negotiate the different codes used in his workplace. Other subjects mentioned that when they encounter unintelligible items, they "just let it pass" (EV; Zimbabwe, male, social worker in Sheffield). EV also mentioned a compensatory strategy to ensure intelligibility. He follows up the conversation with a written record, through an email. Amare later said that she achieves "common understanding" by speaking "slowly and clearly." Tadese (Ethiopia, male, health professor in Seattle) said that he would use "patience and tact" to negotiate differences. Subjects in 13–15 above exploit the layers of mediating social scales (i.e., professional, educational, class) to recontextualize the interaction in their favor.

We also have to be aware that it is their strong ownership over their codes and envoicing strategies that motivates my subjects to both use their own codes in these contexts and to be respectful of the voices of others in their interactions. Through these effective strategies, the language resources they bring gain new indexicality. They are not treated as deficient or low prestige codes, but index legitimate difference. It is also clear that migrants bring different dispositions to these encounters to succeed in their attempt to rescale talk. They are informed by a collaborative ethic, language ideologies that favor pluralized norms, and a functional view of language that accommodates intelligibility rather than correctness. These dispositions motivate them to adopt appropriate negotiation strategies for voice and favorable footing in their interactions.

Whatever the strategies used, it is clear that the communicative norm expected in these translocal spaces is not a uniform conformity to one order of indexicality. It is expected that there will be mutual accommodation to the norms of the other. From the findings emerging from the data, I have to also question Blommaert's notion of portable resources. Such resources are not elite varieties of English. They are not even codes. The status of these codes shifts according to changing and fluid orders of indexicality in diverse translocal spaces. What seems to help migrants are the strategies and dispositions that enable them to shuttle across scales and negotiate diverse norms for intelligibility and communication. How are these dispositions acquired and developed in a context where formal language instruction focuses on grammar? OI (in 7) indicates above that they are socialized into these language ideologies, dispositions, and strategies in their multilingual home communities. We will consider in Chapter 9 how multilinguals develop this translingual competence.

Conclusion

The narratives from the migrants help us to adopt a different orientation to macro-level social spaces and power from Blommaert's model. They encourage us to perceive social spaces as laminated by competing and overlapping scales with different orders of indexicality. The scales themselves are diverse, spanning temporal, spatial, social, and institutional domains. Multilingual migrants focus not on form or language norms, but on practices, as they adopt suitable strategies for voice and intelligibility. We can adopt the metaphor in the previous chapters and say that migrants are *framing* their talk according to more egalitarian norms and succeeding in altered *footing* that enables co-construction of meaning. Such a perspective enables us to appreciate the agency of translinguals, the fluidity of social spaces, and the emergent orders of indexicality in translocal mobility.

Place doesn't emerge as determining the status of migrants. Migrants enjoy agency to negotiate the differing scales and indexical orders to their advantage and reconstruct space. They make spaces for their voices and norms as they contest dominant language ideologies and indexical orders. Often they are able to persuade even native/local speakers who are invested in traditional norms to move to a different scale of interaction where plural norms can be negotiated in more cosmopolitan terms. Scales become useful only in the context of strategies. Scales are not predefined and static, and different scales can overlap and co-exist in talk. The layered simultaneity of scales and norms in any given place is unpacked and renegotiated to construct translocal spaces agentively through the strategies of the participants. The narratives and opinions of skilled migrants then show that they relate to translocal spaces, scales, and indexical orders as open to negotiation, different from the ways theorized by Blommaert. Migrants treat translocal spaces as contact zones, which though implicated in power, are open to negotiation and generation of new norms and indexical orders, as theorized in this book.

These narratives on the negotiation of social spaces outside the classroom complement our findings from classrooms, educational contexts, and the academic communication in previous chapters. Critics may point out that pedagogical contexts are "unreal" or "protected" because of their educational purpose. They may consider the strategies of communication in these contexts as inappropriate for theorizing language contact and politics. However, we find similar strategies of negotiation and translingual practices adopted in social spaces outside the classroom. This connection enables us to theorize the competence of multilingual students and scholars better. It appears as if they are bringing into the classroom the strategies and dispositions they develop outside. It is possible that they are socialized into these strategies from interactions in everyday life and social interactions. In the next chapter, I theorize how translinguals develop competence in these communicative practices.

9

DEVELOPING PERFORMATIVE COMPETENCE

What competence do translinguals bring to help them achieve successful communication in the global contact zones? Communication in these contexts requires a competence for plural language norms and mobile semiotic resources. As there is no homogeneous norm available for preconstructed meanings in the contact zone, competence requires suitable negotiation strategies and reciprocal practices. Traditional models based on predefined grammatical constructs are unable to explain the complexity of translingual communication. In this chapter, we will discuss what kind of competence accounts for this communicative practice, and how translinguals develop it.

Performative competence

The Chomskyan model of grammatical competence dominates discussions of proficiency—even well-meaning efforts to define multilingual competence as different from that of monolinguals. Competence is treated as grammatical, mentalist, and abstract in the Chomskyan tradition, as knowledge of form constituted as a system and shared by the community is treated as accounting for successful communication. What Chomsky (1988) defined as having only secondary importance for putting into practice the basic grammatical competence, performance, was given greater importance by Dell Hymes (1974) in his formulation of communicative competence. Hymes makes a space for social knowledge without which grammatical knowledge is unhelpful in communication. Though this is a useful clarification, Hymes' communicative competence also doesn't come close to addressing the competence displayed by translinguals. The dichotomies of grammar and practice, and cognition and context, are still preserved in Hymes' model. Communicative competence is defined as a form of knowledge and located in cognition, facilitating the application of grammatical competence. Adopting Byram's (2008) useful distinction, we can say that what translinguals bring is a form of *procedural knowledge*, not the *propositional knowledge* of either grammatical or communicative competence. Their competence isn't constituted of the *what*, but of the *how* of communication. This type of knowledge is developed in and through practice, shaping both cognition and form in terms of one's ongoing experiences. The dynamic and reciprocal strategies translinguals adopt, based on their knowledge of *how*, motivate them to respond strategically to unexpected interlocutors and spaces with diverse norms in contact zones. I label this form of competence *performative competence* in an effort to emphasize its practice-based nature. Though this has a cognitive dimension and implications for grammatical awareness, it treats both as shaped by locally situated performance.

In some ways, performative competence is similar to *strategic competence*, the last of the three components which Canale and Swain (1980) identify in an effort to unpack Hymes's communicative competence. This kind of competence constitutes strategies that enable interlocutors to deal with breakdowns and trouble spots in interactions. However, I see this kind of strategic competence as forming the basic component of all communication, and shaping the other components of grammatical or socio-linguistic competence in the model of Canale and Swain. Another term that relates closely to performative competence is *interactional competence* (see Kaur, 2009). It is used largely in CA to refer to the ability to conduct conversational interactions, with an awareness of the interpersonal strategies that accompany the use of language. Though it usefully focuses on the practical nature of conducting everyday inter-actions, I define this kind of interactional competence as going beyond the micro-structure of conversational turns to include negotiation of broader social and ecological dimension. It also has implications for meaning-making and the construction of new indexicalities, contributing to the intrinsic semiodiversity of all language interactions.

What does performative competence consist of? The key feature of this competence is *alignment*. As I mentioned earlier, there is a remarkable confluence of scholarship on this strategy from social cognitive theorists (Atkinson *et al.*, 2007) and South Asian linguists (Khubchandani, 1997). Alignment involves connecting semiotic resources, environmental factors, and human subjects in relation to one's own communicative needs and interests in order to achieve meaning. In fact, the alignment between mind, body, and the environment is itself changing all the time. Alignment enables translinguals to respond to such highly diverse, unexpected, and changing contexts and codes by strategically combining ecological resources. Alignment is adaptability. It calls for alertness, creativity, and strategic thinking and action. It is the ability to find order out of chaotic and ever-changing environmental stimuli. There are implications for grammar and form. Alignment is the ability to create new grammars and indexicals from diverse semiotic resources through repeated situated use, co-constructed meaning, and sedimentation. Alignment is behind the strategies of envoicing, recontextualization, interaction, and entextualization which translinguals use to produce and interpret codes in contact zones. In short, translinguals have the ability to align diverse semiotic resources to create meaning and achieve commu-nicative success when words in isolation are inadequate and homogeneous norms are not available in contact zones.

How does performative competence work in conversational and literacy interactions? I first offer a simplified model of performative competence as it emerges from South Asian linguists, lingua franca scholars, and my own studies. I will explain how the negotiation strategies I described in the previous chapters fit into this form of competence. I illustrate this model with examples from my subjects.

If we were to offer a template of the procedural knowledge which translinguals bring to contact zone communication, it would appear like the following:

- Start from your positionality;
- Negotiate on equal terms;
- Focus on practices, not form;
- Co-construct the rules and terms of engagement;
- Be responsive to joint accomplishment of goals;
- Reconfigure your norms and expand your repertoire.

To begin with, translinguals start their communication from the contexts they are located in, and the language resources and values that they bring with them. In the African migrants, for example, we don't see a desire to move to elite forms of English, even in Inner Circle contexts. Nor do they strive for a value-free or neutral form of English, as theorized by ELF or EIL scholars. Translinguals bring a strong sense of voice and locus of enunciation. The motivation for their *envoicing strategies* and their negotiatory effectiveness is explained by their ability to start from their social positioning.

However, one's own resources are only the starting point and basis for negotiation. What enables translinguals to achieve meaning despite the fact that they all start with their own codes is their openness to negotiate on equal terms. Though they understand that in certain contexts the norms of certain participants enjoy more status, they expect everyone to be open to co-constructing meaning. In other words, though they acknowledge the reality of power, they treat it as negotiable. They adopt suitable strategies to persuade their interlocutors to adopt this openness to negotiation. Without disregarding local orders of indexicality, they engage in constructing new indexicals in situational terms. Also, as the forms and norms which the parties bring to the interaction may be very diverse, they don't depend on them as the sole or primary sources of meaning; they depend on practices that are adaptive, reciprocal, and dynamic to co-construct meaning. These are the *interactional strategies* which I have described in the previous chapters, such as "let-it-pass," make it normal, clarification, and confirmation.

As they bring these orientations to the interaction, an important step in the negotiation process is a suitable framing and footing for the context of communication. I cover this domain under *recontextualization strategies*. They help define the ground rules and terms of interaction. The South Asian linguist Khubchandani calls this a "mutuality of focus" (Khubchandani, 1997, p. 49). If the interlocutors are confused or conflicted in terms of the relevant ecological features and contextual conditions informing the interaction, they won't have a suitable context to frame the interaction or shape the meaning of their semiotic resources. The frame and footing have to be mutually established. The contextual cues in their text and/or talk will help interlocutors signal to each other the features that they consider relevant for this interaction. Obviously, translinguals will define the footing and frames to favor negotiation and resist monolingual ideologies.

To succeed in communication, interlocutors have to be responsive throughout to the moves of the other parties and respond accordingly. Negotiation is a "two-way street" as one of the African migrants observes in Chapter 8. This not only means constant monitoring of the framing and footing of the talk so that adjustments can be made as required, but also responsiveness means making concessions to the other and adopting the best strategy for uptake. The speaker/writer has to sequence the semiotic resources in such a way that the interlocutor can process them effectively for meaning. The notion of *entextualization strategies* addresses this dimension of the competence. Translinguals have the ability to constantly monitor and adjust their text and talk to structure them to suit the alignment needs of their interlocutors. Here again, there is no easy recipe to structure syntax or discourse for success. As we observe in Buthainah, she compels her readers to adopt certain strategies and perform certain outcomes, but she herself also makes concessions and facilitates alignment in different contexts, to suit her objectives and interlocutors.

As for the outcomes of the talk, translinguals don't assume that their meanings and objectives for the communicative interaction will be unconditionally accomplished. They are open to hybrid, qualified, and negotiated outcomes. This orientation makes the interaction truly dialogical. In this manner, there is an opportunity for both parties to gain from the contribution of the other. Thus translinguals are able to connect *learning* with *use* in their language interactions—constructs that are kept separate in other models of competence. It is this orientation that enables them to add to the repertoires that they bring with them. It enables them to sharpen, refine, and add to their negotiation strategies as well. As I will show in the next section, it also contributes to their *cooperative disposition*. It enables them to acquire tastes, values, and skills that favor co-existence with others. In this sense, their performative competence doesn't make them remain where they started but moves them to a higher proficiency and awareness. The performative competence that they bring with them is made more advanced. Translinguals thus develop a more complex language awareness and metalinguistic competence. This is especially important, as there is no end-point or threshold for proficiency in contact zone communication, which is always new, diverse, and unpredictable.

Though performative competence is not defined in terms of form, as traditional linguistic schools might do, it does have implications for form. Through this process, translinguals co-construct indexicals with shared meanings, values, and norms, which through sedimentation can lead to new dialects, registers, or discourses. Performative competence thus enables translinguals not to master one language system at a time, but to develop an ever-expanding repertoire of codes. Their focus is not mastery but open-ended development of more semiotic resources. Similarly, rather than focusing on a mastery of grammar, translinguals focus on developing a language awareness or metalinguistic competence that enables them to deal with any grammar which they might encounter in contact situations. In performative competence, proficiency in languages is not conceptualized individually, with separate competencies developed for each language. What is emphasized is the repertoire—the way in which the different language resources constitute an integrated and ever-widening competence. Furthermore, equal or "advanced" proficiency is not expected in all the languages. Using different languages for distinct purposes qualifies as competence. One doesn't have to use all the languages involved in one's repertoire as all-purpose languages.

It should be clear that performative competence goes against many other dichotomies, beyond the grammar/practice or cognition/context framing of traditional models of language competence. In similar ways, traditional models have also distinguished between individual versus community, treating the former as the locus of learning and competence. They have distinguished between fixity versus fluidity, rational versus multisensory, and linear versus multilateral, considering the first construct in each pair as ensuring superior learning and competence (see Canagarajah, 2007, for a fuller discussion). They also have an end-point to learning, distinguishing the target language from interlanguages, which are supposed to be non-functional and imperfect till they reach the target of native speakers. This distinction depends on another hierarchy, native versus non-native, treating the competence and norms of the former as the target to be reached. Evidently, these binaries are based on monolingual ideologies that treat the learning and proficiency of the native speaker in a homogeneous environment as the norm, as is typical of Chomskyan competence. Furthermore, while traditional models treated the speech community as the locus of learning, I am considering contact zones as the domain for consideration. As is to be expected, the types of competence necessary and the modes of learning taking place in these contexts are different from those in purportedly bounded and homogeneous contact. I am not arguing that performative competence is an alternative model which is relevant for certain special types of communication. Since all contexts are contact zones, and bounded/homogeneous communities are an ideological contruct, I am arguing that performative competence characterizes all communication.

We must also question the very notion of "acquisition" used in traditional models of language learning and competence, as in the term "second language acquisition". "Acquisition" assumes the learning of a system that is out there, almost as a product. It assumes a filling-in, with little personal participation or modification from the resources one already possesses. The target of acquisition also remains unchanged by the acquirer. What we see in translingual practice is that learning is invested and personal. The learner shapes the target. Neither the learner nor the system remain unchanged by the communicative and learning activity. Some scholars prefer the term "development" instead (see Larsen-Freeman, 2011). This term also accommodates the possibility that the learning of different repertoires is ongoing, multidirectional, and sometimes parallel. Hence my choice of title for this chapter.

The strategies we see among translinguals are so intuitive and unlearned that many consider them universal. What is impressive is that students and migrants who might be considered to display imperfect control over the form of English still demonstrate complex negotiation strategies. Kaur therefore argues that these practices "are utilized in ways that are similar to how native speakers use them to negotiate understanding" (Kaur, 2009, p. 241). Along these lines, other scholars also consider translingual competence deriving from a universal cognitive mechanism (Franceschini, 2011). Though I agree that performative competence is displayed by all people, regardless of their native/non-native or monolingual/multilingual status, I must make a few clarifications. As I have indicated above, I don't see performative competence as being primarily cognitive. As I will go on to develop below, I see this competence as being based on socialization in contact zone communication. In this sense, I diverge from Kaur's position that this competence is developed in "native" (or L1) and presumably homogeneous and bounded contexts. Also, my orientation is influenced by the perspectives of social cognitive theorists (see Tomasello, 2008) that cognition is embedded, embodied, and works in alignment with ecological resources. Such cognitive orientations posit that the mind does not constitute structures to work independently, but strategies to work in alignment with others and other environmental resources. Performative competence is informed by such orientations to social cognition that treat environment and practice as constitutive of meaning-making activities of humans.

Cooperative disposition

The above orientations to language development find inspiration from models theorized in ways different from traditional SLA by many scholars and schools today (see Atkinson, 2011a). For example, sociocultural theory develops models that show how environment mediates language learning in productive ways (see Lantolf, 2011). Sociocognitive theory explores how embedded and extended cognition enables language learners to align mind, body, world relationships in their competence (see Atkinson, 2011b). Dynamic systems theory accommodates knowledge of a system that is open yet stable, and diverse yet patterned (Larsen-Freeman, 2011). Language socialization models theorize how learners develop their competence in ecologically embedded language resources through everyday social relationships and practice (Duff and Talmy, 2011). All these schools situate the previously dominant constructs such as form, cognition, and the individual in a more socially sensitive, ecologically embedded, environmentally situated, and interactionally open model.

Despite the positive influence, these models differ slightly from performative competence as developed in this book. All of these models still assume languages to have their own independent systems, different from the translingual orientation of languages as mobile resources. Most of them (excluding dynamic systems theory) also assume that learners acquire the system without at the same time changing the system. Though dynamic system treats the system as diverse and open, it still considers language system as independently patterned and located in order to produce meaning. In treating the system as capable of producing meaning by itself, the model is somewhat impersonal. The orientation in this book is that it is practices and social negotiations that generate meaning out of fluid and hybrid codes. Performative competence emphasizes human agency and social practices in producing meaning. More importantly, while these models are busy developing alternate learning and cognitive models at a theoretical level, we lack adequate information on the learning strategies and processes that will help us translate these models for pedagogical purposes. We need more information on the interface between competence and learning to develop effective pedagogical practices. I consider below the ethnographic and qualitative data in the previous chapters to account for the development of performative competence.

How do my subjects develop performative competence? Their answers point to socialization. The African skilled migrant OI (#7 in Chapter 8) in her interview attributes her competence to the multilingual environment in her home community in Nigeria. There she shuttled between diverse languages, enabling her to develop the negotiation strategies that help her achieve intelligibility across diverse varieties of English in the USA. She considers those in the USA as having a different kind of disposition that doesn't help them to negotiate differences but insists on their own norms. Similarly, when I commented that Buthainah was probably codemeshing in her essay under the influence of other American peers who were doing so in my course, she corrected me in her member check comments. She attributed her pre-paredness to socialization through Arabic religious texts and family interactions which made her treat communication as multilingual and multimodal. Furthermore, the African migrants and my multilingual students often commented on the unhelp-fulness of classroom learning. They complained about being placed in ESL and remedial classes which were irrelevant for their needs and proficiencies. These featured teacher-led, norm-based, and product-oriented pedagogies, treating students as linguistically deficient. My subjects had to resort to finding their own resources to develop their language repertoires and negotiation strategies.

What exactly helps my subjects to tap into the affordances in the environment to develop their performative competence and translingual proficiency? My reading of the narratives and opinions of my subjects points to certain dispositions that they bring to contact zone interactions to achieve communicative success and further develop their performative competence. These dispositions provide the aptitude for translingual practices. They explain how my subjects don't wait for their performative competence to be developed inside the classroom or by teachers. They already bring certain advanced levels of performative competence with them, as is clear from Buthainah's writing strategies (Ch. 7) and the conversational strategies of the Hertfordshire students (Ch. 4). Their socialization in multilingual environments and contact zones has helped them adopt these strategies in classrooms.

What makes translinguals open to negotiating diversity and the co-construction of meaning, I call the *cooperative disposition*. I borrow this metaphor from Tomasello (2008) who views cooperation and collaboration as the basic principles behind the human biological development of communication and cognition. What do these dispositions consist of? These dispositions constitute a specific set of tastes, values, and skills, similar to the way Bourdieu (1977) defines *habitus*. In relation to language learning, these three components can be defined more specifically as language awareness, social values, and learning/communicative strategies, respectively. Translinguals bring a specific set of language assumptions, social orientation, and strategies of negotiation and learning that help them to develop performative competence and to engage in translingual practice. These dispositions are developed in social contexts through everyday experiences, as in habitus. However, there is also space for agency and personal development in habitus (Navarro, 2006). How similar social experiences in contact zones fail to help some to develop these dispositions, or to develop them to a higher degree than others, cannot be explained by social environment alone. Therefore, these dispositions are not treated in socially deterministic ways. For example, while Buthainah codemeshed, Keiko (a student from Japan in the same class) adopted less agentive writing strategies, though coming from a similar multilingual environment. We need to accommodate personal experiences, investments, and positionality (often unavailable in all their complexity to outside researchers) to explain how dispositions develop in relation to social environment. Note also that many NES subjects in my data (Mark and Tim in Ch. 7, and Milne in Ch. 5) display such openness to negotiation and performative competence. This is not surprising, as all of us inhabit contact zones and enjoy affordances to develop such dispositions. It is possible that some NES enjoy personal investments and agency to develop such dispositions further when many others succumb to monolingual ideologies. For such reasons, it is important for dispositions to be defined with a cognitive and affective component that is not socially overdetermined. As cooperative dispositions have a psychological dimension then, I adopt a practice-based orientation toward subjective life, different from the innate and transcendental orientation of traditional Cartesian models. Dispositions provide subjective processes of a social and material cast.

I highlight three key features for each domain of language awareness, social values, and learning strategies that constitute the dispositions of the more successful translinguals we have met in the previous chapters. Though the third component of strategies consists of both communicative and learning strategies, I focus on learning strategies in this chapter as I have articulated communicative strategies in previous chapters.

The dispositions that emerge from the data are as follows:

1. *Language awareness:*

    a. language norms as open to negotiation;
    b. languages as mobile semiotic resources;
    c. a functional orientation to communication and meaning.

2. *Social values:*

    a. openness to diversity;
    b. a sense of voice and locus of enunciation;
    c. a strong ethic of collaboration.

3. *Learning strategies:*

    a. learning from practice;
    b. adaptive skills;
    c. use of scaffolding.

Let me illustrate.

Language awareness: Translinguals treat language norms as open to negotiation. They don't come with rigid and predefined norms for their own languages or for those of others. They are open to reconstructing meanings and values in context, in collaboration with their interlocutors. As we saw in the case of African skilled migrants, they assume that norms are multiple, diverse, relational, and changing in contact zones. While not imposing their own norms on others, they resist (to the extent that is practically possible) the imposition of other people's norms on them, even in cases where the interaction occurs in Inner Circle institutional contexts. Similarly, Buthainah repeatedly challenges my invocation of native speaker norms in my feedback to criticize her idiomatic and syntactic choices. She expects readers to negotiate her language norms, even in a literacy event in the US academic context. Such an orientation, which translinguals bring from socialization in multilingual environments, encourages them to both apply and further to develop performative competence to renegotiate norms, when others resort to their own norms.

Secondly, translinguals treat languages as mobile semiotic resources. Each of these three words is important, as we discussed in Chapter 2. Translinguals treat languages as *resources* that they can mix and mesh in unusual patterns to construct meaning. The economic metaphor emphasizes the way language is used in relation to one's social and material interests. Translinguals also see these resources as not owned by any one community or place, as they are *mobile*. It is this assumption that enables them to appropriate resources traditionally defined as untouchable or owned by others. It also explains their strong sense of agency, as they are prepared to appropriate codes from diverse communities even in elite contexts to accomplish their purposes. Finally, they treat language as part of a broader set of multimodal *semiotics*. Language combines with other symbol systems, diverse modalities of communication, and environmental resources to create meaning. As we saw in the case of Buthainah, she adopts an aesthetic and material orientation to words, as she expects readers to factor in such a holistic response to facilitate meaning. Like the others we saw in the preceding chapters, she is prepared to mesh English with other codes in her repertoire for her voice and interests.

Thirdly, translinguals adopt a functional orientation to communication and meaning. Note how Buthainah labels herself as a "functional bilingual." In doing so, she foregrounds what she can do with language resources, and downplays formal correctness. Recall also how the Zimbabwean physician (#12 in Chapter 8) says that what is important is not the English variety used or the level of formal proficiency, but the ability to "deliver." With this disposition, translinguals consider form as the servant of meaning. Form changes meaning and value according to the purposes they are put to use for. Translinguals are open to the possibility of emergent grammar and new indexicalities. Hence a functional orientation encourages translinguals to focus on negotiation strategies and communicative practices rather than formal correctness. Note how African skilled migrants say that it is not correctness that they are after but getting across their message, even if they concede that they speak what others might consider "broken English" (as TW does in #13).

Social values: Language assumptions and ideologies are complemented by certain social values that enable translinguals to develop their interactional skills. A key social value is their openness to diversity. As the South Asian linguist Khubchandani affirms, it is this disposition that motivates translinguals to treat "deviation as the norm," whether in social life or grammar (Khubchandani, 1997, p. 94). It is remarkable that the skilled migrants consider translocal social spaces as shared by all, wherever they come from. They expect NES, the traditional owners of English, to also assume difference as the norm and to focus on negotiating meaning. Interestingly, for some, "The beauty of America is the difference" (Gabra, #2). Though they understand the dominant ideologies of the *place*, they strive to co-construct *spaces* of diversity.

This radical openness to others is complemented by a strong sense of voice and locus of enunciation. Translinguals base their interactions on their own positionality. It is their openness to diversity that makes them comfortable with their own voice and difference. They don't feel that their peculiarity should be suppressed for the sake of social harmony or communicative success. This explains the envoicing strategies of translinguals. They develop diverse practices for envoicing their difference in the resources they choose for communication. At times, this need for voice can take overly insistent and agentive proportions, as in the case of Buthainah's justifications for her unconventional idiomatic and word choices. Note also the ethic of not asking for repetitions among skilled migrants (#8, and #9 in Chapter 8). This is treated as an insult to one's voice.

What enables translinguals to deal with this paradox—that is, insisting on their own difference and being open to other people's difference—is their strong ethic of collaboration. They collaborate with others to co-construct meaning. For Buthainah, literacy is "negotiated" (MC) and, for skilled migrants, communication is "a two-way street" (see MA #4). Strategies such as interactional, entextualization and recontextualization depend heavily on a collaborative ethic. ELF scholars House (2003) and Seidlhofer (2004) have also observed such solidarity among translinguals. This conversational ethic doesn't mean that disagreements and resistance are impossible in the messages. Even disagreement can be communicated effectively (and receive uptake) only through collaborative effort. The ethic also doesn't mean ignoring the reality of power and dominant ideologies. The interactional strategies of translinguals are calculated to persuade those in power to adopt a different footing based on collaboration.

Learning strategies: Translinguals combine these linguistic and social values with effective learning and communicative strategies to develop their performative competence. An important skill they bring is to learn from practice. Language use and learning are not separate processes for translinguals. Communication in everyday life provides them with opportunities for purposive and meaningful learning. Such learning is of course challenging and brings its own difficulties. Learning has to take place in ecological contexts where input is embedded and constantly evolving with the environment. Translinguals bring the disposition to decode and form rules from such holistic input. My students and adult migrants all affirm that they developed their performative competence from everyday interactions. PZ, an elderly priest from Zimbabwe now living in Leeds, conveyed how he was learning four other languages he needed for his work after migration to the UK: "by talking to people, I listen when they are speaking in their own languages and I learn that way. I also use the computer to learn new languages." For translinguals, learning is "lifelong and lifewide" (Duff, 2008, p. 257). They have to respond to unpredictable situations in global contact zones where the set of interlocutors or languages cannot be controlled and they cannot always be prepared. It is through engaging in these contexts that translinguals learn while communicating. It is not surprising that House (2003) argues that those who succeed in these contexts bring with them the ability to do on-site and instantaneous decoding of their interlocutor's norms and conventions to frame their own contributions accordingly. Perhaps translinguals have a heightened language awareness and metalinguistic competence to be able to decode norms and conventions from embedded ecological resources. As I will show below, this is also a multisensory learning. Translinguals learn language not purely from a rational orientation but with the aid of diverse sensory scaffolds and affordances.

What enables translinguals to progress in these contexts is their adaptive disposition. This disposition is aided strongly by their reflective skills, motivated by an openness to learning. They also bring the humility to make mistakes, acknowledge their failures or limitations, and engage in self-correction. They can apply lessons learnt in one context to a new context. They can infer lessons from past mistakes for improved performance in the next context. They can be self-critical and bring a keen sensitivity to criticism. They have the ability to thrive and develop from feedback, implicit or explicit, in their communicative encounters. There is remarkable adaptation to the norms of the local context from practice-based learning. For example, Buthainah engages with the responses of her peers, and often seeks their feedback to revise her strategies. The Nigerian university administrator discusses how he not only got over his initial difficulties with accent differences, but gradually learnt to cope with the accents of other nationals he interacted within his work ("now my ear is tuned towards different accents" in #6). Adaptive skills also contribute to skills of alignment, enabling subjects to bring together shifting configurations of language, body, mind, and environment for meaning-making.

Thirdly, translinguals bring the learning strategy of scaffolding to develop their performative competence. They use scaffolds of many kinds to develop their proficiency. Buthainah's literacy autobiography reveals that her parents provided multimodal cues from the environment to learn new words. Buthainah herself refers to using her knowledge of one language to develop proficiency in another—as in the case of using online dictionaries in English and guessing from similar roots to learn French. She uses various caregivers and agents (i.e., parents, cousins, American friends, and multilingual classmates) to help her in learning. She also seeks new resources as scaffolds. When her Arabic teacher provides only form-based assignments for her writing, Buthainah focuses more on the teacher's personal and highly expressive commentary to develop her rhetorical competence. Many African migrants shared how they developed competence in NES varieties by comparing notes with their spouses at home after they encountered new problems or gained new insights during their work during the day. Such learning strategies, in combination with the communicative strategies we saw in the previous chapters, provide translinguals with the aptitude to develop their performative competence.

Pedagogical implications

Arguing that cooperative diposition provides the aptitude for performative competence doesn't mean that there is no room for improvement and further development among students. Translinguals can develop their proficiency through favorable pedagogical strategies and resources. In fact, if translinguals are always open to learning, lifelong and lifewide, they would have the disposition to treat classroom relations and activities also for their development. The fact that we see effective socialization into performative competence in everyday situations in social contexts doesn't mean that the classroom cannot be transformed to provide similar resources. Teachers can welcome and encourage cooperative disposition to further develop the performative competence of their students.

We must be aware though that traditional classroom relations and pedagogical approaches have the potential to stifle the dispositions and competences which students bring with them. A form-focused, teacher-led, product-oriented pedagogy will contradict the learning strategies and dispositions students bring for performative competence. Such a pedagogical environment can counter-socialize students into monolingual ideologies and norms. Moreover, it can fail to exploit the affordances the classroom ecology has for situated and practice-based learning. We have to consider what pedagogies can open up the classroom as a space for social negotiations, ecological affordances, and practice-based learning. Rather than asking what we can offer to deficient or novice students, we have to ask how we can let students bring into the classroom the dispositions and competencies which they have richly developed outside the classroom. This involves turning the classroom into a site for translingual socialization. Teachers have to permit, as much as they can, the conditions, resources, and affordances students find outside the classroom for the development of their performative competence. In this enterprise, teachers should be prepared to learn from their students.

I amplify below the pedagogical features I have adopted in my classes (as shared in Chapter 7) to develop performative competence. I find useful what Halasek labels a Bakhtinian *dialogical pedagogy* (Halasek, 1999, pp. 178–93). Dialog is enacted in diverse ways. The readings and writings emerge out of dialog and dialectical interactions with one's peers and the instructor. Often web-based instructional systems facilitate the frequent and open interactions between everyone in the class. The peers and the instructor are expected to read one's course products and post their feedback into the author's folder. The authors have an opportunity to respond to the feedback, reflect on their writing challenges, and pose further questions in their weekly journal entries as they revise the drafts or products for another review. Learning from textbooks is also collaborative, with classroom and online discussions and group activities complementing reflections, journaling, and writing. In addition to the negotiation of language and literacy artefacts of the course, the very classroom interaction is modeled on collaborative interaction. Classroom discourse is not modeled on the IRF routine controlled by the teacher for purpose of knowledge display. A dialogical pedagogy encourages the development of strategies for meaning negotiation, in addition to critical reflection and language awareness.

In such a pedagogy, teachers should scaffold students' translingual practices in creative ways. The course described in Chapter 7 on literacy was set up in such a way that it generated fascinating products and processes of translingual communication. The fact that students had an opportunity to work on a single writing project over a long period of time, in a protracted manner, helped them to experiment with modes of representing their voice. The possibilities of negotiating their text with others in the class and in relation to the readings also helped them to reconsider the rhetorical effects and intentions of their texts. For example, the fact that I didn't control the assessment excessively through a teacher-fronted pedagogy meant that writers also had to depend on their peers for their response. They thus gave more value to peer feedback. The widening of the potential readership of their texts helped students consider their rhetorical intentions and voice in relation to their peers. It turned out that students started to influence each other through their writing strategies. Though the assignment didn't ask them to codemesh, and didn't provide any expectations on form, it was interesting that many of the essays began to explicitly codemesh as the semester progressed.

Teachers should also give models for students to emulate. Textbooks like *Critical Academic Writing and Multilingual Students* (Canagarajah, 2002b) critique dominant orientations to normative writing and consider codemeshing as an option. The codemeshed article by Smitherman (1999) that my students analyzed also provided a model for emulation. My own literacy autobiography (Canagarajah, 2001), provided in the beginning of the course as a model for their own writing, may have influenced the students. Though it didn't codemesh explicitly, the essay combined literate and oral discourses and showed how hybrid texts are acceptable in the academy and can break into print. Later in the semester, Buthainah would acknowledge that my openness to codemeshing made her comfortable with this form of writing.

Teacher feedback can help scaffold students' language production. In my response to student writing, I adopted the approach of a sympathetic but curious listener or respondent. I negotiated meanings with the student writers to co-construct meanings as in a contact zone of diverse conventions and codes. We had multiple occasions for meaning negotiation through serial drafts. They also gave me ample opportunities to clarify meaning and to understand the intentions and goals of the writers before having to assign a grade and judge them. In addition to this enactment of dialogical engagement in classroom communication, the fact that I was open to codemeshing (which students gradually discovered in my scholarship and writing practice) also helped students to accommodate their language resources into their writing.

The dialogical pedagogy also helped me as a teacher to navigate some of the ethical questions teachers face in teaching translingual communication. Since translingual practice is a collaborative achievement, teachers may wonder how they can stand outside the interaction and critique/assess their students' performance. Furthermore, teachers who don't come from the students' language backgrounds may wonder how they can assess the performance in languages they don't share or understand. However, a dialogical teaching approach can help to resolve these dilemmas. By helping students critically reflect on their choices through peer critique and intensive teacher feedback, teachers can help multilingual students develop a better self-awareness and understanding of their language potential. This way, teachers can help students develop translingual practice according to their chosen trajectory rather than impose lines of development that are foreign to them. Teachers can also become learners and understand students' communicative strategies. They don't have to adopt the posture of authorities who have to tell students how to communicate. Though my questions to students in the feedback provided a space to bring in authoritative information and scholarship on the expectations of writing, it wasn't so intrusive and invasive as to stifle their choices. My feedback was one among many that they received for consideration. It was also framed as curious questions for answers which I was genuinely seeking about their strategies and choices.

Should we teach the four strategies I highlighted in my analyses of contact zone communication in the previous chapters? We must remember that these strategies of communication have been framed at an etic and macro level. The precise way in which they find realization in specific situations will be different in relation to different communicative objectives and interlocutors. Furthermore, teaching these strategies explicitly and formulaically for deductive application is distorting. These strategies are situated and practice-based. They cannot be implemented in a product-oriented and a priori manner. However, it is certainly useful to create an awareness of these strategies among students. It can be done best after the fact, by explicating the strategies students are themselves using in classroom negotiations. Students should also note that these strategies can be further developed through classroom practice and through a more reflective and critical awareness.

Does valuing the resources which translinguals bring with them mean that their choices are always correct or perfect? In some circles, these intuitive choices have been valorized and affirmed to such an extent that it has begun to appear that multilingual students cannot err and that there is nothing further to be taught (see Lin and Martin, 2005; and Heller and Martin-Jones, 2001). However, as pointed out earlier, it is in the nature of translingual competence to fuse language use and learning. Translinguals are always ready to learn the new patterns, conventions, and norms of their interlocutors even as they engage in communication. From this perspective, learning never stops for them. Performative competence is based on dispositions such as humility toward communicative challenges, tolerance toward the norms and expectations of others, and a self-critical attitude toward one's own biases and limitations. Such dispositions are conducive to critical learning and language awareness. My position is that though students come with intuitive and socially developed competence for translingual practice, they can develop their competence in reflective and critical ways through pedagogical scaffolding.

In order to teach, one should be able to distinguish ineffective choices and identify areas for improvement. However, distinguishing errors from creative translingual practices can be difficult. Whose and which norms do we use to define error? From my experience with students, it became clear that they themselves make a distinction between appropriate and inappropriate choices. For example, there might be textual inconsistencies which suggest that students are not always in control of their choices. In one case of possible misspelling, I asked Buthainah: "You misspell verses as versus. Since you have been very careful with your choice of Arabic and other stylistic devices in this essay, I was wondering how you would explain these spelling mistakes. Did you think these issues were less important? Did you think the readers will easily understand your meaning and therefore you don't have to worry too much about editing problems?" Buthainah answered: "I am quite embarrassed about this *error* (and another *mistake* below). I had multiple drafts of this essay, but did not notice this *error*" (SR; emphasis added).

Buthainah didn't elaborate on the distinction between error, mistake, and code-meshing. However, intentionality seems to make a difference in some cases. In the instance above, Buthainah didn't use these spellings consciously. They are therefore *mistakes*. Features that have been systematically and consciously used by the author, but fail to gain uptake for several reasons, I treat as *errors*. In linguistic terms, some interlocutors may have problems negotiating the meaning of certain grammatical or vocabulary choices. In others, their effectiveness may be limited or insignificant. This mode of defining an error is practice-based, not norms-oriented. There is also a sociality to this notion of error. Uptake is important for a potential error to become a new indexical. If a usage failed to gain uptake, both parties have to ask what could be done differently. Writers/speakers have to ask how they could facilitate more effective uptake. Readers/listeners have to ask how they could negotiate better for meaning. Of course, what is an error in one context may not be so in another; for a different set of interlocutors, it could be a new indexical. In this sense, there is also a relativity to error. More importantly, error is also rhetorical, as some deviations are performative. We have to therefore take into consideration the context, interlocutors, modality, and objectives in deciding the appropriateness of linguistic and textual choices. The point here is that deviations from dominant norms that gain uptake in a situated interaction may be a new indexical, and not errors or mistakes.

Though some of Buthainah's choices fail to gain wide uptake (consider, for example, the cases of mixed metaphors and unconventional idioms which some readers had problems with), what is important is that the feedback which her peers and I gave may have helped Buthainah consider her choices from diverse perspectives. Our questions about her choices might have helped her develop a reflexive awareness of her choices and consider other alternatives in her successive drafts. There is a key here to the development of a pedagogy for translingual practice. If teachers and students are prepared to negotiate texts and language according to the expanded and more interactional pedagogy enacted in my courses, a lot of learning will take place. Students will learn to engage imaginatively and collaboratively in meaning-making; they will judge as errors not those which deviate from NES norms, but those that fail to gain collective uptake; they will assess the effectiveness of the text based on the way it marshals other contextual resources and communicative modalities for the construction of meaning. Teaching and assessment in this regard is a case of negotiation—that is, learning to find the right balance between writers' voices and readers' uptakes, between authorial intentions and readers' backgrounds, between author's design and space for readers to roam—all leading to the appropriate sense of coherence, meaning, and rhetorical effectiveness.

From this perspective, the negotiations we see around the texts and talk in classrooms are already pedagogical as they help interlocutors assess uptake, learn each other's backgrounds and assumptions, recalibrate their own strategies, and experiment with more effective choices. Features such as peer review, serial drafting, and teacher feedback facilitated a lot of negotiations among us. There was constant negotiation of texts (both student drafts and readings from publications) as we exercised our willingness and capacity to co-construct meaning and learn from each other. Such a dialogical pedagogy will help both readers and writers develop a more reflective and critical awareness of their negotiation strategies and practices, and facilitate their own paths of rhetorical development.

Such a pedagogy can enhance the cooperative disposition students bring with them to develop performative competence. Many scholars interested in developing translingual practices among students work primarily at the level of strengthening these dispositions (see Gutiérrez, 2008; Hornberger, 2003). This makes sense. If students develop the appropriate dispositions for performative competence, they will learn in whatever context they encounter, even outside the classroom. Such dispositions keep alive lifelong and lifewide learning. In a sense, cooperative dispositions are the most rewarding portable resource in contact zones and globalization. As students encounter unpredictable interlocutors and atypical codes, they will apply their dispositions to develop performative competence and co-construct meaning. Portable resources for migration and globalization are not the elite and prestigious codes that can jump scales, as Blommaert (2010) theorizes, but appropriate dispositions and strategies for translingual negotiation.

Toward translingual awareness

A translingual orientation doesn't mean that there is a valorized end-product for either conversation or writing. There will be diverse outcomes based on the contexts and backgrounds of the students. The translingual orientation will approximate "standard language" in some occasions and vernacular in others, both mediated by the diverse other language repertoires which students bring with them. Translingual practice can approximate conventional uses in some (as in Smitherman's writing) and resist them in others (as in Buthainah's). As I have been demonstrating in the earlier chapters, it can be realized by both NES and multilingual students alike. While codemeshing often characterizes the end-product of many multilinguals, translingual practice can lead to products approximating SWE also. What is more important in every case is a reflective *awareness* of the potential of language resources and the negotiation of meanings, transcending the limiting monolingual and normative ideologies of society or classroom.

I will conclude my pedagogical reflections with an example of how translingual awareness is cultivated despite the different textual outcomes for different students. I reinterpret an event in the class of a colleague, Min-zhan Lu (1994). Lu's student, a Chinese undergraduate from Malaysia, used an unconventional verb construction in her English essay: "can able to." What was puzzling was that the related modals "can" and "may" were used with their conventional meaning. It appeared therefore that the student was using the new construction with a meaning not conveyed by the other available modals. The following are some examples of the student's usage (note the highlighted modals):

> "As a Hawaiian native historian, Trask *can able to* argue for her people;"
>
> "Most of the new universities' students are facing new challenges like staying away from family, peer pressure, culture shock, heavy college work, etc. I *can* say that these are the 'obstacles' to success. If a student *can able to* approach each situation with different perspectives than the one he brought from high school, I *may* conclude that this student has climbed his first step to become a 'critical thinker.'"

Lu's response was motivated by the distinction I made earlier between errors and mistakes. The consistency with which the unusual modal was used suggested to her that the author had a systematic meaning behind that usage and perhaps intended some rhetorical effects. It was not a mistake. As Lu spoke to her student in her office, she realized the intention behind this unconventional usage. In the student's first language, "can" and "be able to" have interchangeable meanings. However, the student showed with the help of her *Random House Dictionary* that "can" has an additional meaning of "have permission to" that is not connoted by "be able to" in English. Therefore, she had constructed "can able to," she argued, to connote "ability from the perspective of the external circumstances" (Lu, 1994, p. 452). This construction was an alternative to the individual transcendence and personal power connoted by "be able to." It was also an alternative to the fatalism and deference to authority connoted by "may." It emerged that the student sought an alternative to the American "can do" attitude of individual agency. She also wanted an alternative to the fatalism of her native community. She had personally overcome the barriers set by her family and community to migrate to the USA for education. It is this positionality of resisting external constraints to develop an earned agency that she wanted to convey through her neologism. She saw this orientation to power in the native American historian Trask and the first-year college students she was writing about. Therefore, she was struggling to find a different modal unavailable in the language to express her specific meaning. We might say that the student was seeking a new indexical for an unusual meaning.

However, intentions and desires are not enough for translingual practice. The author has to achieve uptake through creative strategies that negotiate the dominant norms. In developing a translingual awareness, Lu went beyond celebrating any atypical usage as creative. She planned to engage all her students with the unusual modal to generate a critical language awareness in the writer as well as in the readers. Lu presented to her students the dilemma experienced by the writer to examine their uptake. There was a diversity of responses, which suggested the development of a critical language awareness. Many multilingual students didn't see "can" and "be able to" as interchangeable in meaning, similar to the writer. However, they explored other ways in which the writer's desired meaning can be captured and facilitate more successful uptake. Some suggested "may be able to." Others suggested adding an "if" clause to "be able to." In offering such options, they considered how the meaning of the writer can be indexed by more widely shared and already existing grammatical forms. A few mavericks suggested using "can able to" with a parenthetical explanation (or with a footnote) to explain the need for such usage. In discussing these options, students not only developed sensitivity to the ideological implications of grammatical choices, they also developed a richer stock of vocabulary and strategies.

In the end, the choices adopted by the students varied according to their expressive needs and social positioning. In her final product, the writer chose to adopt "may be able to." She was interested in working within SWE norms, even as she expressed her agency. A Vietnamese student, on the other hand, opted to use "can" and "be able to" interchangeably because their connotations of agency inspired modes of resistance and individual empowerment that were a corrective to the fatalism of his own community. It is important to note here that the choices of *both* these students are part of translingual practice. Their options emerge from negotiating the choices that they have in relation to diverse codes, contexts, ideologies, and rhetorical considerations. The fact that the writer eventually decided to use a conventional structure ("may be able to") was not a cop out in deference to power and exigency. This choice was borne out of critical reflection. There is a new resonance to the "standard English" item in the context of her social positioning and writing process. Similarly, the Vietnamese student's choice of treating "can" and "be able to" interchangeably should be given complexity. Though it affirms dominant usage, what is more important is the language awareness generated and the translingual practice accompanying the choice. In opting for this structure, the student considered the social position of his community, the ideological implications, and his rhetorical objectives in relation to the diverse language choices available for him.

The example also shows how "sameness" can have "difference" (Pennycook, 2010, pp. 34–51). Even "standard language" can be used with critical thinking for empowering purposes. The students' examples show that grammar items don't have rigid ideological meanings attached to them. They gain new meaning in relation to the social positioning and rhetorical purposes of the users. Though the Malaysian and Vietnamese students opted eventually for modals that are fairly normative, these forms gain new indexicality. They gain slightly different meanings and values, given the background of the writers and the process of their choice in this class. Though the Anglo-American students in the class expressed that they treated "can" and "be able to" as interchangeable in meaning, the Vietnamese student's similar option has a different resonance. It indexes his empowering and resistant meanings in the context of his background and writing. Therefore, the mere appearance of SWE norms in a textual product shouldn't mean a lack of voice or criticality.

Interestingly, though the student writers chose safer options, the unusual modal ("can able to") gained new indexicality. Lu goes on to say that after the class discussion, the modal "became a newly coined phrase we shared throughout the term" (Lu, 1994, p. 454). The students referred to "can able to" as an inside joke at opportune moments. It achieved a shared meaning and became a new indexical. Through the class discussion and repeated reference, its indexicality became sedimented. This eventuality reveals the slow process of language and discursive change. What is considered a non-standard item or erroneous use becomes "standardized" when it serves social purposes for language users. Though the Anglo-American students in the class didn't see any problems in using "can" and "be able to" as being interchangeable in meaning, it is possible to imagine that they too ended up with a reflexive translingual awareness through the process of this writing practice and classroom negotiations. If they did share in using the new indexical with their multilingual peers, the NES probably gained some insights into the ideological implications behind normative grammatical items in different rhetorical and textual contexts. They also sharpened their negotiation strategies as they struggled for uptake in relation to the different choices of the multilingual students.

This example shows that translingual practice doesn't necessarily lead to breaking grammar rules all the time. Developing a critical awareness of how norms are constituted, negotiating the norms to find what suits one's purposes, and engaging creatively to use language in relation to one's context are more important. It is in this sense that translingual practice is relevant for "monolingual"/NES students as well. Though codemeshing is the way in which voices and identities will be represented effectively for some students, for others a critical use of language will imbue normative grammatical and idiomatic structures with new meanings and values. In this way, the demographic group that has been left out of consideration in ELF research (i.e., NES) makes its own contributions to semiodiversity, if not glossodiversity. As they negotiate meanings with multilinguals, NES will engage in language contact and change, developing translingual competence.

Conclusion

Pedagogy can be refashioned to accommodate the modes of performative competence and cooperative disposition we see outside the classroom. Rather than focusing on a single language or dialect as the target of learning, teachers have to develop a readiness in students to engage with the repertoires required for transnational contact zones. While joining a new speech community was the objective of traditional pedagogy, now teachers have to train students to shuttle between communities by negotiating mobile semiotic resources in contact zones. To this end, they have to focus more on negotiation strategies, rather than on form. Or rather they should treat form as negotiable. Students would develop language awareness to cope with the new indexicalities and emergent grammars of contact situations, rather than focusing only on mastering the preconstructed grammars of a single variety. In the context of plural forms and conventions, it is important for students to be sensitive to the relativity of norms. Therefore, by going beyond the pedagogies for constructing prefabricated meanings through words, students will consider *shaping* meaning in actual interactions and even *reconstructing* the rules and conventions to represent their interests, values, and identities. In short, it is not what we know as much as the versatility with which we can do new things with words that defines proficiency in the global contact zones.

10
TOWARD A DIALOGICAL COSMOPOLITANISM

> In the beginning is the deed: practices and not principles are what enable us to live together in peace. Conversations across boundaries of identity ... begin with the sort of imaginative engagement you get when you read a novel or watch a movie or attend to a work of art that speaks from some place other than your own ... Conversation doesn't have to lead to consensus about anything, especially not values; it's enough that it helps people get used to one another.
>
> *(Appiah, 2007, p. 85)*

The constructs developed in the preceding pages—that is, translingual communicative practice, performative competence, and cooperative disposition—facilitate modes of global citizenship that have always been important for all of us. In this chapter, I adopt a broad lens to view the communicative interactions discussed in the previous chapters to consider their implications for effective forms of cosmopolitanism debated by scholars in diverse disciplines. I explicate the principles and orientations behind the model developed in this book to resolve some of the pressing questions in cosmopolitanism.

The new forms of communication, technology, and travel suppress space/time differences and intensify inter-community contact, impressing upon us the fact that our fates are intertwined. International economy, politics, and industrial production require a remarkable level of collaboration between diverse and distant communities today. The very local has become open to translocal influences. One doesn't have to travel to experience cosmopolitanism. We experience it in our neighborhoods, in forms of super-diversity constructed by people of different language and cultural backgrounds. These developments make our lives intensely interconnected and motivate us to search for meaningful forms of co-existence. However, we mustn't think of this cosmopolitan outlook and relationships as a new feature of late modernity. After all, the wandering philosopher Diogenes declared his identity as *kosmopolites* in the fifth century BC. We will therefore discuss below how effective forms of cosmopolitanism have existed in other times and places, such as the precolonial South Asia (see Pollock, 2006).

Yet, it is possible to understand why the search for cosmopolitan models has gained new vigor in academic and policy circles today. After framing academic discourses and socio-political models under narrowly bounded notions of community, influenced by the Herderian triad, there is now a need to discover new models that frame relationships in more inclusive and plural terms. There is a search on for new models of flexible citizenship, international law, regional economy, trasnational production networks, and urban planning to facilitate co-existence (see Vertovec and Robins, 2003). While these macro-level models are being constructed in some fields, scholars in the humanities and social sciences are searching for the ethics, interaction styles, and dispositions that would enable cosmopolitan relationships. It is to this inquiry that this book contributes.

Though linguistics has not actively engaged with cosmopolitan models, it has a lot to offer. As we see from the epigraph of philosopher Anthony Appiah above, conversation is a common analogy for cosmopolitan relationships. However, conversation is not just a useful metaphor—for language scholars, it is a practice. The findings on effective conversational strategies for negotiating difference can provide insights into the achievement of cosmopolitan relationships in everyday life. Other scholars in cultural studies have also recently called for the micro-social orientation of linguistics to throw more light into a relationship that is becoming romanticized. Adopting the term creolization (as a less elitist term for cosmopolitanism and drawing attention to the subaltern modes of multilingual contact that counter the jet-setting and globe-trotting cosmopolitanism of the super-rich), Dominique Chance (2011) warns of the danger that terms like cosmopolitanism may become essences, thereby losing their critical edge. Adopting the theorization of Glissant (1997), she proposes that we treat cosmopolitanism as a verb rather than a noun, or a process rather than a state. She argues that linguists might be able to unveil the strategies and practices that enable these relationships. She goes to the extent of suggesting that the micro-level orientation of linguistics can demystify the processes and practices that have been ignored in cosmopolitan discourses: "To be sure, linguists destroy certain fantasies that utopians take pleasure in cultivating. ... If the whole world is on its way to creolization, then it is all the more useful to understand with precision the processes and the conditions that underwrite such a movement" (p. 267).

The translingual practice we see in this book, in classrooms and work places, in conversation and literacy events, reveals the strategies informing everyday forms of cosmopolitanism that are being practiced as a verb and not a noun. Rather than theorizing cosmopolitan relationships deductively or from the abstract, it is better to derive our models from the practices which have been evolving for generations in many multilingual communities and contact zones.

Models of cosmopolitanism

Hollinger (2002) usefully summarizes the competing orientations to cosmopolitanism into two broad models: universalism and pluralism. Universalism searches for common values that connect diverse people into cosmopolitan relationships. The assumption is that these shared values will motivate people to engage in harmonious inter-community relations and enjoy human solidarity. However, as Appiah's (2007) book-length exploration suggests, finding common values is not easy. Cultures are different, and presumed similarities may have shades of difference that defy generalization. Furthermore, communities often accentuate their difference in inter-group relations for purposes of identity. Any effort to look for commonalties should take account of such performative acts of members who might distance themselves from others for strategic reasons. A claim of shared values can also have coercive effects. What history shows is that certain dominant communities have imposed their own values on others in the name of shared values. It is unwise to rely on commonalities or shared values to bring people together. More importantly, difference matters, and people are not prepared to sacrifice their difference for inter-group solidarity. In a perceptively titled book, *Jihad vs. McWorld*, Ben Barber (1995) shows how the increasing homogeneity of globalization (McWorld) also encourages people to separate themselves from others to preserve their identity, autonomy, and integrity (Jihad).

Pluralism acknowledges the difference between cultures and identities while finding modes of social cohesion to accommodate the difference. In such models, people maintain their difference and occupy their own niches while coming together for collective life and shared goals. The separate ethnic enclaves we see in big metropolises might be an analogy for this sense of pluralist cosmopolitanism. The glue that holds these separate collectivities together needs consideration. At best, these are pragmatic arrangements designed to manage difference for the sake of social harmony. But these forms of collective life are superficial in quality and realization. The separate communities aren't provided spaces or motivation to engage with each other, develop a reflexive and critical awareness of their mutual differences, and further develop their social values and cultural resources. In fact, the types of super-diversity we see in many urban spaces show a mixing and meshing of people and values that defy the compartmentalization of pluralist approaches.

There are certain common tendencies in both approaches. Power differences between groups are ignored, as both pluralism and universalism project a romanticized state of togetherness, either in the name of shared universals or unity-in-diversity. Another common orientation behind both approaches is the grounding of cosmopolitanism in terms of essences, that is, values that are common or different to communities. They identify communities in terms of values and treat cosmopolitanism as a state of being. In this sense, these orientations are product-oriented and somewhat static.

The practice-oriented approach of translingual communication in this book offers some advantages to help resolve the dilemmas of the above models. Since values are shifting, fluid, and conflicting, the translingual orientation doesn't rely on values—whether shared, common, or neutral—to achieve cosmopolitan relationships. Cosmopolitanism is treated as a process, achieved and co-constructed through mutually responsive practices. Practices help negotiate the shifting, fluid, and hybrid values in changing situations and interlocutors to achieve community. In this sense, practices help side-step the search for shared values. It is perhaps for this reason that Appiah (2007) eventually opts for "practices and not principles" (p. 85) to base his conversations across boundaries of difference. In particular, Appiah holds up the strategy of "engagement" that enables people to align diverse and competing resources for meaning and collaboration. This is analogous to the practice of alignment developed in this book. It is remarkable that Appiah is prepared to see these forms of alignment leading to collaboration without "consensus about anything." This is a radically practiced-based orientation.

I interpret the performative competence and cooperative disposition of translinguals presented in the last chapter to show the implications for what I consider to be a practice-based *dialogical cosmopolitanism*. Note that translinguals always start from their positionality. In this sense, their voice and difference matters in this form of cosmopolitan relation. There is no neutral standpoint available for cosmopolitan relationships. There is no need to abandon one's difference for the sake of harmonious cosmopolitan relationships. Cosmopolitanism is vibrant when one's difference and voice are affirmed. This model thus enables a rooted cosmopolitanism, one based on a firm grounding on one's location, biography, and interests.

However, translinguals bring a disposition that is open to the difference of others and collaborates in achieving solidarity around mutual objectives. What enables translinguals to hold their values, be open to others' difference, and yet achieve community is their negotiation strategies. The practice that holds these strategies together is alignment. One can align the different values and identities of the participants around objects, people, and ecological factors to achieve meanings and goals. In this sense, it is not uniformity of values that achieves community, but the ability to align disparate values and features for common goals. This openness of the cooperative disposition distinguishes dialogical cosmopolitanism from past forms of *imperial cosmopolitanism* that imposed one's values on others for community building. This doesn't mean that dialogical cosmopolitanism ignores the reality of power. It treats power as open to negotiation and realignment.

In adopting this practice, translinguals are open to negotiated and hybrid outcomes. In this manner, they keep themselves open to change. Performative competence, then, doesn't focus on maintaining and preserving difference. It is engaged and progressive. The ability of the interlocutors to closely engage with each other's difference generates a reflexive self- and other-awareness. The participants develop the ability to perceive their own values and interests from the other's point of view. This kind of engagement provides avenues for change as participants develop hybrid new values and positions based on such dialogical interactions. More importantly, such interactions provide possibilities for co-constructed values that align people in situated interactions and objectives. They also provide possibilities of strategic community-building, as people come together for focused interests, with the freedom to align with multiple communities.

It should be now clear why I label this model *dialogical cosmopolitanism*. This form of cosmopolitanism is interactive and negotiated. It is not given, but is achieved in situated interactions. It is based on mutual collaboration, with an acceptance of everyone's difference. It enables self-awareness and self-criticism, as communities don't just maintain their difference and identity but further develop their cooperative dispositions and values.

Before we conclude this theorization of dialogical cosmopolitanism, it is important to address a thorny issue. Are practices free of values? More importantly, are practices by themselves adequate to ensure cosmopolitan relationships without the motivation of any ethical or moral values? I consider everything as value-ridden. The values informing dialogical cosmopolitanism are motivated by the cooperative dispositions I described in Chapter 9. They constitute the modes of language awareness and social orientation that favor translingual practice. I prefer to call them dispositions rather than cultural values for a reason. They function at a meta-cultural and meta-community level. That is, while communities have their particular values emerging from the sedimentation of their local and in-group practices through a shared history (and the identities celebrated through these values are to be respected), the values motivating dialogical cosmopolitanism emerge at and for the contact zones. The term disposition favors the practice-based orientation to embedded and embodied cognition, developed by scholars like Tomasello (2008). If we amplify the orientation of such social cognition theorists, we might say that we are "wired" for dialogical cosmopolitanism. We cannot function other than by seeking alignment with others, and between disparate values, communities, objects, and semiotic resources. If this is a claim of universality for dialogical cosmopolitanism and translingual practice, it is paradoxically practice-based, social, ecological, and situated.

I must emphasize that dialogical cosmopolitanism is not new. As I made clear in Chapter 9, the procedural knowledge of performative competence is motivated by my understanding of modes of social and language interaction in precolonial South Asia and other multilingual communities. Pollock's (2006) treatment of the dialogical relationship between the Sanskrit universal and vernacular particularism in the region in South Asia approximates the model I have outlined above. Pollock argues that although this kind of cosmopolitanism was not theorized into explicit discourses, the practices of South Asians provide a model for present day cosmopolitanism. Pollock concludes:

> To know that some people in the past could be universal and particular in their practices of culture and power without making their particularity ineluctable or their universalism compulsory is to know that better cosmopolitan and vernacular practices are at least conceivable, and perhaps even—in a way those people themselves never have fully achieved—eventually reconcilable.
>
> *(p. 580)*

It is important to recover such forms of world citizenship in other times and places, especially in subaltern communities, as they feature a form of vernacular cosmopolitanism that constitutes local traditions which provide alternatives to elite versions of cosmopolitanism predicated on international travel, flexible citizenship, and mobile capital in late modernity.

It is important to remind ourselves that what Pollock presents of precolonial South Asia is still practiced in social relationships, as it emerges in the publications of regional linguists reviewed earlier. My data in the previous chapters bring out the strategies informing such cosmopolitan relationships in media scapes, classrooms, and work places today. Dialogical cosmopolitanism is therefore not an abstract theoretical construction. It is developed from forms of lingua franca encounters and contact zone interactions taking place both in the East and in the West. The model thus gives dignity to the everyday forms of cosmopolitanism practiced by ordinary people.

Recovering community and identity

As we move away from perceiving language, community, and place as bounded and isomorphic along Herderian discourses and orientate to cosmopolitan relationships, we have to redefine notions of community and identity. Some interpretations of the fluidity of postmodern community and social identity have been exaggerated and romanticized, generating opposition from minority communities and critical scholars who bring a keen sense of power, heritage, and rights. I will consider ways of developing more balanced forms of community and identity that resolve the competing discourses of global citizenship and local integrity.

Post-Herderian discourses don't do away with "communities." They theorize people's ability to align with multiple communities, treating them as mobile, constructed, hybrid, and heterogeneously constituted. Such are the diverse lifestyle, diaspora, and virtual communities formed in the age of migration, social media, and transnational connectedness today. These communities are not based on the rigid identification criteria of traditional markers such as language, ethnicity, or place. People come together, united by tentative interests or goals, from diverse backgrounds and places. Papastergiadis (2000) is open to the possibility that what he calls "clusters" can be formed around "inessential features" (p. 210), not treating essences such as language, ethnicity, or place as the main criteria. Scholars are now borrowing metaphors from chaos theory (see Appadurai, 1996) and aesthetics (Papastergiadis, 2000) to define communities in a more open manner, where there could be stability despite fluidity, harmony despite difference, and structure despite flux.

I have offered a practice-based explanation for the possibility of such communities. Shared values or languages are not required for such communities of practice to work. Members are able to adopt diverse negotiation strategies and alignment practices to find coherence, meaning, and functionality beyond their heterogeneous codes and values. It is from such perspectives that we can understand the very functional collectivities we see in the chapters above. Skilled African migrants can achieve community with local inhabitants (NES) and other migrants in their places of work in the West, despite the still-evolving repertoires they bring with them. Native English students and international students can do problem solving or interpret texts, achieving shared outcomes and meanings, despite the different levels of proficiency in their languages.

Such a perspective also has important implications for identity. We are able to enjoy identities that transcend our native language, ethnicity, or place of birth. We recognize identities as constructed and performed. They are situational and strategic.

From our layered subjectivities, we display relevant identities to both form alliances and resist dominant discourses for voice. Languages don't determine or limit our identities, but provide creative resources to construct new and revised identities through reconstructed forms and meaning of new indexicalities. It is from this perspective that we are able to understand how skilled migrants and international students are able to achieve voice and agency in even the high-stakes contexts of work and education with disprivileged varieties of English or vernaculars.

Despite the value of such redefined communities and identities, there are also exaggerations that need to be checked in the current discourses. To begin with, such processes of community and identity formation are treated as if they are free and uninhibited in some circles. They are considered "ludic" (Maher, 2010, p. 584; Pennycook, 2010, p. 133; Rampton, 1999b, p. 499), giving the impression of a playfulness that lacks serious purposes or objectives. Maher's definition of "metroethnicities" takes to an extreme the playful, ironic, and parodic forms of community and identity: "Ethnicity can be a toy. Something you play with" (2010, p. 584). It is important to emphasize that power and dominant ideologies restrict possibilities of community and identity in diverse social contexts. Any effort toward voice and resistant identities has to strategically negotiate power structures and discourses. So, in my analysis above, Smitherman recognizes the power of SWE in academic communication as she adopts qualified uses of AAVE in well-defined recontextualized spaces in the text. Buthainah understands the power of autonomous literacy as she adopts creative entextualization and interactional strategies to prepare, invite, and coax her readers to negotiate her codemeshed writing. The African skilled migrants understand the power of NES norms in translocal spaces of work as they invoke alternate language ideologies and dispositions for a more egalitarian footing. Though they acknowledge the authority of the employers to define them as unproficient, send them to remediation classes, and offer lower salary or designation, they keep alive a critical awareness ready to be realized in interactions they recontextualize in their favor. Their agency doesn't disregard power.

A second problem with notions such as metroethnicities is that they are framed in opposition to traditional and autochthonous communities and identities. Maher argues: "Metroethnicity rejects the logocentric metanarrative of traditional ethnicity. It sidesteps the bruised-n-battered ethnic bollard around which an ethnic group assembles in order to construct an internally validated description of itself. It is no longer the rhetoric of contrast—here is majority society and there is minority society" (2010, p. 584). Such an argument exacerbates the suspicions diverse indigenous communities and scholars of language rights have with postmodern discourses. They see these discourses not as empowering but as compromising. Statements that languages cannot be owned, communities cannot be identified by claims to traditional land, or that identities cannot be tied to specific values can be perceived as a threat to the struggle many communities have been waging for language rights, heritage language preservation, and sovereignty in their traditional lands. An example of a counter-discourse to translingual practices is that of Scott Lyons, a Native American scholar. He argues against codemeshing in American literacy classrooms as he sees them leading to reduced proficiency in heritage languages, dilution of traditional cultural practices, and weakening of the integrity of native languages. He therefore argues for models of diglossia and bilingualism for Native American students: "Codemeshing is hybridity and violates the elders' rule of mutually assured separatism" (Lyons, 2009, p. 102). In other words, he favors codeswitching rather than codemeshing, in terms of the debate articulated in Chapter 6.

The challenge for many critical minority scholars, however, is that they also sympathize with notions of language contact, mediation, and hybridity. Lyons, for example, accepts that native languages have already appropriated many language resources from English, French, and other colonial languages, that Native Americans today have hybrid identities and cultural practices, and that language/cultural contact is necessary and good for the community. His recommendation for language separation in school contexts, therefore, appears theoretically unintegrated with his postmodern position on the creolization of native cultures. Is there a way to acknowledge cosmopolitan relations and yet make a space for language rights, heritage languages, and community sovereignty? The theoretical position informing translingual practices and dialogical cosmopolitanism in this book has elements that can make such a space for the importance of community solidarity and rights.

My position is that if it is ideologies that give identity to semiotic resources, as they get labeled as specific languages or representing specific ethnicities, it is left to the agency of the community on how it defines its heritage language and ethnicity. Heritage languages and identities are also ideological constructs. From this perspective, ideologies are not always evil or limiting; they are also enabling. One can marshal a diverse collection of semiotic resources and "perform" one's identity and community through strategic practices. These personal and community identities can become sedimented through historical processes. I use the term *strategic constructivism* to capture this activity of constructing languages and identities that favor one's interests and purposes. It is modeled after Spivak's (1993) notion of strategic essentialism. Spivak's term connotes how subaltern communities may adopt essentialized positions of community or place for purposes of struggle. I adopt strategic constructivism to draw attention to the constructed nature of this identity, and the processes involved in such construction, when Spivak's term focuses on the product. Furthermore, beyond subaltern communities, I consider the term useful for diaspora and lifestyle communities in late modernity.

Consider how strategic constuctivism helps my own diasporic community of Sri Lankan Tamils celebrate their ethnic identity and heritage language while engaging in cosmopolitan relationships. After leaving their traditional homeland in Sri Lanka, the community finds that the younger generation is fast losing its proficiency in the Tamil language. This has created concerns about the future of Tamil identity and language in diaspora locations among some community elders. However, what I find the younger generation and community members doing *in practice* is that they have redefined Tamil ethnic identity and heritage language for diaspora contexts (see Canagarajah, 2013). Though they cannot claim the same type of Tamil language proficiency or language ideologies as practiced in traditional homelands, and they have developed proficiency in new languages and cultures in diaspora settings, they claim that their ethnic identity and heritage language are vibrant.

How is this possible? In diaspora contexts, the community has redefined what it means by heritage language proficiency and identity. People adopt many different semiotic resources and practices to perform situated in-group identities (as I illustrated in the example discussed in the opening chapter). The Tamil words they mesh in their English matrix syntax, the receptive proficiency they have for understanding the Tamil of their elders, the words they have appropriated into Tamil from diverse languages, and the multimodal resources they adopt in in-group conversations in Tamil to both understand and communicate (through gestures, situational cues, and objects), all index Tamil identity and heritage language for them. In other words, for most people in the diaspora, such communicative practices have combined through sedimentation, a constructivist language ideology, and continued shared practices to index Tamil identity and language proficiency. We might say that the community has "colonized" other language resources and cultural values for the reconstruction of Tamilness. This is strategic constructivism.

Scholars are now open to the possibility of heritage being a construct, though this notion sounds like an oxymoron. Agnes He (2010) writes: "HL [heritage language] is not static but dynamic; it is constantly undergoing transformation by its learners and users, so that at the same time it serves as a resource for the transformation of learner identities, it is also transformed itself as result of learners' and users' language ideologies and practices" (p. 77). Diaspora Tamils, for example, know that what they consider to be their heritage language is already a construct even before migration. "Tamil" language accommodates many resources from Sanskrit and later colonization by English, Dutch, and Portuguese, that even purists in Sri Lanka sometimes treat them as part of Tamil language. Members of the diaspora are open to continuing this reconstruction of heritage language and culture, and including other semiotic resources into their formation. In this manner, they are able to engage with other communities and their semiotic resources, borrow from them, develop their own linguistic and cultural resources, and yet maintain their heritage language and ethnic identity. Through such strategic constructivism, it is possible to affirm the right of communities to celebrate their heritage without becoming isolated, purist, or ossified. They are able to perform in-group Tamil identities and represent traditional identities for strategic purposes, while having the freedom and resources to adopt other identities. They are also able to maintain a vibrant ethnic community life, while enjoying the ability to join diverse situated communities of practice and broader cosmopolitan relationships.

Conclusion

While this book opens up more complex ways of looking at communication, identity, and community from the perspective of translingual practices, we have to be mindful of the monolingual ideologies and modernist discourses identified in the first two chapters. These ideologies are powerful, and have the possibility of being reproduced in social relationships, educational settings, and language interactions. In this sense, my reliance on dispositions for developing the performative competence for translingual communication needs to be qualified. It is possible for dominant ideologies to resocialize people into monolingual practices and colonizing relationships. For this reason, critical intervention by informed scholars and committed teachers is always necessary. While research that articulates the strategies and practices which translinguals adopt to negotiate cosmopolitan relationships and new indexicalities is important, we need constructive pedagogies for classroom purposes. Teachers are in the front lines of the ideological battle to construct effective forms of global citizenship and cooperative dispositions. I hope that this book has expanded our perspectives on both research and pedagogy. My aim has been to provide new research insights into the ways in which mobile semiotic resources are negotiated for meaning in global contact zones, and also to suggest pedagogical approaches to develop such cooperative dispositions and performative competence for cosmopolitan relationships.

NOTES

1 Introduction

1 The following special transcription conventions are used in the data cited in this book:

(.) significant pauses
[ ] explanations by the transcriber
= latched utterances
xxx indecipherable
@@ laughter
Italics: author's translation
Bold: items meshed into another matrix code

3 Recovering Translingual Practices

1 In transcriptions of Tamil, I use upper case to distinguish retroflex sounds from dental alveolars (in lower case). Thus I distinguish between T/t, N/n, R/r, and L/l.

5 Translingual Negotiation Strategies

1 I thank Paul Roberts for sharing the data and results of his corpus-analysis of form-based features.

6 Pluralizing Academic Writing

1 I recognize that Smitherman is using "code switching" broadly for a practice I consider to be codemeshing.

7 Negotiating Translingual Literacy

1 Some of the typographical idiosyncrasies in the transcripts are explained by the fact that the interviews were conducted through email.

8 Reconfiguring Translocal Spaces

1 This is a multi-sited qualitative study, funded by the Worldwide Universities Network. Interviews were carried out between February 2010 and February 2011 by a multi-disciplinary group of scholars from universities in different countries under my role as principal investigator. All face-to-face and telephone interviews were audio-recorded and transcribed. Each interview ran for around 45–90 minutes. A few interviews were conducted by email. I thank the following Co-PI's for their help in collecting data: Adrian Bailey, Leeds University, UK; Frances Giampapa, Bristol University, UK; Margaret Hawkins, University of Wisconsin, USA; Ellen Hurst, University of Cape Town, South Africa; Ahmar Mahboob, University of Sydney, Australia; Paul Roberts, York University, UK; and Sandra Silberstein, University of Washington, USA.

2 I identify the informants by their country of origin, gender, profession, and current/migrant location, in that order.

BIBLIOGRAPHY

Abrahams, R. D. (1985). *Afro-American folk tales: Stories from Black traditions in the New World*. New York: Pantheon.

Adsera, A. and Pytlikova, M. (2010). The role of language in shaping international migration: Evidence from OECD countries 1985–2006. www.cepr.org/meets/wkcn/2/2429/papers/Adserafinal.pdf. (Accessed 24 February 2011)

Agha, A. (2003). "The social life of cultural value." *Language & Communication*, 23, 231–73.

Ammon, U. (2007). "Global scientific communication: Open questions and policy suggestions." *AILA Review*, 20, 123–33.

Annamalai, E. (2001) *Managing multilingualism in India*. New Delhi: Sage.

Anzaldúa, G. (1987). *Borderlands, la frontera: The new mestiza*. San Francisco: Aunt Lute.

Appadurai, A. (1996). *Modernity at large: Cultural dimensions of globalization*. Minneapolis: University of Minnesota Press.

Appiah, K. A. (2007). *Cosmopolitanism: Ethics in a world of strangers*. New York: Norton.

Ashcroft, B. (2009). *Caliban's voice: The transformation of English in post-colonial literatures*. New York: Routledge.

Atkinson, D., Churchill, E., Nishino, T. and Okada, H. (2007). "Alignment and interaction in a sociocognitive approach in second language acquisition." *Modern Language Journal*, 91, 2, 169–88.

Atkinson, D. (ed.). (2011a). *Alternative approaches to second language acquisition*. Oxford: Routledge.

Atkinson, D. (2011b). "A sociocognitive approach to second language acquisition: How mind, body, and world work together in learning additional languages." In D. Atkinson (ed.), *Alternative approaches to second language acquisition*, Oxford: Routledge, pp. 143–66.

Auer, P. (1999). "From codeswitching via language mixing to fused lects: Toward a dynamic typology of bilingual speech." *International Journal of Bilingualism*, 3 (4), 309–32.

Baca, D. (2009). "Rethinking composition, five hundred years later." *Journal of Advanced Composition*, 29, 229–42.

Bailey, C.-J. and Maroldt, K. (1977). "The French lineage of English." In J. Meisel (ed.), *Langues en contact: Pidgins, creoles*. Tubingen: TBL-Verlag Narr, pp. 21–53.

Bakhtin, M. M. (1986). *Speech genres and other late essays*. Trans. V. W. McGee. Austin: University of Texas Press.

Barber, B. (1995). *Jihad vs McWorld*. New York: Times Books.

Barbour, S. (2002). "Language, nationalism and globalism: Educational consequences of changing patterns of language use." In P. Gubbins and M. Holt (eds), *Beyond boundaries: Language and identity in contemporary Europe*. Clevedon: Multilingual Matters, pp. 11–18.

Barthes, R. (1974). *S/Z*. Trans. Richard Miller. New York: Hill and Wang.

Baugh, J. (1983). *Black street speech*. Austin: University of Texas Press.

Bauman, R. and Briggs, C. L. (2000). "Language philosophy as language ideology: John Locke and Johann Gottfried Herder." In P. V. Kroskrity (ed.), *Regimes of language: Ideologies, polities, and identities*. Oxford: James Currey, pp. 139–204.

Bernstein, B. (1971). *Class, codes and control*, Vol. 1. London: Routledge & Kegan Paul.

Bhatia, T. K. and Ritchie, W. C. (2004). "Bilingualism in South Asia." In T. K. Bhatia and W. C. Ritchie (eds), *The handbook of bilingualism*. Oxford: Blackwell, pp. 780–807.

Biber, D. (2006). *University language: A corpus-based study of spoken and written registers*. Amsterdam: John Benjamins.

Bizzell, P. (2010). English Only? Composition Instruction in a Multilingual, Competitive Liberal Arts College. Paper presented in the Thomas R. Watson Conference, University of Louisville, 14 October 2010.

Bleakley, H. and Chin, A. (2004). "Language skills and earnings: Evidence from childhood immigrants." *Review of Economics and Statistics*, 86 (2), 481–96.

Block, D. (2010). "Speaking *romance-esque*." In D. Nunan and J. Choi (eds), *Language and culture: Reflective narratives and the emergence of identity*. New York and Oxford: Routledge, pp. 23–29.

Blommaert, J. (2010). *The sociolinguistics of globalization*. Cambridge: Cambridge University Press.

——(2008). *Grassroots literacy: Writing, identity and voice in Central Africa*. Oxford: Routledge.

——(2005). "Situating language rights: English and Swahili in Tanzania revisited." *Journal of Sociolinguistics*, 9 (3), 390–417.

Blommaert, J. and Verschueren, J. (1992). "The role of language in European nationalist ideologies." *Pragmatics*, 2 (3), 355–76.

Bolton, K. (2008). "English in Asia, Asian Englishes, and the issue of proficiency." *English Today* 24 (2), 3–12.

——(2003). *Chinese Englishes: A sociolinguistic history*. Cambridge: Cambridge University Press.

Bourdieu, P. (1977). *Outline of a theory of practice*. Cambridge: Cambridge University Press.

Bourdieu, P. and Passeron, J.-C. (1977). *Reproduction in education, society and culture*. London: Sage.

Braunmüller, K. (2006). "On the relevance of receptive multilingualism in a globalised world: Theory, history and evidence from today's Scandinavia." Paper read at the First Conference on Language Contact in Times of Globalization. University of Groningen. 28 September 2006.

Bright, W. (1984). *American Indian linguistics and literature*. The Hague: Mouton.

Brown, C. (1966). *Manchild in the promised land*. New York: Penguin.

Butler, J. (1990). *Gender trouble*. Oxford: Routledge.

Byram, M. (2008). *From intercultural education to education for intercultural citizenship*. Clevedon: Multilingual Matters.

Calvert, L.-J. (1998). *Language wars and linguistic politics*. Trans. M. Petheram. New York: Oxford University Press.

Canagarajah, A. S. (2013). "Reconstructing heritage language: Resolving dilemmas in language maintenance for Sri Lankan Tamil migrants." *International Journal of Sociology of Language*. (In Press)

——(2009). "The plurilingual tradition and the English language in South Asia." *AILA Review*, 22, 5–22.

——(2007). "Lingua franca English, multilingual communities, and language acquisition." *Modern Language Journal*, 91 (5), 921–37.

——(2006a). "The place of World Englishes in composition: Pluralization continued." *College Composition and Communication*, 57, 586–619.

——(2006b). "Toward a writing pedagogy of shuttling between languages: Learning from multilingual writers." *College English*, 68 (6), 589–604.

——(2002a). *A geopolitics of academic writing.* Pittsburgh: University of Pittsburgh Press.
——(2002b). *Critical academic writing and multilingual students.* Ann Arbor: University of Michigan Press.
——(2001). "The fortunate traveler: Shuttling between communities and literacies by economy class." In D. Belcher and U. Connor (eds), *Reflections on multiliterate lives.* Clevedon: Multilingual Matters, pp.23–37.
——(2000). "Negotiating ideologies through English: Strategies from the periphery." In T. Ricento (ed.), *Ideology, politics, and language policies: Focus on English* Amsterdam, Philadelphia: John Benjamins, pp. 107–20.
——(1997a). "Safe houses in the contact zone: Coping strategies of African American students in the academy." *College Composition and Communication*, 48 (2), 173–96.
——(1997b). "Challenges in English literacy for African-American and Lankan Tamil learners: Towards a pedagogical paradigm for bidialectal and bilingual minority students." *Language and Education*, 11 (1), 15–37.
——(1996). "From critical research practice to critical research reporting." *TESOL Quarterly*, 29 (2), 320–30.
Canale, M. and Swain, M. (1980). "Theoretical bases of communicative approaches to second language teaching and testing." *Applied Linguistics*, 1 (1), 1–47.
Chambers, I. (2002). "Citizenship, language, and modernity." *PMLA*, 117 (1), 24–31.
Chance, D. (2011). "Creolization: Definition and critique." In F. Lionnet and S-M. Shi (eds), *The creolization of theory.* Durham, NC: Duke University Press, pp. 262–78.
Chelliah, J. (1922). *A century of English education.* Vaddukoddai: Jaffna College.
Chiswick, B. R. and Miller, P.W. (2007). The international transferability of immigrants' human capital skills. IZA Discussion Papers 2670, Institute for the Study of Labor (IZA). ftp://repec.iza.org/RePEc/Discussionpaper/dp2670.pdf. (Accessed 24 February 2011)
——(2002). "Immigrant earnings: Language skills, linguistic concentrations and the business cycle." *Journal of Population Economics*, 15 (1), 31–57.
——(1995). "The endogeneity between language and earnings." *Journal of Labour Economics*, 13 (2), 246–88.
Cilliers, P. (2010). "Difference, identity, and complexity." *Philosophy Today*, 54 (1), 55–65.
Clemente, A. and Higgins, M. (2008). *Performing English with a postcolonial accent.* London: Tufnell.
Cook, V. (1999). "Going beyond the native speaker in language teaching." *TESOL Quarterly*, 33(2), 185–209.
Cope, B. and Kalantzis, M. (eds). (2000). *Multiliteracies: Literacy learning and the design of social futures.* London and New York: Routledge.
Council of Europe. 2000. *Common European framework of reference for languages: Learning, teaching, assessment.* Language Policy Division. Strasbourg. http://www.coe.int/t/dg4/linguistic/Source/Framework_EN.pdf (accessed 24 November 2010)
Chomsky, N. (1988). *Language and problems of knowledge.* Cambridge, MA: MIT Press.
Creese, A. and Blackledge, A. (2010). "Translanguaging in the bilingual classroom: A pedagogy for learning and teaching?" *Modern Language Journal*, 94 (1), 103–15.
Creese, A. and Blackledge, A. (2008). Flexible bilingualism in heritage language schools. Paper presented at *Urban Multilingualism and Intercultural Communication*, Antwerp, Belgium.
Crystal, D. (2004). *The language revolution.* Cambridge: Polity.
——(1997). *English as a global language.* Cambridge: Cambridge University Press.
Cummins, J. (2008). "Teaching for transfer: Challenging the two solitudes assumption in bilingual education." In J. Cummins and N. H. Hornberger (eds), *Encyclopedia of language and education*: Vol. 5. Boston: Springer Science-Business Media, pp. 65–75.
de Certeau, M. (1984). *The practice of everyday life.* Trans. Steven Rendall. Berkeley: University of California Press.
DeGraff, M. (2003). "Against creole exceptionalism." *Language*, 79 (2), 391–410.
de Souza, L. M. (2002). "A case among cases, a world among worlds: The ecology of writing among the Kashinawa in Brazil." *Journal of Language, Identity, and Education*, 1 (4), 261–78.

Delpit, L. (1995). *Other people's children: Cultural conflict in the classroom.* New York: New Press.

Dirks, N. B. (2001). *Castes of mind: Colonialism and the making of modern India.* Princeton: Princeton University Press.

Dorian, N. (2004). "Minority and endangered languages." In T. K. Bhatia and W. C. Ritchie (eds), *The handbook of bilingualism* Oxford: Blackwell, pp. 437–59.

Dong, J. and Blommaert, J. (2009). "Space, scale and accents." In J. Collins, M. Baynham, and S. Slembrouck (eds), *Globalization and language in contact: Scale, migration, and communicative practices,* London: Continuum, pp. 42–61.

Duff, P. A. and Talmy, S. (2011). "Language socialization approaches to second language acquisition: Social, cultural, and linguistic development in additional languages." In D. Atkinson (ed.), *Alternative approaches to second language acquisition,* Oxford: Routledge. pp. 94–116.

Duff, P. A. (2008). "Language socialization, higher education, and work." In P. Duff and N. Hornberger (eds), *Language socialization: Encyclopedia of language and education,* Boston: Springer, pp. 267–70.

Dustmann, C. and van Soest, A. (2002). "Language and the earnings of immigrants." *Industrial and Labor Relations Review,* 55 (3), 473–92.

Dustmann, C. and Fabbri, F. (2003). "Language proficiency and labour market performance of immigrants in the UK." *Economic Journal,* 113, 695–717.

Dustmann, C. (1994). "Speaking fluency, writing fluency and earnings of migrants." *Journal of Population Economics,* 7, 133–56.

Eastman, C. M. (ed.). (1992). *Codeswitching.* Clevedon: Multilingual Matters.

Elbow, P. (2002). "Vernacular literacies in the writing classroom? Probing the culture of literacy." In C. Schroeder, H. Fox, and P. Bizzell (eds), *ALT DIS: Alternative discourses and the academy,* Portsmouth, NH: Boynton/Cook, pp. 126–38.

——(1999). "Inviting the mother tongue: Beyond 'mistakes,' 'bad English,' and 'wrong English.'" *Journal of Advanced Composition,* 19 (2), 359–88.

Erling, E. (2002). "'I learn English since ten years': The global English debate and the German university classroom." *English Today,* 70, 8–13.

Fennell, B. (2001). *A history of English: A sociolinguistic approach.* Oxford: Blackwell.

Firth, A. and Wagner, J. (2007). "Second/foreign language learning as a social accomplishment: Elaborations on a reconceptualized SLA." *Modern Language Journal,* 91, 798–817.

——(1997). "On discourse, communication, and (some) fundamental concepts in SLA research." *Modern Language Journal* 81, 285–300.

Firth, A. (1990). "'Lingua franca' negotiations: Towards an interactional approach." *World Englishes,* 9, 69–80

——(1996). "The discursive accomplishment of normality. On 'lingua franca' English and conversation analysis." *Journal of Pragmatics,* 26, 237–59.

——(2009). "The lingua franca factor." *Intercultural Pragmatics,* 6 (2), 147–70.

Fishman, J. A. (1967). "Bilingualism with and without diglossia; diglossia with and without bilingualism." *Journal of Social Issues,* 32, 29–38.

Flower, L. (1994). *The construction of negotiated meaning: A social cognitive theory of meaning.* Carbondale: Southern Illinois University Press.

Fox, H. (1994). *Listening to the world: Cultural issues in academic writing.* Urbana, IL: NCTE.

Franceschini, R. (2011). "Multilingualism and multicompetence: A conceptual view." *The Modern Language Journal,* 95 (3), 344–55.

Garcia, O. (2009). *Bilingual education in the 21st century: A global perspective.* Oxford: Wiley-Blackwell.

Gates, H. L. (1990). *Signifying monkey: A theory of African-American literary criticism.* Oxford: Oxford University Press.

Giles, H. (ed.) (1984). "The dynamics of speech accommodation." *International Journal of the Sociology of Language* 46. (Special issue).

Glissant, E. (1997). *Poetics of relation.* Trans. B. Wing. Ann Arbor, MI: University of Michigan Press.

Goffman, E. (1981). *Forms of talk*. Oxford: Blackwell.

Gorlach, M. (1990). *Studies in the history of English language*. Heidelberg: Carl Winter.

Graddol, D. (1999). "The decline of the native speaker." *AILA Review*, 13, 57–68.

Gramkow Andersen, K. (1993). *Lingua franca discourse: An investigation of the use of English in an international business context*. Unpublished MA thesis, Aalborg University, Denmark.

——(2001). *The joint production of conversation*. Aalborg University: Denmark.

Gunasekera, B. (1893). *Glossary of native and foreign words occurring in official correspondence and other documents*. Colombo: The Government Printer.

Gunasekera, M. (n.d.) *The postcolonial identity of Sri Lankan English*. Colombo, Sri Lanka: Katha Publishers.

Gutiérrez, K. (2008). "Developing a sociocritical literacy in the third space." *Reading Research Quarterly*, 43 (2), 148–64.

Halasek, K. (1999). *A pedagogy of possibility*. Carbondale: Southern Illinois University Press.

Hall, S. (1997). "The local and the global: globalization and ethnicity." In A. D. King (ed.), *Culture, globalization, and the world system*. Minneapolis, MN: University of Minnesota Press, pp. 19–40.

Halliday, M. A. K. (2002). Applied linguistics as an evolving theme. Plenary address at the International Association of Applied Linguistics, Singapore. December.

Harris, R. (2009). *Integrationist notes and papers: 2006–2008*. Gamlingay: Bright Pen.

He, A. (2010). "The heart of heritage: Sociocultural dimensions of heritage language learning." *Annual Review of Applied Linguistics*, 30, 66–82.

Heath, S. B. (1983). *Ways with words*. Cambridge: Cambridge University Press.

Heller, M. and Martin-Jones, M. (eds) (2001). *Voices of authority: Education and linguistic difference*. Westport, CT, and London: Ablex

Hesford, W. (2006). "Global turns and cautions in rhetoric and composition studies." *PMLA*, 121 (3), 787–801.

Hesse, D. (1999). "Saving a place for essayistic literacy." In G. E. Hawisher and C. L. Selfe (eds), *Passions, pedagogies and 21st century technologies*. Logan: Utah State University Press, pp. 34–48.

hooks, b. (1989). *Talking back: Thinking feminist, thinking Black*. Boston: South End Press.

Hollinger, D. (2002). "Not universalists, not pluralists: The new cosmopolitans find their own way." In S. Vertovec and R. Cohen (eds), *Conceiving cosmopolitanism* Oxford: Oxford University Press, pp. 227–39.

Hornberger, N. (ed.). (2003). *Continua of biliteracy: An ecological framework for educational policy, research, and practice in multilingual settings*. Clevedon: Multilingual Matters.

Hopper, P. (1987). "Emergent grammar." *Berkeley Linguistics Society*, 13, 139–57.

Horner, B., Lu, M., Royster, J. J. and Trimbur, J. (2010). "Language difference in writing: Toward a translingual approach." *College English*, 73 (3), 303–21.

House, J. (2003). "English as a lingua franca: A threat to multilingualism?" *Journal of Sociolinguistics*, 7 (4), 556–78.

——(2002) "Developing pragmatic competence in English as a lingua franca." In Knapp, Karlfried, Meierkord, Christiane (eds). *Lingua franca communication*. Frankfurt: Peter Lang, pp. 245–67.

Hyland, K. (2003). *Second language writing*. Cambridge: Cambridge University Press.

Hymes, D. (1974). *Foundations in sociolinguistics: An ethnographic approach*. Philadelphia: University of Pennsylvania Press.

Jenkins, J., Cogo, A. and Dewey, M. (2011). "Review of developments in research into English as a lingua franca." *Language Teaching*, 44 (3), 281–315.

Jenkins, J. (2009). "English as a lingua franca: Interpretations and attitudes." *World Englishes* 28 (2), 200–207.

——(2006). "Current perspectives on teaching world Englishes and English as a lingua franca." *TESOL Quarterly*, 40, 157–81.

——(2000). *The phonology of English as an international language*. Oxford: Oxford University Press.

Johnson, S. (1755). *A dictionary of the English language.* London: Strahan.

Johnson-Eilola, J. (2004). "The database and the essay: Understanding composition as articulation." In A. Wysocki, et al. (eds), *Writing new media,* Logan: Utah State University Press, pp. 199–235.

Jørgensen, J. N. (2008). "Poly-lingual languaging around and among children and adolescents." *International Journal of Multilingualism,* 5 (3), 161–76.

Kachru, B. (1986). *The alchemy of English: The spread, functions and models of non-native Englishes.* Oxford: Pergamon.

Kandiah, T. (1984). "'Kaduva': Power and the English language weapon in Sri Lanka." In P. Colin-Thome and A. Halpe (eds), *Honouring E. F. C. Ludowyk.* Colombo: Tisaro Prakasayo, pp. 117–54.

Kaur, J. (2009). *English as a lingua franca: Co-constructing understanding.* Berlin: Verlag.

Kell, C. (2010). "Literacy practices, text/s and meaning making across time and space." In M. Baynham and M. Prinsloo (eds), *The future of literacy studies.* Basingstoke: Palgrave Macmillan, pp. 75–100.

Kellman, S. G. (2000). *The translingual imagination.* Lincoln: University of Nebraska Press.

Khubchandani, L. M. (1997). *Revisualizing boundaries: A plurilingual ethos.* New Delhi: Sage.

Kirkpatrick, A. (2010). *English as a lingua franca in ASEAN.* Hong Kong: Hong Kong University Press.

Kossoudji, S. A. (1988). "The impact of English language ability on the labor market opportunities of Asian and Hispanic immigrant men." *Journal of Labour Economics,* 6 (3), 205–28.

Kramsch, C. (2006). "The traffic in meaning." *Asia Pacific Journal of Education,* 26 (1), 99–104.

Kroskrity, P. (ed.) (2000). *Regimes of language: Ideologies, polities, and identities.* Oxford: James Currey.

Lantolf, J. (2011). "The sociocultural approach to second language acquisition: Socio-cultural theory, second language acquisition, and artificial L2 development." In D. Atkinson (ed.), *Alternative approaches to second language acquisition* Oxford: Routledge, pp. 24–47.

Larsen-Freeman, D. (2011). "A complexity theory approach to second language development/acquisition." In D. Atkinson (ed.), *Alternative approaches to second language acquisition* Oxford: Routledge, pp. 48–72.

Lave, J. and Wenger, E. (1991). *Situated learning: Legitimate peripheral participation.* Cambridge: Cambridge University Press.

Levinson, S. (1983). *Pragmatics.* Cambridge: Cambridge University Press.

Li, David. (2002). "Pragmatic dissonance: The ecstacy and agony of speaking like a native speaker of English." In David Li (ed.), *Discourses in search of members: In honor of Ron Scollon.* Lanham, MD: University Press of America, pp. 559–95.

Lillis, T. and Curry, M. J. (2010). *Academic writing in a global context: The politics and practices of publishing in English.* London: Routledge.

Lin, A. and Martin, P. (eds). (2005). *Decolonisation, globalisation: Language-in-education policy and practice.* Clevedon: Multilingual Matters.

Lyons, S. (2009). "The fine art of fencing: Nationalism, hybridity, and the search for a Native American writing pedagogy." *Journal of Advanced Composition,* 29, 77–106.

Lu, M-Z. (2009). "Metaphors matter: Transcultural literacy." *Journal of Advanced Composition,* 29, 285–94.

——(1994). "Professing multiculturalism: The politics of style in the contact zone." *College Composition and Communication,* 45 (4), 442–58.

McArthur, T. (1987). "The English languages?" *English Today,* 3 (3), 9–13.

Maher, J. C. (2010). "Metroethnicities and metrolanguages," in N. Coupland (ed.), *The handbook of language and globalization.* Oxford: Wiley-Blackwell, pp. 575–591.

Makoni, S. (2002). "From misinvention to disinvention: An approach to multilingualism." In G. Smitherman, A. Spear and A. Ball (eds), *Black linguistics: Language, society and politics in Africa and the Americas.* London: Routledge, pp. 132–53.

Matsumoto, Y. (2012). The role of speech-gesture interface in ELF speaker interaction. Paper presented at the Fifth Conference of the International Society for Gesture Studies, July 24–27, Lund, Sweden.

Mauranen, A. (2009). "Introduction." In A. Mauranen and E. Ranta (eds) *English as a lingua franca: Studies and findings*. Newcastle upon Tyne: Cambridge Scholars Publishing, pp. 1–9.

Meierkord, C. (2004). "Syntactic variation in interactions across international Englishes." *English World-wide*, 25 (1), 109–32.

Mesthrie, R. and Bhatt, R. M. (2008). *World Englishes*. Cambridge: Cambridge University Press.

Mignolo, W. D. (2000). *Local histories/global designs: Coloniality, subaltern knowledges, and border thinking*. Princeton: Princeton University Press.

Miller, S. (ed.). (2009). *The Norton book of composition studies*. New York and London: Norton.

Modiano, M. (2004). "Monoculturalization and language dissemination." *Journal of Language, Identity, and Education*, 3 (3), 215–27.

——(1999). "Standard English(es) and educational practices for the world's lingua franca." *English Today*, 15 (4), 3–13.

Moerman, M. (1988). *Talking culture*. Philadelphia: University of Pennsylvania Press.

Mohanty, A. (2006). "Multilingualism of the unequals and the predicaments of education in India: Mother tongue or other tongue?" In O. Garcia, T. Skuttnab-Kangas, and M. Torres-Guzman (eds), *Imagining multilingual schools*. Clevedon: Multilingual Matters, pp. 262–83.

Murata, K. and Jenkins, J. (eds) (2009). *Global Englishes in Asian contexts*. New York: Palgrave Macmillan.

Navarro, Z. (2006). "In search of cultural intepretation of power." *Institute for Development Studies Bulletin*, 37 (6), 11–22.

Nicotra, J. (2009). "'Folksonomy' and the restructuring of writing space." *College Composition and Communication*, 61 (1), 259–76.

Norton, B and Early, M. (2011). "Researcher identity, narrative inquiry, and language teaching research." *TESOL Quarterly*, 45 (3), 415–39.

Papastergiadis, N. (2000). *The turbulence of migration: Globalization, deterritorialization and hybridity*. Cambridge, UK: Polity Press.

Parakrama, A. (1995). *De-hegemonizing language standards*. Basingstoke: Macmillan.

Pattanayak, D. P. (1984). "Language policies in multilingual states." In A. Gonzalez (ed.), *Panagani: Language planning, implementation, and evaluation*. Manila: Linguistic Society of the Philippines, pp. 75–92.

Pennycook, A. (2010). *Language as a local practice*. Oxford: Routledge.

——(2007). *Global Englishes and transcultural flows*. Oxford: Routledge.

Pennycook, A. and Makoni, S. (2005). "The modern mission: The language effects of Christianity." *Journal of Language, Identity, and Education*, 4 (2), 137–55.

Pitzl, M-L. (2010). *English as a lingua franca in international business*. Saarbrucken: VDM-Verlag.

Planken, B. (2005). "Managing rapport in lingua franca sales negotiations: A comparison of professional and aspiring negotiators." *English for Specific Purposes*, 24 (4), 381–400.

Pollock, S. (2006). *The language of the gods in the world of men: Sanskrit, culture, and power in premodern India*. Los Angeles: University of California Press.

Posner, R. (1991). "Der polyglotte dialog." *Der Sprachreport*, 3, 6–10.

Pratt, M. L. (1991). "Arts of the contact zone." *Profession*, 91, 33–40.

——(1987). "Linguistic utopias." In N. Fabb, D. Attridge, A. Durant, and C. MacCabe (eds), *The linguistics of writing: Arguments between language and literature*. Manchester: Manchester University Press, pp. 48–66.

Rampton, B. (2008). *Language in late modernity: Interaction in an urban school*. Cambridge: Cambridge University Press.

——(1999a). "Styling the Other: Introduction." *Journal of Sociolinguistics*, 3 (4), 421–27.

——(1999b). "*Deutsch* in Inner London and the animation of an instructed foreign language." *Journal of Sociolinguistics*, 3 (4), 480–504.

Ratcliffe, K. (1999). "Rhetorical listening: A trope for interpretive invention and a 'Code of Cross-Cultural Conduct.'" *College Composition and Communication*, 51, 195–224.

Reid, J. M. (1989). "English as a second language composition in higher education: The expectations of the academic audience." In D. M. Johnson and D. H. Roen (eds), *Richness in writing: Empowering ESL students*, New York: Longman, pp. 220–34.

Roberts, P. and Canagarajah, S. (2009). "Broadening the ELF Paradigm: Spoken English in an International Encounter." In F. Sharifian (ed.), *English as an international language: Perspectives and pedagogical issues*. Clevedon: Multilingual Matters, pp. 209–26.

Romaine, S. (1989). *Bilingualism*. Oxford: Blackwell.

Royster, J. J. (1996). "When the first voice you hear is not your own." *College Composition and Communication*, 47 (1), 29–40.

Rubdy, R. and Saraceni, M. (eds) (2006). *English in the world: Global rules, global roles*. London: Continuum.

Sampson, H. and Zhao, M. (2003). "Multilingual crews: Communication and the operation of ships." *World Englishes*, 22 (1), 31–43.

Schegloff, E. (2000). "When 'others' initiate repair." *Applied Linguistics*, 21, 205–43.

Schroeder, C., Fox, H. and Bizzell, P. (eds.). (2002). *ALT DIS: Alternative discourses and the academy*. Portsmouth, NH: Boynton/Cook.

Seidlhofer, B. (2009). "Common ground and different realities: world Englishes and English as a lingua franca." *World Englishes*, 28 (2), 236–45.

——(2004). "Research perspectives on teaching English as a lingua franca." *Annual Review of Applied Linguistics*, 24, 209–39.

——(2001). "Closing a conceptual gap: The case for a description of English as a lingua franca." *International Journal of Applied Linguistics*, 11 (2), 133–57.

Silverstein, M. (1996). "Monoglot 'standard' in America: Standardization and metaphors of linguistic hegemony." In D. Brenneis and R. Macaulay (eds) *The matrix of language: Contemporary linguistic anthropology*, Boulder: Westview Press, pp. 284–306.

Silverstein, M. and Urban, G. (eds.). (1996). *Natural histories of discourse*. Chicago: University of Chicago Press.

Smitherman, G. (2003). "The historical struggle for language rights in CCCC." In G. Smitherman and V. Villanueva (eds), *From intention to practice: Considerations of language diversity in the classroom*, Carbondale: Southern Illinois University Press, pp. 7–39.

——(1999). "CCCC's role in the struggle for language rights." *College Composition and Communication*, 50 (3), 349–76.

——(1998). "'Dat teacher be hollin at us'—What is ebonics?" *TESOL Quarterly*, 32 (1), 139–43.

——(1990). *Talkin and testifyin: The language of Black America*. Detroit: Wayne State University Press.

——(1974). "Soul 'n' style." *English Today*, 63 (3), 14–15.

Sohan, V. K. (2009). "Working English(es) as rhetoric(s) of disruption." *Journal of Advanced Composition*, 29 (1/2), 270–75.

Spivak, G. (1993). *Outside in the teaching machine*. New York: Routledge.

Stark, R. (2008). "Some aspects of Christian mystical rhetoric, philosophy, and poetry." *Philosophy and Rhetoric*, 41 (3), 260–77.

Street, B. (1984). *Literacy in theory and practice*. Cambridge: Cambridge University Press.

Swales, J. (1990). *Genre analysis: English in academic and research settings*. Cambridge: Cambridge University Press.

Swyngedouw, E. (1997) "Neither global nor local: glocalization and the politics of scale." In K. R. Cox (ed.), *Spaces of globalization: Reasserting the power of the local*. New York: Guilford Press, pp. 137–77.

Tannen, D. (1982). *Spoken and writing language: Exploring orality and literacy*. Norwood, NJ: Ablex.

Tardy, C. (2011). "Enacting and transforming local language policies." *College Composition and Communication*, 62 (4), 634–61.

Thaiss, C. and Zawacki, T. M. (2002). "Questioning alternative discourses: Reports from across the disciplines." In C. Schroeder, H. Fox, and P. Bizzell (eds), *ALT DIS: Alternative discourses and the academy* Portsmouth, NH: Boynton/Cook, pp. 80–96.

Tomasello, M. (2008). *Origins of human communication*. Boston: MIT Press.

Tompkins, J. P. (1980). *Reader-response criticism: From formalism to post-structuralism.* Baltimore: Johns Hopkins University Press.

Trimbur, J. (2010). "Linguistic memory and the uneasy settlement of US English." In B. Horner, M-Z. Lu, and P. K. Matsuda (eds), *Cross-language relations in composition.* Carbondale: Southern Illinois University Press, pp. 21–41.

Uitermark, J. (2002). "Re-scaling, 'scale fragmentation' and the regulation of antagonistic relationships." *Progress in Human Geography*, 26 (6), 743–65.

Vertovec, S. (2007). "Super-diversity and its implications." *Ethnic and Racial Studies*, 29 (6), 1024–54.

Vertovec, S. and Cohen, R. (eds), (2002). *Conceiving cosmpolitanism.* Oxford: Oxford University Press.

Villanueva, V. (2011). "Reflections on style and the love of language." *College Composition and Communication*, 62 (4), 726–38.

——(1993). *Bootstraps.* Urbana, IL: NCTE.

Wallerstein, I. (2001). *Unthinking social science.* Philadelphia: Temple University Press.

Wenger, E. (1998). *Communities of practice.* Cambridge: Cambridge University Press.

Widdowson, H. G. (1997). "EIL, ESL, EFL: Global issues and local interests." *World Englishes*, 16, 135–46.

Wysocki, A. (2004). "Opening new media to writing: Openings and justifications." In A. Wysocki, et al. (eds), *Writing new media* Logan: Utah State University Press, pp. 1–41.

Young, V. (2004). "Your average nigga." *College Composition and Communication*, 55 (4), 693–715.

INDEX